FOREIGN POLICY MAKING IN DEVELOPING STATES

Foreign Policy Making in Developing States

A comparative approach

edited by
CHRISTOPHER CLAPHAM

PRAEGER PUBLISHERS
Praeger Special Studies

New York • London • Sydney • Toronto

British Library Cataloguing in Publication Data

Foreign policy making in developing states.
  1. Underdeveloped areas —Foreign relations
  1. Clapham, Christopher
  327'.091712'4   D849   77-71401

PRAEGER PUBLISHERS, PRAEGER SPECIAL STUDIES
383 Madison Avenue, New York, N.Y. 10017, U.S.A.

Published in the United States of America in 1979 by Praeger Publishers
A Division of Holt, Rinehart and Winston, CBS, Inc.

© 1977 by Christopher Clapham

Library of Congress Catalog Card Number: 77-71401

Printed in Great Britain

Contents

List of tables   vi
List of maps   vi
The contributors   vii
Preface   ix

1   Theories of foreign policy making for the developing
    countries   1
    Christopher Hill

2   South-east Asia   18
    Michael Leifer

3   The Middle East   42
    A. I. Dawisha

4   Sub-Saharan Africa   76
    Christopher Clapham

5   The Commonwealth Caribbean   110
    Vaughan A. Lewis

6   Latin America   131
    Edy Kaufman

7   Comparative foreign policy and developing states   165
    Christopher Clapham

Index   179

List of tables

3.1 Total arms transfers of major suppliers to ten core Middle
Eastern states, 1965–74   46

3.2 Trade balance of ten core Middle Eastern states, 1974   57

3.3 Defence expenditures of ten core Middle Eastern states in
1974   59

4.1 Population, gross domestic product, and diplomatic representation of sub-Saharan African states   102

6.1 Embassies and Legations of Latin American states   142

List of maps

2 South-East Asia   18

3 The Middle East   43

4 Africa   76

5 The Caribbean   111

6 Latin America   132

The contributors

Christopher Clapham is Senior Lecturer in Politics at the University of Lancaster. Born in 1941, he read Philosophy, Politics and Economics at Keble College, Oxford, and completed a DPhil there on Ethiopian politics, subsequently teaching in the universities of Addis Ababa, Manchester, and the West Indies. His publications include *Haile-Selassie's Government* (1969) and *Liberia and Sierra Leone: An Essay in Comparative Politics* (1976).

A. I. Dawisha is currently Research Associate of the International Crisis Behaviour Research Project. Born in Baghdad, Iraq, he received his undergraduate training at the University of Lancaster, and his PhD from the London School of Economics. He has published widely in the fields of foreign policy analysis and Middle East politics, including articles in the *British Journal of International Studies, Political Studies,* and the *Middle East Journal.* He is the author of *Egypt in the Arab World: The Elements of Foreign Policy* (1976).

Christopher Hill was born in 1948. He read Modern History at Merton College, Oxford, and afterwards spent three years as a Student of Nuffield College. He was the Noel Buxton Student in the Department of International Relations at the London School of Economics, where he has been a Lecturer since 1974. He is currently completing a detailed case-study of the British foreign policy process, and has written articles on the theory of foreign policy and the domestic dimensions of international behaviour.

Edy Kaufman is Lecturer in International Relations and past Chairman of the Department of Latin American Studies at the Hebrew University, Jerusalem. He was born and brought up in Argentina, and studied at Santa Fe University, Argentina, the Hebrew University, and the Sorbonne, where he received his doctorate. He has written extensively on international relations with special reference to Latin America, including *La Politica Exterior del Gobierno de la Unidad Popular (Allende) en Chile (1970–1973) (1975),* and *The Superpowers and their Spheres of Influence: a comparative analysis of the foreign policies of the Soviet Union and the United States in Eastern Europe and Latin America* (1976).

Michael Leifer is Reader in International Relations in the University of London, and teaches in the Department of International Relations at the London School of Economics. He received his BA from Reading University and his PhD from London. He has taught at the Universities of Adelaide, South Australia, and Hull, and has been Visiting Professor of Government and Asian Studies at Cornell University. His numerous publications include *Cambodia: The Search for Security* (1967), *Dilemmas of Statehood in South East Asia* (1972), and *Foreign Relations of the New States* (1974).

Vaughan A. Lewis is acting Director of the Institute of Social and Economic Research at the University of the West Indies, Jamaica. Born in St Lucia, he received his BA from the University of the West Indies and his PhD from Manchester University. He is the author of *Models of Political Systems* (with M. Davies), and has written extensively on problems of small states in international relations, including *Size, Self-determination and International Relations: the Caribbean* (1976).

William Wallace, general editor of this series, is a Research Fellow at the Royal Institute of International Affairs, and Lecturer in Government at the University of Manchester. He is the author of *Foreign Policy and the Political Process* (1972), and of *The Foreign Policy Process in Britain* (1975).

Preface

This book is one of a projected series of three volumes on the comparative analysis of foreign policy making, under the general editorship of William Wallace. The other volumes, edited by W. Paterson and William Wallace and by Hannes Adomeit respectively, will examine the making of foreign policy in Western Europe and in the socialist states. The aim of all these volumes is to combine an informative and empirical analysis of foreign policy making in the region with an awareness of the theoretical approaches to the subject which have proliferated in recent years, such that each illuminates the other and the more useful points of contact between them can readily be seen.

This volume, accordingly, starts with an introductory chapter on theories of foreign policy making, with a particular concern for the adaptations or replacements of theories devised for industrial states which may be necessary for the analysis of developing countries. (We decline to be drawn into sterile controversies over whether this part of the world should be referred to as developing, underdeveloped, or less developed, as the Third World, or whatever.) The five following chapters consider the salient features of foreign policy making in Southeast Asia, the Middle East, Sub-Saharan Africa, the Commonwealth Caribbean, and Latin America. The volume thus represents a very wide spectrum both of domestic and of external environments. The authors, all of whom are specialists in (and three of whom are natives of) their particular areas, have been asked to consider domestic, regional and global influences on policy, and the decision-making process, but have been left free to order this material as they saw best, within the common concerns of the book as a whole. They have not taken for granted any previous knowledge of the region, and each chapter is provided with a bibliographical appendix, to enable interested readers to pursue the subject further. The concluding chapter continues the comparative theme by drawing together threads from the regional chapters, and examining the levels at which, and techniques through which, the comparative analysis of third world foreign policies may profitably be undertaken.

We should like to express our thanks to the Political Science Association of the United Kingdom, at whose Lancaster conference in 1974 the idea for this series first took root; to many friends and colleagues with whom the project and individual contributions to it have since been discussed; to Mr John Irwin of Teakfield Limited; and to Lesley Hoyle of Lancaster University for undertaking the major part of the typing.

WILLIAM WALLACE   March 1977
Royal Institute of International Affairs
CHRISTOPHER CLAPHAM
Department of Politics, University of Lancaster

1 Theories of foreign policy making for the developing countries*

CHRISTOPHER HILL

Foreign policy theorists interested in the Third World, or, equally, students of the developing countries [1] inclined to relate their work to the field of comparative foreign policy, may adopt one of three approaches. The choice lies between (1) applying to new states the models constructed during the study of the already-modernised countries, even though the concepts concerned may be culture-bound; (2) employing a special frame of reference which focuses exclusively on the behaviour of young states with little experience or weight in international politics, and as yet only small industrial sectors; (3) effectively combining the first two approaches by treating different types of state within the same set of concepts, but within a wider set than that generally used in the US-based school of foreign policy analysis.

It is this third option which is taken here to provide the most useful approach. The variety of problems and decision making procedures encountered by states hardly seems justification for the kind of intellectual separatism that would hive off developing countries into special conceptual categories. On the other hand, it also seems to make nonsense of attempts to apply narrowly Western models to radically different cultures. Consequently the minimum requirement of an open-minded student must be the elaboration of pre-theories wide enough in scope to preclude identification with any particular class of state, whether liberal or communist, developed or developing, closed or open. Inevitably, analysis will concentrate at first on a straightforward specification of all the variables that might conceivably affect foreign policy decisions, according to what we know or theorise about domestic and international politics at present. The ultimate ambition, of course, is that of being able to state with some confidence which factors tend to be most influential in what circumstances, and why. But although the 'why' questions are fundamentally the

* I am grateful for the helpful comments of Dr Michael Leifer on an earlier draft of this paper.

most important of all, they cannot be answered without establishing beforehand exactly what phenomena need to be explained. And by extension, none of these stages of reasoned enquiry can be followed unless all kinds of states are deemed suitable cases for the same kind of scholarly treatment until proved otherwise.

Yet if theory does not help us to sort out the interesting and answerable questions from the rest, it is nothing. Taxonomies in themselves are sterile, and a taxonomy of the influences on foreign policy, world-wide, may be so general as to be self-defeating. [2] As a result, what follows does accept that some areas of enquiry are more fruitful than others in the contemporary study of foreign policy making in the Third World. The basis of the discrimination, however, is not the common assumption that there must inevitably be a sharp contrast between decision making in complex industrial societies, and in elitist developing countries. Instead, some areas of research are simply seen as potentially more relevant to the study of developing countries than others, within a basic argument that no model can be excluded from the outset unless one wishes only to fulfil initial prophecies about perceived intrinsic contrasts between new and old states; the converse is obviously true, that no model proved in the context of an industrialised country can provide, *ipso facto*, an acceptable global generalisation.

If we begin with those factors likely to be less prominent in the policies of new states than in countries like Britain, the United States, and the Soviet Union, it takes little sophistication to see that bureaucracy will be among the first of them. It is well-known that in recent years the roles of large departments and the routines of administrative procedure have increasingly been related to what happens in foreign policy. [3] Disagreement has been rife over the precise evaluation of bureaucracy, but there has been a growing consensus recently over the inapplicability of the insights of Allison, Halperin, Destler et al. to foreign policy making inside less modernised states. [4] J. S. Migdal has stated bluntly that 'these states do not ... have enough stability of structure or form in their organisational routines or bargaining processes for the researcher to employ these conceptual models usefully'. [5] Likewise, F. B. Weinstein, when discussing the foreign policy of Indonesia, discounts the 'Snyder framework', because it 'is really designed for the analysis of policy-making in complex organisations'. [6] In another detailed study Maurice East argues, on the evidence available from Uganda, where the Foreign Ministry is shown to be of low political importance and intellectual calibre, that small states are indeed a special case as far as the making of foreign policy is concerned. [7] Finally, by way of illustrating the current

2

view, McGowan and Shapiro's painstaking collection of explicitly comparative findings contains almost nothing about bureaucracy in the developing countries – an indication that the subject is considered of little relevance to the explanation of their foreign policies. [8]

This tendency to associate organisation exclusively with developed states is perfectly understandable. Our image of the new states is conditioned by what we know about capricious dictators, about poverty, and about lack of expertise. But while it may be futile to expect studies of bureaucracy in, say, Kenya or Thailand or Pakistan to provide the key to an understanding of those countries' foreign policies, it would be just as absurd to neglect the area. In the fields of comparative politics and development, after all, it is common to assume that it is the administrative elite above everything that holds together societies aiming for both industrialisation and independence under conditions of great internal strain. Whether through sheer organisational professionalism or the monopolisation of key decision making positions, it is clear that such exercises as the planning of modern cities and communications, and the fostering of an education system, depend heavily on such trained administrators as are available. [9] No doubt foreign policy in these states is a different matter altogether; it may be a lesser priority because of the paradoxical security and lack of power experienced by many developing countries, while decisions will always be subject to the ambitions of individual leaders to make their mark in world politics. On the other hand, it can be argued that, because of their very smallness and disabilities, bureaucracies are important negative influences on the foreign policies of presidents such as Amin or Neto, and thus deserve attention. Failures to collect and process information thoroughly, or to achieve effective liaisons between the various arms of government, can mean the difference between success or failure when the actual resources behind policy are as stretched as they were, for example, with Uganda's failure to prevent the Israeli raid at Entebbe in July 1976, or with President Numeiry's difficulties over tracing the links between outside elements and those plotting against him inside the Sudan. [10]

Less pedantically, an important reason for not discarding the administrative perspective in this context is the positive impact that bureaucracy can have on foreign policy, the potential for which is growing at the same pace as development itself. In Indonesia during the late 1960s and early 1970s, after Suharto came to power and ended the period in which Sukarno, the Army and the Communist Party had all manoeuvred for influence over policy, there still seem to have been definite distinctions between the role of the so-called technocrats and that

3

of the Army, even though the latter was always ultimately dominant. In 1970, for example, military pressure for a move against Cambodia was successfully nullified by the professional diplomatic service, headed by Foreign Minister Malik. The hawks were headed off by the holding in Jakarta of an international conference to discuss Cambodia. [11]

Indonesia has not been alone among new states in having both a sufficiently active foreign policy and a sufficiently sophisticated political process to deserve analysis that goes beyond the rational actor approach. It should hardly need stating that North Korea could not build secret tunnels towards the South, nor co-ordinate a publicity campaign in the West, without a reasonably effective administrative machine; [12] India could not develop the potential for nuclear weapons or handle her complicated relations with such powers as China and the Soviet Union, let alone run her huge and heterogeneous society, if government depended purely upon the energies of Mrs Gandhi and a few courtiers; Nigeria would not be capable of the successful leadership she displayed in the negotiations over the Lomé agreement, or of the effective diversification of her foreign currency holdings, without the kind of foresight and expertise that an established bureaucracy can provide. [13] We should remember that although Egypt and Senegal may have similar *per capita* national incomes (and thus be classed as poor) it does not follow that the study of organisation will be marginal for either or both. [14] For the analyst the problem is less the existence (or not) of bureaucracies, than the dearth of useful information about them.

If we now cast the net rather wider over the domestic sources of foreign policy, we find that the same theme recurs: while it would be perverse and wasteful to concentrate energies on the kind of subject familiar to students of the State Department or Quai D'Orsay, it does not follow that the internal affairs of a new state have little impact on its international position. It is true that the complex of pressure groups found in Britain is hardly paralleled in even the most developed of the new states (because of both their youth and their fears about factionalism); that the West provides enough journalists and commentators for the world over and cannot be matched by states still struggling to achieve mass literacy; [15] that the gap between mass and elite can be so great that tribal language simply does not possess the words with which to communicate the phenomena encountered by modern governments. [16] It is not surprising, therefore, that the detailed legislative interest in foreign policy that is the practice in some industrialised democracies, or the comprehensive party network that exists in the Warsaw Pact countries, each providing at least some potential for inputs into policy making, are not to be found in many states of the Third World.

On the other hand, it is also true that economic issues are even more crucial for LDCs than they are for the already industrialised. [17] Consequently, their foreign policies are very directly constrained by the need to conserve resources and are themselves in large part composed of the external aspects of economic policy, [18] a fact which applies just as much to the oil-rich as the poor states. Further, their foreign policies are intimately concerned with the problems of nation-building and nationalism; a sense of being Cambodian may well be fostered by pursuing a foreign policy of strict independence, while the unity of Nigeria may be served by establishing the country's prominence inside the African bloc. Less significantly, individual rulers can use foreign policy as a weapon in their competition with political rivals at home, in the style of the mediaeval European kings. Mr Bhutto's progresses around the diplomatic capitals of the world help to present an image of dignity and achievement to the people of Pakistan. [19] In sum, what goes on inside a developing country is of the greatest relevance to its foreign policy, and vice versa, even if the interaction between internal and external does not take the form of administrative infighting or wide-spread public debate as often as it does in the West.

It should be clear by now that those approaches to foreign policy analysis which least repay application to developing states are only *relatively* inappropriate. Any delving beyond initial impressions will probably discover the same processes at work in both developed and developing countries, even if operating in different contexts and at different stages of maturity. An excellent example of this is the area that may be termed capability analysis. Highly detailed cost-benefit projections of the economic or military instruments available to new states are obviated both by the present small scale of their available resources (however broadly construed), and by the particularly dynamic quality of their economies, which can make such statements rapidly out-of-date. [20] But again it is largely a matter of degree. Heavily armed states such as Iran, Syria and India are as much meat for the defence analysts as are France or the United States. [21] Likewise, OPEC countries have recently absorbed as much of the attention of western economists as the OECD states themselves. Leverage of the kind enjoyed by Saudi Arabia is not an option for most LDCs, [22] but for a substantial minority the run of history means a swift realisation of their potential to join the ranks of the middle powers, some of whom in their turn are being forced to take the part of the declining gentry, unable to meet the challenge of new conditions.

5

To the extent that there is a contrast between decision making in rich and poor states, some concepts will fit the poor far more than the rich, and it is to these that we now turn. Of those perspectives especially relevant to the LDCs, the most commonly encountered is that of charismatic leadership. Since Max Weber's initial formulation, the idea of charisma has been associated with the populist appeal enjoyed by individual leaders of heroic personality, people who are by their very nature forces for change and instability. [23] It is easy to understand why this has been taken up as a ready-made explanation for foreign policies in the Third World. Ignorant masses, societies under transformation, leaders enjoying the glory of newly-won independence: these are ready ingredients for a theory based on the notion of charisma. In 1966, Henry Kissinger wrote that 'The charismatic leader needs a perpetual revolution to maintain his position', while 'the new nations, in so far as they are active in international affairs have a high incentive to seek in foreign policy the perpetuation of charismatic leadership.' [24] He saw the West as 'deeply committed' to Newtonian rationalism, while new states had still to free themselves from a revolutionary 'fervour and dogmatism' fuelled by 'cultures which escaped the early impact of Newtonian thinking'. As a result they were vulnerable to the seductions of leader-prophets. [25]

Although the simplifications and paternalistic tone of this view will be apparent, it cannot be denied that the study of individual leadership finds good material among the developing countries. The lives of Nehru, Nasser and Nkrumah, and the continuing careers of Nyerere, Makarios and Ghaddafi, all testify to the importance of explaining the impact of great men, if not to the accuracy of the view that charismatic leadership necessarily involves the triumph of risk over reason. [26] Nonetheless, erratic, idiosyncratic and charismatic behaviour by world statesmen is not restricted to points south of the Mediterranean, or to early European history. It is generally accepted that even in pluralist societies, foreign policy is an area of great executive freedom for Presidents, Prime Ministers and Foreign Secretaries. Churchill, Franco, Adenauer, De Gaulle and Kissinger alone provide sufficient examples to remind us uncomfortably that strong personalities and personal views may account for a significant percentage of all international behaviour. Doubtless, if we were to count up, more leaders in new states have more opportunities to define for themselves their countries' foreign policies, simply through the smaller size of their establishments, but we know from the familiar debates about world historical individuals from Napoleon through Stalin to John F. Kennedy that bureaucracy has rendered policy making no more impersonal than has democracy. In some respects a more complicated society may even place a greater premium on personal initiatives, to counteract inertia. [27]

As a spin-off from his work on Indonesia, F. B. Weinstein has suggested that we should approach developing countries through a 'central organising concept — the uses of foreign policy'. [28] By this he means the functions that foreign policy performs, whether internationally or at home, for the nation as a whole, and for sectional interests. This proposal builds on Robert Good's argument a decade before that foreign policy was being 'recruited to the state-building task'. Good considered that foreign policy often served four purposes: to continue the revolution against colonial rule; to establish the identity of new states; to keep an in-group in power; and to reduce foreign influence at home. [29] It is certainly true that the first two of these functions are by definition restricted to newly independent states. Beyond that, it is difficult to see why 'the uses of foreign policy' should be accepted either as an adequate theoretical approach or as a concept peculiar to one class of states. The idea of 'uses' distracts us from the various environmental constraints under which decision makers have to operate, as well as from the origins of the values implicit in their goals. It implies too much manipulative intent and capability. Furthermore, the usual argument can be levied against it. Foreign policies are pursued to help in-groups stay in power in modernised states no less than elsewhere; indeed it is almost an intrinsic attribute of foreign policy that it should help to reduce foreign influence at home.

Far more useful as a special framework is the concept of dependence. This goes beyond both the simple listing of functions and the truism about asserting independence to the undoubted fact that those developing countries that are without hope of escaping from poverty or low international status [30] (the majority) share a very real condition of reliance on the developed world. Expertise, trade and capital are all vital and are all supplied on the donor's, or major partner's, terms. Dependence will be particularly acute if a country wishes, as almost all do, to modernise quickly and to attain at least the appearance of international influence. Certainly foreign policy will be no less powerfully affected by the condition than the country's domestic life. While struggles against actual colonialism are becoming more and more residual, awareness of neo-colonialism does not abate. Indeed, it produces a sense of shared interests among the Third World states that falls far short of creating an under-privileged block, but does lead to their increased self-confidence and to assertiveness in the General Assembly of the UN. This, and in particular the demands for a 'new international economic order', have certainly changed the current language of world politics. It remains to be seen whether in this instance ideas and rhetoric will help to shape reality, but it is clear that most developing countries do appreciate now the extent to which they are have-nots. Their foreign policies will be formulated in the light of this image as long as the domestic and world conditions which produced it survive.

Structural dependence will affect foreign policy in two ways, according to the viewpoint taken. The two interpretations are best seen as forming the opposite ends of a continuum. Dependence will either impose acquiescence in the interests and dogmas of capitalism (and/or state capitalism, if the USSR is included), via the mechanisms of trade, aid, and investment, or it will breed a determination to resist, to achieve solidarity with those similarly placed, and to create a world order based on different socio-economic values from those which currently hold sway. [31] Whatever the outcome, one of the main tasks of the individual state's foreign policy will be to deflect the pressures exerted by countries interested in protecting their overseas investments or in getting political returns for their aid. The more positive requirements of achieving greater freedom of choice over production and social organisation, or of significantly narrowing the wealth gap, even within one country, are beyond the scope of single states not favoured with natural resources. Revolution and autarchy, if practicable possibilities, might help to attain independence, but are unlikely to raise standards of living in the short term. To most LDCs then, a realistic foreign policy means exerting pressure for the common interests of poor states, avoiding retaliatory action from the powerful, and working to satisfy the particular needs of their own country. This balancing act symbolises the precariousness of the average new state's foreign policy. [32]

By way of conclusion, we come to those concerns of foreign policy analysis which cannot be focused on certain types of state more than others. Unlike the areas considered above, where there is at least a case to be made for a greater or lesser degree of relevance to the developing countries, these are completely open-ended. The first illustrates more clearly than any why it is both patronising and short-sighted to regard policy analysis as appropriate largely for the fully developed society, whatever that may be. The 'psychological environment' encapsulates the notion that how decision makers perceive the world is at least as important for explaining their actions as is the world's actual condition. [33] In consequence the personalities of statesmen and the dynamics of group behaviour become central factors in the analysis. The potential repercussions of Great Power foreign policy and the relative availability of data in the West have meant that the United States and the European powers between them have monopolised the attention of scholars working in this field. The persistence of stereotypes, the origins of misperception, and the nature of behaviour under crisis conditions have all been examined closely and fruitfully in the context of relations between the major states. [34] There is no reason, other than the paucity of data and the complexion of current academic interests, why this situation should not be extended elsewhere. In every nation groups of politicians or advisers meet to discuss policy and are automatically subject to the pressures of conformity and over-simplification. And wherever politics is talked about the notion of image will be pertinent. The perceptual dimension of foreign policy exists independently of degrees of modernisation. This means that it would be equally absurd for the pendulum to swing to the other extreme, where the pathology of charismatic leadership in the Third World is sometimes taken to be peculiarly suitable for psychological appraisal. Michael Brecher's work on Khrishna Menon and on Israel highlights the genuine comparative utility of many concepts from psychology, which is arguably less bound by time and culture than many branches of the social sciences. [35]

Another model which seems applicable to all modern states is that of transnationalism. The most cursory reader of academic literature about politics over recent years will have noted the widespread view that industrialised societies are becoming increasingly penetrated and inter-dependent as economic growth continues, and that the ability of even established states to exercise their legal sovereignty is being called into question. Governments are being by-passed and their freedom of manoeuvre is being circumscribed − although to what extent is a matter of hot debate. [36] Opinions such as these need only a little cosmetic altera-tion to be immediately applicable to the developing countries. They are intimately related to the discussion about neo-colonialism, in that some of the parent countries of multinational companies themselves suffer from the consequences of transnational business activity. Britain and Japan are obvious recent examples of middle-range powers embarrassed by large companies; [37] societies of all types are affected (if to differing degrees) by cultural penetration; South Africa and the Soviet Union can be affected by a drop in the price of gold just as Zambia would suffer from the production of copper substitutes. The operations of the contemporary world economy affect all the participants within it. Some are undeniably more independent than others, but very few are isolated from the effects of such international phenomena as fluctuating commodity prices or technological change.

The last perspective of obvious universal relevance is that of elites. Although we have known at least since Mosca and Pareto that elites may take different forms according to time and place, it is still reasonable to argue that all types of polity are prone to rule by dominant minorities. [38] In developed societies subtle processes of socialisation and recruitment make access to policy making circles difficult for those who do not share the mores and aspirations of the establishment. In younger countries power falls inevitably into the hands of that educated minority which has the opportunity to achieve personal wealth and important contacts abroad. Whether or not elitism is an iron law of politics, it is clear that the questions raised by its study get to the heart of the issues of power, accountability, and participation in any society. Development will be one factor affecting our answers to these questions, as will all elements of circumstance, but there is no reason why it should pre-determine the uses of a theory that makes such fundamental statements about human behaviour.

There is one aspect of the study of elites, however, which may be a special case. The proliferation of military governments has largely taken place in the Third World, and clearly results in part from the centrifugal forces which independence unleashed inside societies created by outsiders. But if it is possible that there is a correlation between underdevelopment and a propensity to military rule (and exceptions such as Greece, Chile, and Spain spring easily to mind) this is a long way from saying that military governments in new states share a distinctive form of foreign policy, except perhaps in the sense that these governments are often sympathetic to the West. [39] And this in itself, of course, coupled with the fact that traditional social elites have generally been supplemented by the forces of modernisation, only strengthens the argument for using the same models for the analysis of both rich and poor states.

In summary then, we have stressed how important it is not to foreclose avenues of enquiry before the enquiry begins. It is more difficult to break down an initial presumption of the differences between states than to shake a generalisation about similarities. The instinct for empirical study is strong and has built-in tendencies towards qualification and contrast. [40] If the comparative approach is thought at all worthwhile, then it is an illogical procedure 'if each researcher devises his own framework, using what he can from others, but assuming above all that his model is suited to his own data and his own theoretical concerns'. [41] Findings and methods will be non-commensurable and theories based on them not susceptible to refutation.

To make this argument it has been necessary to protest too much about the common factors affecting developing and developed countries. The many points of difference should not be ignored, and universal generalisations will always be broken down as they become more detailed. In particular, foreign policies in the Third World must always be considered in the light of dependence. But the basic conclusion drawn from a survey of theory still remains valid: that while empirical work may ultimately demonstrate the validity of this or that assumption, empiricism will only be hindered if we pre-judge its findings by treating certain questions as irrelevant from the outset. For existing concepts are so broad and nebulous that any theory employing too partial an approach risks building castles in the air. It is sometimes said, for example, that the foreign policies of the developing countries are ultimately shaped by the external environment, and to this extent come into a special category. [42] But what is meant by the statement? It contains implicit assumptions about determinism and about special characteristics which are questionable as well as sweeping. It is the kind of mono-casual explanation pilloried for its crudity when applied to the complexities of industrialised states. It does not specify which external factors are decisive, or why developed states are in a qualitatively different position. Such errors are not important in themselves. They do matter, however, when they become accepted as conventional wisdoms, thereby simplifying the quality of discussion about developing states. Important omissions or distortions can result.

In terms of methodology then, there is no *a priori* justification for assuming that certain kinds of behaviour will not be found outside conditions of industrialisation. Such an assumption elevates development prematurely from the status of variable to that of explanation. The remnants of a *de haut en bas* prejudice towards immature societies probably account for such eager compartmentalisation, but whatever the reason, it does not promote the comparative study of foreign policy. All states have to face the same problems of reconciling domestic values and requirements with external circumstances. There are limits to the ways in which any government can handle foreign policy, and therefore all should be treated by academics as inhabitants of the same world.

Notes

[1] In the interests of readability the terms 'developing countries', 'new states', 'Third World', 'unmodernised states' and occasionally 'LDCs' (Less Developed Countries) are used interchangeably.

[2] This is not to down-grade the kind of pioneering work exemplified by Joseph Frankel's *The Making of Foreign Policy*, Oxford University Press, London 1963, and Michael Brecher, Blema Steinberg and Janice Stein's 'A Framework for Research in Foreign Policy Behaviour', *Journal of Conflict Resolution*, vol. XIII, no. 1, March 1969, which by breaking down decision making into its component variables, and by showing how they operate, performed an essential service.

[3] The most notable exponents in this respect have been G. Allison, in *Essence of Decision*, Little Brown, Boston 1971, M. Halperin, in *Bureaucratic Politics and Foreign Policy*, the Brookings Institution, Washington, DC 1974, I. Destler in *Presidents, Bureaucrats and Foreign Policy*, 2nd ed., Princeton University Press, 1974, and more briefly, F. Rourke, *Bureaucracy and Foreign Policy*, Johns Hopkins University Press, Baltimore 1972.

[4] Maurice East argues that writers about international relations have traditionally classified all small states as 'nothing more than ... large states writ small' (see 'Size and Foreign Policy Behaviour', *World Politics*, vol. XXV, no. 4, July 1973, p.558). In the area of foreign policy analysis, this has not been the case in recent years (see below).

[5] Joel S. Migdal, 'International Structure and External Behaviour: Explaining Foreign Policies of Third World States', *International Relations*, London May 1974, p.519.

[6] F. B. Weinstein, 'The Uses of Foreign Policy in Indonesia: An Approach to the Analysis of Foreign Policy in the Less Developed Countries', *World Politics*, vol. XXIV, no. 3, April 1972, p.359. Weinstein is referring to R. C. Snyder, H. W. Bruck and B. Sapin (eds), *Foreign Policy Decision-Making*, Free Press, New York 1962, (but itself based on an earlier version of 1954), a book which stood for a new wave of interest in the 'how' rather than the 'what' of foreign policy.

[7] M. East, 'Foreign Policy-Making in Small States: Some Theoretic Observations Based on a Study of the Ugandan Ministry of Foreign Affairs', *Policy Sciences*, vol. 4, no. 4, 1973 (particularly pp.491–2). East does distinguish between 'small' and 'developing' states, but still tends to use the two terms with a cavalier disregard of niceties.

[8] P. McGowan and H. Shapiro, *The Comparative Study of Foreign Policy*, Sage, Beverly Hills and London 1973. The absence of references to bureaucracy in the developing countries does not indicate that the authors are fundamentally opposed to classifying states according to their wealth and modernisation. Plenty of attention is given to 'development' as a variable in foreign policy, but not in the context of bureaucracy.

[9] See G. A. Heeger, 'Bureaucracy, Political Parties, and Political

Development', in *World Politics*, vol. XXV, no. 4, July 1973. J. White, *The Politics of Foreign Aid*, Bodley Head, London 1974, pp.83–8, contains an interesting discussion of the conflicts which can arise between different departments within an aid-receiving Government's machinery.

[10] It seems clear that better Ugandan intelligence and less lax security at the airport would have made the raid a far more costly affair for the Israelis (see *The Sunday Times* 'Insight' reports of 11 and 18 July 1976). On the Sudan, see p.476 of M. C. Hudson's 'The Middle East' in J. N. Rosenau, K. W. Thompson and G. Boyd (eds), *World Politics*, Free Press, New York 1976, pp.466–501.

[11] F. B. Weinstein, 'The Foreign Policy of Indonesia' in Rosenau, Thompson and Boyd, op. cit., pp.256–60, and M. Leifer, 'Patterns of Indonesian Foreign Policy', in F. S. Northedge (ed), *The Foreign Policies of the Powers* (2nd ed.), Faber and Faber, London 1974, pp.373-4.

[12] See, for example, North Korea's full-page advertisements in *The Times* of 14 August and 25 October 1974; also *The Sunday Times*, 11 May 1975. For the tunnels, see *The Times*, 24 May 1975.

[13] J. Mayall, 'Oil and Nigerian Foreign Policy', *African Affairs*, vol. 75, no. 300, July 1976, p.325. The Central Bank of Nigeria stated in 1976 that it was seeking to diversify from a reliance on sterling into stronger currencies such as the Mark and the Yen. (Information from Nigerian High Commission, 9 September 1976).

[14] In 1973, Egypt's *per capita* national income at market prices was $245, and Senegal's $228. UN *Monthly Bulletin of Statistics* July 1976, vol. XXX, no. 7, pp. xxii–iii.

[15] This fact has recently been recognised by non-aligned countries, and remedial action has begun. At a New Delhi meeting of July 1976 they formulated a plan for setting up combined regional news agencies of their own to rival Reuters, Agence France-Presse and the rest. See *The Guardian*, 14 August 1976 and *The Times*, 17 August 1976.

[16] C. B. Marshall, 'On Understanding the Unaligned' in L. Martin (ed.), *Neutralism and Nonalignment: The New States in World Affairs*, Praeger 1962, pp.13–33, expresses this point graphically. But see also J. Nye, in M. Kilson (ed.), *New States in World Politics*, Harvard 1975, p.167, who points to the relatively broad base of colonial educational systems in Africa.

[17] As clearly shown by R. Vernon's discussion of the balance of payments concerns of LDCs, and the impact of US investment upon them, in *Sovereignty at Bay*, Penguin, Harmondsworth, Middlesex 1973, pp.170–6.

[18] If one needs convincing on this point, East (*World Politics*) op cit.,

pp.573–5 tells us on the basis of the quantified creon data-set that 'economic bureaucracies and economic techniques of statecraft are more frequently involved or utilised in the foreign policy behaviour of small states' (than in that of large states).

[19] In 1974, Prime Minister Bhutto visited Iran, China, Bangladesh and the Soviet Union. On at least three of these occasions he was accompanied by a large retinue. *The Times*, 11 May, 28 June, and 25 October 1974.

[20] As well as by their inability to control resource allocation precisely – White, op.cit., p.93; – a characteristic shared of course by many industrialised states, Britain prominent among them.

[21] *The Military Balance 1975–1976*, International Institute for Strategic Studies, London, pp.76–7, shows that Iran, Syria and India spent in 1975 28.3 per cent, 24.0 per cent, and 21.1 per cent respectively of Government expenditure on defence (compared to 19.1 per cent for France and 26.6 per cent for the USA). Moreover, in absolute terms Iran spent as much as Britain, Syria roughly as much as Romania, and India almost as much as Canada.

[22] Certainly not while 120 countries have to share only 25 per cent of the world's realised wealth. M. Singer, 'The Foreign Policies of Small Developing States' in Rosenau, Thompson and Boyd, op.cit., pp.264–70.

[23] Max Weber, *The Theory of Social and Economic Organisation*, Free Press, Glencoe Ill. 1947 (translation).

[24] H. Kissinger, 'Domestic Structure and Foreign Policy', *Daedalus*, Spring 1966, and reprinted in *The Shaping of Foreign Policy*, H. K. Jacobson and W. Zimmerman (eds), Atherton Press, New York 1969. Here, see pp.152–3.

[25] Ibid, pp.156–8.

[26] Both J. S. Migdal, op.cit., pp.521–2 and F. B. Weinstein, op.cit. warn against such a stereotype.

[27] Particularly in crisis conditions. See D. Kavanagh, 'Crisis, Charisma and British Political Leadership: Winston Churchill as the Outsider', Sage Professional Paper in *Contemporary Political Sociology*, vol. 1, no. 06–001, London and Beverly Hills 1974. F. Greenstein, *Personality and Politics*, Markham, Chicago 1969 is illuminating on the general argument about individual potential.

[28] Weinstein, op.cit., p.366.

[29] R. C. Good, 'State-Building as a Determinant of Foreign Policy in the New States' in L. Martin, op.cit., p.5.

[30] Status may be improved without poverty or dependence necessarily being diminished. See White, op.cit., pp.80–1, for the size of India's

problem in this respect.

[31] For works which discuss dependence in some detail, if with varying degrees of sophistication, see: M. Barratt Brown, *The Economics of Imperialism*, Penguin, Harmondsworth, Middlesex 1974, pp.256–84; J. Galtung, 'A Structural Theory of Imperialism', *Journal of Peace Research*, vol. 2, 1971; R. Jenkins. *Exploitation*, MacGibbon and Kee, London 1970.

[32] White, op.cit., pp.98–103, details these dilemmas. M. Singer, *Weak States in a World of Powers*, Free Press, New York 1972 (especially pp.89–364, and 377–8), argues at length that outside intervention in the affairs of weak countries is inevitable, and almost intrinsic to international relations.

[33] The term was introduced to the study of foreign policy making by H. and M. Sprout in 'Environmental Factors in the Study of International Politics', *Journal of Conflict Resolution*, vol. 1, no. 4, December 1957.

[34] Particularly by J. De Rivera, *The Psychological Dimension of Foreign Policy*, C. E, Merrill, Columbus, Ohio 1968; I. Janis, *Victims of Groupthink*, Houghton Mifflin, Boston, Mass. 1972; R. Jervis, 'Hypotheses on Misperception', *World Politics*, April 1968; and E. May, *'Lessons' of the Past: The Use and Misuse of History in American Foreign Policy*, Oxford University Press, New York 1973.

[35] M. Brecher, *India and World Politics: Krishna Menon's View of the World*, Oxford University Press, London 1968; *The Foreign Policy System of Israel*, Oxford University Press, London 1972; *Decisions in Israel's Foreign Policy*, Oxford University Press, London 1974.

[36] The work which best represents this school is R. D. Keshane and J. Nye (eds), *Transnational Relations and World Politics*, Harvard University Press, Cambridge, Mass. 1971, first published as the summer 1971 issue of *International Organisation*. Recent discussions of the importance of the transnational approach are to be found in *International Affairs*, July 1976, and *Millennium*, Spring 1976, in articles by S. Strange, J. N. Rosenau, and F. S. Northedge.

[37] Britain by Chrysler's thinly veiled threat to close down their plants in Britain if financial aid was not forthcoming, and Japan by Lockheed's payments to prominent politicians in return for securing important contracts. For these see, among many reports, *The Times*, 29 November 1975, and *Keesings' Archives* 1976, pp.C27840–1.

[38] G. Parry, *Political Elites*, George Allen and Unwin, London 1969, is an excellent assessment of elite theories and their current status.

[39] As a generalisation, it is broadly true that the majority of military governments have been anti-communist. In terms of the precise content of

these countries' foreign policies, of course, the generalisation should be qualified considerably.

[40] J. H. Hexter argues that historians divide into 'lumpers' (generalisers) and 'splitters' (qualifiers), but for the former can only cite such untypical figures as Toynbee and Christopher Hill; 'The Burden of Proof', *Times Literary Supplement*, 24 October 1975, pp.1250–2.

[41] Weinstein, op.cit., p.362. But Weinstein is in favour of findings 'using well-known, loosely-defined variables capable of easy translation from one study to the next', p.363.

[42] White, op.cit., p.75; East, *Policy Sciences*, op.cit.; Weinstein, op.cit., and M. Singer, *Weak States in a World of Powers* e.g. pp.38 and 367–70, also see the foreign policies of developing countries as being uniquely and quintessentially reactive.

2 South-East Asia

MICHAEL LEIFER

The regional context

The making and practice of foreign policy within South-East Asia is not unique in relation to the overall experience of Third World countries. Any measure of distinctiveness which the foreign policy process of its resident states might possess arises above all from a regional replication of domestic circumstances which shape external priorities.

The ten states of South-East Asia [1] are situated within regional bounds determined by the eastern marches of the Indian subcontinent, the southern perimeter of China and the northern approaches of Australia. With the exception of Thailand, they have all experienced colonial domination and their independent existence within the contemporary international system dates only from after the end of the Pacific War in 1945. Indeed, a sense of regional definition has emerged also only since the end of that war, which was responsible for the term South-East Asia coming into common usage. South-East Asia escapes tangible definition, however, in terms of such encapsulating features as an integral land mass or a single great cultural tradition. Its common bio-geographical and climatic properties do not compensate for a fragmentation produced by physical and maritime divisions which obstructed pre-colonial attempts at hegemony from within the region. Significantly, pre-colonial intrusions from without not only failed to overcome the fissiparous character of South-East Asia, but also contributed to it through the penetration and movement of migrant peoples, traders and priests.

These somewhat negative aspects of the regional context might appear to obstruct any serious examination of the influence on the foreign policies of the ten states concerned of any so-called common environment. Indeed, it is pertinent to ask what is really common about a regional situation distinguished by manifold diversity, except for a varying propinquity of states. One response to such a question might be to argue that since, with only one exception, all the states of South-East Asia have been subject to direct colonial domination, such a common historical experience provides a basis for contemplating foreign policy formulation and practice. Such a premise is valid in that colonial powers influenced

17

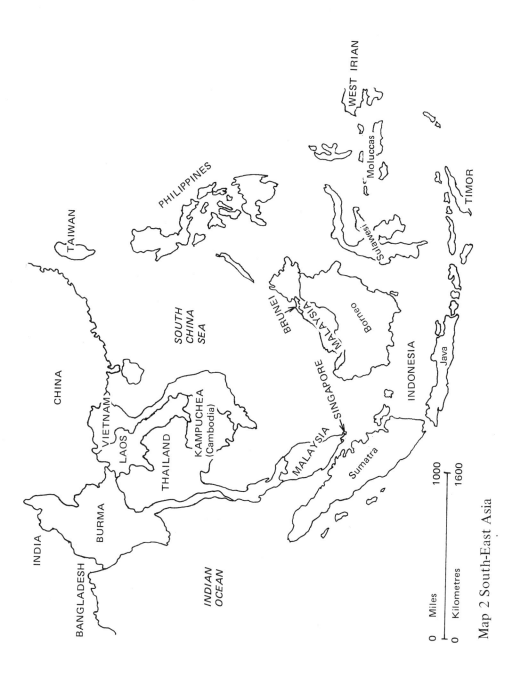

Map 2 South-East Asia

INDIA

BANGLADESH

BURMA

CHINA

TAIWAN

VIETNAM

LAOS

THAILAND

KAMPUCHEA
(Cambodia)

SOUTH
CHINA
SEA

PHILIPPINES

WEST IRIAN

Moluccas

Sulawesi

BRUNEI

MALAYSIA

Borneo

SINGAPORE

MALAYSIA

Sumatra

INDONESIA

Java

TIMOR

INDIAN
OCEAN

Miles   0   1000

Kilometres   0   1600

the societies and especially the economies of their oriental prizes, and integrated them into the international economy so as to shape post-independence relationships. However, without in any way wishing to deny the fact or significance of common consequences arising from economies based on plantation agriculture and extractive industry, this is not a phenomenon peculiar to South-East Asia but is generally characteristic of the post-colonial 'Third World'.

In other important respects, the impact within South-East Asia of what was a multiple, and not a uniform, colonialism, both confirmed the subordinate international position of regional polities, and contributed in turn to an existing kaleidoscopic pattern. Successive Portuguese, Spanish, Dutch, British, French and American intrusions both consolidated the bounds of established political identities and promoted new ones. In the maritime part of South-East Asia, the Spanish and the Dutch welded archipelagos into viable administrative units, though without ever fully domesticating all of the social forces so encompassed. In the mainland, where the course of major river valleys has dictated the pattern of human settlement, colonial administrative divisions more readily corresponded to those separating historical kingdoms, although the experience of the latter had never encompassed the idea of a lineal political boundary. [2] Thus, although one of the major consequences of colonialism was significant administrative fusion of territorial domain, the overall impact of a variety of external intrusions, in a part of the world long influenced by geographic configuration and distinguished by the absence of any dominant cultural or political centre of gravity, was to reinforce an intrinsic diversity. And this diversity was sustained by the characteristic pattern of communication between metropolitan centres and colonial outposts.

A greater sense of regional definition and common environment, though externally imposed, followed the swift eradication by Japan during the Second World War of the multiple colonial position. But what was common in political terms within the territories of the occupied region was an external source of initiative and demands; policies applied were far from uniform. Political participation was promoted and pseudo-independence granted, only in so far as it assisted the Japanese war effort, and to this end also major demands were made on natural and human resources. The Japanese experience brought a more cruel subordination than that of European colonialism and its common feature was a regional debilitation arising from Japanese demands and aggravated by the actual course of the Pacific War. It was shortly after its abrupt termination that the process of independence began with a devastated and prostrate Philippines acquiring sovereign status in July 1946.

The overall experience of the attainment of independence was not at all common as the four major returning colonial powers differed in their willingness to concede nationalist demands which became strident with the successive collapse of alien authorities. Common perhaps was the relatively short period of gestation experienced by the states of the region before attaining independence, but the major significance of sharing a common period of political metamorphosis was the regional high-lighting of domestic order which had been long managed on the basis of mainly administrative priorities. It is in this respect above all that one might suggest that a common regional environment has existed for the new states of South-East Asia: an environment made up of the aggregated characteristics of successor polities whose basic domestic similarities stand out despite innate differences of composition and experience. Once again, it must be pointed out that such a phenomenon is not peculiar to South-East Asia. Nonetheless the expression of a common new state experience within the region has been of an especially intense kind.

The relatively swift retreat of colonial power, whether willingly or enforced, and the replacement of administrative by political relationships often of an intensely competitive kind posed a challenge to the viability of many of the new states from the very outset. The initial strain arising from an evident lack of congruence between diverse and divided societies on the one hand and the formal unity of aspirant modern polities on the other, was aggravated by material and human underdevelopment. In consequence, there existed a striking contrast between the often ready acquisition of international status and personality, and the absence of the requisite domestic supports of a modern state. Indeed, in many respects, the states of South-East Asia possessed at independence an embryonic and premature quality. In general terms their identities were precariously established, and subject to a variety of internal challenges as inheritance elites met with resistance to their rule based either on opposition to the very identity of the state within its given bounds, or on opposition to its actual territorial form. Such challenges to identity succeeded in time in transforming the political character of successor states in Indochina and they persist elsewhere in the region, if with less vigour. By contrast, irredentist and separatist movements have not been in any way as suc-cessful so far, discounting the special circumstances of Indonesia's acquisition of West Irian from August 1962 and the enforced in-dependence of Singapore from Malaysia in August 1965. Irrespective of the mixed success of challenges of an ideological and separatist kind, however, such challenge has been the experience of every South-East Asian state without exception and has produced in consequence the common concern with territorial unification and centralisation of state control which is found in other parts of the post-colonial world.

The new state experience of South-East Asia, expressed at the outset and beyond in a common condition of political fragility, was projected in aggregate form to make up a major constituent of regional environment: one which has served to ensure subordination within the global international system. An aspect of this subordination common to most of the region was the continuation into independence of economic relationships which had distinguished colonial rule. But, in addition, a major determinant of regional environment in foreign policy terms was an arousal of interest, concurrent with the process of independence, on the part of the then sole global power which came to incorporate South-East Asia within its strategic perspective. The incorporation by the United States of South-East Asia within the compass of its policy of the global containment of communism gave the region an imputed importance beyond any intrinsic significance which it possessed as a source of raw materials and as a crossroads of communications. At a time when the Soviet Union was little more than a regional power and China hardly that, the United States coupled intra-elite competition within successor states (and especially those not yet independent) to a view of an interconnected regional and global order which derived from the notion of a monolithic international communism.

The intrusion of a conflict whose source lay outside South-East Asia, and its junction with internal contests within successor states over their political identity, provided a dominant feature of the regional environment for nearly three decades after the termination of the Pacific War. It served as a common reference point for the states of the region, if not a basis for common external policies. That feature of regional environment has been modified considerably as a consequence of the impact of Sino-Soviet antagonism and America's bitter discovery of a sense of limitation of power. Political transformation in Indochina has not brought about an aggregation of the influence of an international communism and the resolution of internal conflict between alternative elite groups in South-East Asia is no longer joined to the global balance of power. Competitive search for access continues within the region but on a less acute and destructive basis on the part of external states. The countries of South-East Asia still experience dependent relationships with external patrons and economic associates but regional environment has assumed more of an autonomous nature. It is not only that its new states have become less embryonic and more entrenched as territorial entities since the transfers of sovereignty, but also that the extra-regional Powers do not enjoy quite the same commanding or intimidating role. The central features of the contemporary regional environment are the change in the balance of external influences, and the emerging relationships between states whose contrasting social orders represent competing political alternatives.

Sources of international outlook

A basic source of the initiatives and responses which make up the foreign policies of the South-East Asian states has been formative experience which has shaped orientations and attitudes to the outside world. One facet of such experience has been governed by the extent to which the colonial power respected traditional identities in establishing units of administrative control. In the case of South-East Asia, such demarcation was not established solely on an *ad hoc* basis. Thus, in certain instances the eventual acquisition of independence may reasonably be interpreted as a reversion to sovereignty in as much as the historical identity of a pre-colonial kingdom was carried over into the post-colonial era. One such state would be Thailand which, although never subjected formally to colonial domination, was a beneficiary of colonial accommodation as well as an object of its territorial acquisitiveness. The Thai state sustained its historic identity by playing off British and French interests, while Burma and Cambodia reverted to sovereignty after a period of colonisation. For Vietnam, unification within bounds beyond its historic core but coincident with those established at the time of French colonisation was delayed not only by the dogged resistance of the colonial power, but also by American intervention arising from global rather than from any intrinsically regional interest.

The significance of an acquisition of independence being equivalent to a reversion to sovereignty is that this experience may play a part in fashioning international outlook. In the case of the former Democratic Republic of Vietnam, which assumed control of Vietnam down to the line of the seventeenth parallel in July 1954, the state media made considerable play of historical precedent in seeking to generate national consciousness, including significantly the heroic resistance of the legendary Trung sisters against the Mongol invaders in the first century AD. It would not seem to be a coincidence that after the fall of Saigon in April 1975 and the subsequent unification of Vietnam, a conflict of interests in part over territory should emerge with neighbouring China despite the social ideals which the two states hold in common. Thus, the legacy of traditional antagonisms, whether between Vietnamese and Chinese or, for example, between Cambodians and Vietnamese, may assume a revived potency should independence be perceived as a reversion to sovereignty rather than as the emergence of a new state. Such is part of the experience of those states of South-East Asia which abut the Asian mainland, with the striking exception of Laos.

A more extensive, if not uniform, impact of the process of state definition and formation with consequences for international outlook has come from the actual experience of attaining independence. This has been significant in two major respects. The first is the actual experience of the transfer of power and its impact on the collective political consciousness. In the case of South-East Asia, the impact of what might be described as the founding moments on the political culture of the post-colonial states was mixed, given the existence of compliant as well as dogged colonial powers. In addition, the endurance of this mixed impact has varied as generational change and succeeding experiences have both reinforced and modified initial outlooks. Nonetheless, the actual experience of acquiring independence did serve to fashion collective attitudes to the international environment. For example, Indonesia underwent a resentful experience of great power policies during a painful and protracted struggle for independence, which served to promote a common view of a hostile outside world. This view was confirmed, if in different ways, for competing elite groups by subsequent experience of external intervention. In the case of Indonesia, it is possible to suggest that the experience of acquiring independence reinforced two contrasting and competing political subcultures which have expressed themselves in alternative approaches to modernisation and in consequence to foreign policy. A different kind of example is provided by Singapore. The experience of having independence thrust rudely upon it in August 1965, and then of suffering within a matter of months an alarming political reconciliation between former antagonists Indonesia and Malaysia, was a major determinant of its government's initial outlook. The transformation, virtually overnight, from being a constituent unit of Malaysia — then confronted by Indonesia — to becoming a small, vulnerable and conspicuously Chinese island state, and then of suffering the rapprochement of its more powerful Malay neighbours was politically traumatic. The Socialist Republic of Vietnam provides a more recent example of the relationship between the experience of attaining independence and foreign policy formulation; its government's attitude towards other South-East Asian states is inevitably coloured by the close association between some of these states and the external power which sought to deny its conception of independence.

For other states of the region, the experience of the transfer of power was very different. Thus, while it served to shape a particular view of state legitimacy on the part of a country like Indonesia where revolutionary struggle came to be associated with just political succession, it induced a sense of ambivalence in the international outlook of the Philippines, which had also secured territorial definition through colonial enterprise. In the case of the Philippines, a pacific accession to independence, against a background of Japanese invasion, occupation and exploitation and also internal class-based challenge to a neo-traditional elite produced at the outset an amicable and dependent relationship with the former colonial power, if combined in time with a growing awareness of being regarded widely as the dutiful client of the United States. Although progressive governmental concern with acquiring international recognition of a more legitimate status and greater national self-respect has encouraged a willingness to expand both regional and wider relationships, the Philippines has yet to repudiate fully the premises which comprised its post-independence outlook and which were shaped by the experience and circumstances of the acquisition of independence.

A second major consideration of relevance to international outlook and foreign policy has been the nature and related interests of the respective elite groups who have succeeded in changing governments within South-East Asia. Above all, their approaches to the common goal of modernisation have had a direct bearing on the actual practice of foreign policy, reflected in both intra-regional and extra-regional associations. For example, where ruling elite groups are evidently tolerant towards the inflow of foreign capital and the repatriation of profits as part of the process of economic development, as in the case of the five member countries of the Association of South-East Asian Nations (ASEAN), foreign policy while not necessarily uniform tends to be governed by similar priorities which link conservative political orders to external associations.

One factor in determining the character of some of these elite groups has been the practice of colonial powers who provided the territorial frame of reference for their successors. Some consciously went to pains to foster the emergence of groups of an accommodating nature with requisite educational qualities, either to facilitate the administration of colonial society or to ensure that post-independence political succession would produce both stability and continued economic access. This was very much the case in the Philippines, where an accommodation was reached at the outset of American colonisation between an indigenous *mestizo* elite with a base in landholdings and the new administrators, which served to protect mutual interests up to and beyond the transfer of sovereignty in July 1946. A similar example is to be found in Malaysia, where pre-selected members of an administrative and subsequently ruling class were educated in an oriental version of an English public school. The beneficiaries of this regime, conscious of the desirability of asserting independence by means other than revolutionary struggle, perceived a direct connection between an economic system open to international access and the maintenance of a political system which catered for their group interests. In partial contrast to Malaysia, one can cite the example of Indonesia, where the aspirant inheritance elite, although rejected politically by the Dutch before the onset of the Pacific War, was composed of educational beneficiaries of colonial rule drawn from the lesser nobility and native administrative class. This class not only survived the convulsions of the national revolution but also inherited the reins of power from the Dutch on the morrow of independence. Although dislodged in time by a military junta whose leading figures originate from more humble origins, the social values and economic priorities, with attendant international outlook of the inheritance elite, have been reaffirmed since the displacement of the late President Sukarno.

It is important to understand, however, that while European educational and formative experience is a common factor linking inheritance elites, and indeed may have been provided consciously by colonial powers, such experience does not automatically produce common social and economic attitudes and priorities. In the case of Cambodian beneficiaries of an educational experience which linked colonial rule and the post-colonial period, one outcome was an attraction to a marxism in a French ambience, which led to a total rejection of post-independence political orders and the establishment of a political system characterised by an internal self-reliance expressed stridently in foreign policy.

International outlook is not consistently determined by factors of the kind indicated above. In the case of Burma, for example, if one were to consider only the experience of the transfer of power, and the social priorities and economic interests of the ruling military junta which seized power from the inheritance elite in March 1962, without taking fully into account the factor of external environment, a misleading picture of foreign policy priorities might ensue. Nonetheless, the two major constituents of international outlook discussed above are of undoubted relevance to the making of foreign policy in the South-East Asian states. Their particular significance, as with all general factors relevant to the analysis of foreign policy, will depend upon their impact on circumstances which in South-East Asia are characteristically diverse.

The domestic environment of foreign policy

The domestic predicament of the states of South-East Asia has been emphasised in some generality as a common problem and even challenge to governments in the region. Obviously, there are differences between individual circumstances, but in so far as an inheritance elite or its successors are acutely concerned with sustaining or promoting a sense of national identity, foreign policy can be both an expression of such concern and a means with which to overcome it. In this respect, a common source of foreign policy making within the region has been the domestic condition of the state. Great emphasis has been attached to sustaining intact the territorial legacy of colonialism, irrespective of the cultural and political diversity encapsulated, by opposing any precedents which might open up a Pandora's box of centrifugal forces. Thus Indonesia, given its experience of regional dissent, was most reluctant to welcome the advent of Bangladesh in December 1971, because it had been hived off from Pakistan as a direct consequence of external intervention. Earlier, Indonesia's longstanding and successful pursuit of its irredentist claim to West New Guinea was justified in terms of the liquidation of colonialism and the completion of the national state, but it was sustained also because continued Dutch occupation leading to its separate political existence was regarded as a menacing precedent for the fissiparous archipelago. Indeed, Indonesia's enforced incorporation of Portuguese Timor in December 1975, which violated the conventions of colonial succession, was promoted in part by a concern in Jakarta lest the self-determination of this vestige of empire in the Lesser Sundas encourage a renewal of separatist tendencies in the outer islands of the Republic.

Within South-East Asia, incipient separatism has been widespread and matched by irredentist claims of varying intensity. And although they have not posed a major challenge to territorial integrity, they have been of undoubted relevance in the foreign policies of states prosecuting and resisting such claims. The most striking, if exceptional, example has been that of Vietnam. In this case the territorial division which provoked what can be construed as a form of irredentism was brought about and sustained as a consequence of external power intervention rather than as a consequence of the specific policy of the former colonial power. In general, irredentism whether formally or tacitly pressed has been

26

resisted vigorously not only because of a common jealous attachment to sovereign prerogative but also because of related apprehension of the impact of any concessionary precedent on socially heterogeneous societies. It is significant, as was indicated above, that the most successful irredentist claim pursued within the region was at the expense of a former colonial power and not a successor state. Also, the only example of successful separatism within South-East Asia has been that of Singapore, which became independent in unique circumstances when the Federal Government of Malaysia decided that the presence of the island within the Federation was a greater threat to communal harmony than its presence outside as a separate state would be to territorial unity. Against all precedents, separate existence was foisted on a small island whose leadership was reluctant to assert independent status and was certainly not pressing for separate political identity.

Resistance to claims whose successful prosecution would erode territorial integrity has been matched by a corresponding assertion of claims as an instrument of foreign policy designed to shore up a domestic political order beset by a variety of destabilising influences. Thus, the territorial claim by governments of the Philippines to the Malaysian state of Sabah was promoted in part by internal considerations, and was managed at one stage in a manner designed to forestall separatist activity by the concentration of Moslems in the south of the country. Of course, where foreign policy initiatives of this kind have been undertaken to bolster the internal position of individual governments by sustaining the fragile balance of forces upon which it may rest, uniformity of policy is once again not to be expected. What is likely to be common in South-East Asia and the greater part of the decolonised world is a tendency to utilise foreign policy to serve a domestic political function.

It should be stressed then that while within South-East Asia common conditions of domestic weakness have influenced the function of foreign policy guiding the manner of its use, such common conditions have not necessarily given rise to uniformity of governmental responses. Alternative policies of alliance association with an external power or an ostentatious non-alignment, for example, have been influenced by the perception of domestic advantage involved on the part of ruling groups. Thus one reason why some states in South-East Asia opted for non-alignment was because such a policy served to demonstrate the independence of the successor state in the face of opposition charges of governmental subservience to the former colonial power or to an external major power. This was certainly the experience of Cambodia from the outset of independence, when Prince Sihanouk faced political challenge both from within the neo-traditional elite and from a radical grouping which had been associated closely with the Viet-Minh during the First Indochina War. The late President Sukarno's foreign policy, though expressed in romantic slogans, possessed an evident external rationale in its rejection of the conventional wisdom of non-alignment and its challenge to the established structure of the international system. As such, it expressed the frustration of those nationalists like Sukarno who resented the contrast between Indonesia's effective capability and its sense of regional self arising from size, population and natural resources. But this radical foreign policy which sought to substitute for the orthodoxy of non-alignment was also and importantly linked to the political system of Guided Democracy, whose projected aura of solidarity did not conceal an acute and even destructive competitiveness. These competitive political forces were maintained in balance for a time through their separate willingness and need to defer to romantic revolutionary values articulated by Sukarno and justified in great part in foreign policy terms. As such the practice of confrontation against Malaysia and the vindicating ideology of the 'New Emerging Forces' was utilised to manage domestic political conflict and also to sustain the position of President Sukarno at the apex of the political system of which he was the prime beneficiary between July 1959 and October 1965. Of course, such use of foreign policy can rebound to domestic political disadvantage where its exponent's standing is explicitly linked to successful practice. Thus, to return to the case of Cambodia, Prince Sihanouk's right-wing opponents used his alleged failings in foreign policy to inspire the anti-Vietnamese agitation which paved the way for his deposition in March 1970.

The use of foreign policy in order to preserve and perpetuate internal political order possesses an evident external dimension. Resort to foreign connections may serve a similar purpose to the examples cited above. Indeed, many external relationships established by governments within South-East Asia have been contemplated above all as rendering access to a source of countervailing power to contain internal challenges. Vietnam south of the seventeenth parallel while it survived as an international entity represents a notable example, if of a special kind, in that its external patron and benefactor was primarily responsible for the establishment of the truncated state. The significance of external connection for domestic political purpose assumes a more common feature in the case of Thailand. Thus, shortly after the termination of the Pacific War, approval from the American Government for the political rehabilitation of a formal ally of Japan helped to fend off, if only for a limited period, the ambitions of a discredited military. Subsequent alterations in the political criteria regarded as acceptable by the United States and prompted by the onset of the Cold War then enabled the military to resume power with continuing external approval and material benefaction, which contributed to the maintenance of its primacy in politics until October 1973, by which time the Thai bureaucratic elite had begun a major reappraisal of the utility of the post-war relationship with the external patron.

In addition to foreign policy practice arising out of a felt need to bolster the position of government and an associated social structure, it may also relate to domestic political order where that order is affected by the domicile of expatriate ethnic minorities who possess an affinity with either a neighbouring regional state or an extra-regional power. Such minorities are extensive within South-East Asia in varying concentrations. Their economic role tends to be a major factor in commercial life. It arose from colonial priorities and practice and has been a source of domestic tension which in cases has exploded into inter-communal violence with attendant consequences for foreign policy. In such circumstances foreign policy tends to be a function of the size and role of the minority in question and importantly of the prevailing perception of the neighbouring state or extra-regional power. One should distinguish, however, between policy which may arise out of a dispute between a government and a local minority and in consequence government and external state (for example, the antagonism which erupted between Burma and China in 1967 during the course of the Cultural Revolution), and that not necessarily preceded by such circumstances but designed specifically to encourage an ethnic minority to come to terms with the prevailing political order.

Malaysia offers an example of a state where the local Chinese community, whose ancestors settled in the main under colonial auspices, have been perceived not only in terms of cultural separateness and resented economic role but also in relation to locally based communist insurgents and the People's Republic of China. Indeed, the public initiative of May 1961 by the Malayan Prime Minister, Tunku Abdul Rahman, in suggesting the establishment of a federation of Malaysia to include Singapore and the then colonial territories of North Borneo, was inspired by the problem of how to ensure the internal security of Malaya while incorporating within it a politically turbulent Singapore whose population was more than 75 per cent ethnic Chinese. A more recent foreign policy initiative which also related to domestic political order was the decision of the Malaysian Government in 1974 to establish diplomatic relations with China. A stimulus for this change of course in foreign policy came from environmental factors within Asia but it derived also and importantly from a governmental concern to demonstrate to the overseas Chinese community and to the insurgent and predominantly ethnic Chinese Malayan Communist Party that the legitimacy of the Administration in Kuala Lumpur was both recognised and approved in Peking. Confirmation of such a concern was provided in the course of the general elections held in Malaysia in August 1974, when the ruling coalition made considerable use of wall posters showing Prime Minister Tun Abdul Razak in the company of Chairman Mao.

It is possible to contrast the above example of the relationship between domestic order and foreign policy with two others where foreign policy initiatives have been constrained because of the imperatives of domestic political order. In the case of Singapore, there is the unusual circumstance within South-East Asia of a resident Chinese majority, some of whose members are regarded by the predominantly ethnic Chinese government of the island-state as possibly susceptible to undue influence from their resurgent motherland. In consequence, the government of Singapore, while maintaining official contact with China, including visits by its Foreign Minister and Prime Minister, has sought successfully to delay the establishment of diplomatic relations with China because of apprehension about the strength of the local political identity of its majority community. A related reason for Singapore's reluctance is that any fervent welcome given by the people of the island-state to the first diplomatic representatives of China might have consequences for her relations with neighbouring states, especially Indonesia, which has long regarded Chinese minorities in the region as a source of subversion and as the likely tool of Peking. Indeed, on the part of the government of Indonesia there has existed an equivalent reluctance to normalise diplomatic relations suspended since October 1967. This reluctance arises from an exaggerated concern about subversive consequences, lent substance by the conduct of the first Chinese communist diplomatic mission to take up residence in Jakarta following the initial establishment of relations after independence.

The presence of ethnic minorities is common throughout South-East Asia, but the problems and practices of foreign policy to which they give rise are certainly not uniform. For example, the experience of Burma in dealing with its once economically powerful Indian community and the neighbouring state of India has been very different from that of Indonesia in dealing with both its overseas Chinese community and the People's Republic when it sought to dispossess Chinese traders working in the rural areas. However, where ethnic minorities are perceived by regional governments as linked to the interests of an external power, foreign policy decisions may arise not only as a consequence of internal tensions, but also as part of a conscious decision to manage the domestic political system. In this respect, a common feature of foreign policy can be associated with common circumstances but, of course, in a way not peculiar to South-East Asia alone.

A similar relationship of linkage between foreign policy and domestic order may obtain where there is an absence of firm consensus about the actual identity of a state, separate from its concrete territorial form. To illustrate this point one can contrast the differing attitudes of the Malaysian and Indonesian Governments to signature of the Islamic Charter, a document produced at a conference of Islamic states held in February 1972. In the case of Malaysia, although its population is multi-ethnic, Islam is entrenched in the constitution as the state religion and its special status, together with other symbols of Malayan-Muslim dominance, is an indication of an established hierachical political system. In such circumstances the signature by a Malaysian plenipoten-tiary of the Islamic Charter expressed a commitment to a domestic political pecking order because of the special relationship between adherence to the Islamic faith and social status as a Malay.

In the case of Indonesia, however, its present government is acutely conscious of the absence of any one great cultural and religious tradition, and a corresponding absence also of internal consensus about the essential identity of the state. The Government of Indonesia is dominated by a coterie of generals of a predominantly secular disposition whose experience and political outlook has been shaped by recurrent conflict with the forces of Islamic radicalism, whose vocal demands for a theo-cratic state were expressed formally just prior to the proclamation of Indonesian independence and also in insurgent action in West Java, North Sumatra and South Sulawesi during the 1950s. In consequence, the Indonesian Government has refused to countenance any international view of the country which might serve in any way to validate Islamic claims. It refused to permit its representative to sign the Islamic Charter on the grounds that its very designation 'would definitely mean that the signatories would be Islamic countries'. On the other hand, sensitivity to the internal political force of Islam, which expressed its strength in the general elections of July 1971, led the Indonesian Government to ensure the cancellation of a meeting of the World Council of Churches originally scheduled to be held in Jakarta during 1975.

The use of foreign policy to serve domestic needs, in order to repair or contain domestic cleavage and also to maintain the dominant position of a ruling administration, is a common feature of South-East Asia and elsewhere. But in some circumstances governments may be obliged to respond to genuine domestic pressures which may arise, for example, from a popular resentment of an external association. Such pressure may come from local entrepreneurs who resent the undue and ubiquitous economic presence of alien businessmen, as for example within a number of South-East Asian countries where extensive Japanese economic involvement has taken place, although the foreign policy response has been of a limited kind given the value placed on that involvement by governments in the region. Similarly undue political penetration has provoked domestic responses reflected in foreign policy initiatives. For example, in the Philippines there had long been agitation against American military bases represented by opposition nationalists as an affront to national sovereignty. Ironically, such pressures were resisted in great part while the democratic political system endured. It is only since the advent of the martial law regime of President Marcos that demands have been expressed by the Philippine Government that the status of the bases should be changed so that sovereignty could be shown to rest in Manila. This example, while taking cognisance of domestic pressures on government, is not intended to demonstrate any special relationship between such pressures and foreign policy. It is most apposite in illustrating an attempt by an administration to utilise an issue concerning which domestic interest has receded in order to serve its own ends. In the main, the domestic setting of foreign policy does not contain directing pressures which ordain the precise course of state action. It is much more often the case that foreign policy is directed to serve an internal goal which is essentially an adjunct of state-building.

The decision making process

Within the states of South-East Asia, the domain of foreign policy is normally the preserve of a few individuals and in some cases effective decisions are made by only one man. This practice has become increasingly commonplace within the region with the dismantling of political systems inherited from former colonial powers which provided greater opportunity for the articulation of extra-governmental interests. This has been the case in Burma, Indonesia and the Philippines, where military or quasi-military rule has been established with ultimate decision making of a highly personalised nature, given the respective positions of President Ne Win, President Suharto and President Marcos.

It is true to a great extent in Malaysia and Singapore — more in the case of the latter where there is no parliamentary opposition — where little more than the trappings of the Westminster Model have been maintained, and where the press is effectively emasculated. In the revolutionary states of Indochina which emerged during 1975, collective decision making of a kind is the exclusive preserve of politburos, although how it operates remains a mystery. Ironically, in Thailand, the one country not provided with a political model by a colonial power, and for so long identified with autocratic rule, but transformed politically between October 1973 and October 1976, there was a measure of opportunity for popular and parliamentary influence to be exerted on foreign policy issues. The prime example was that of the residual relationship with the United States after the Indochina War.

In the main, foreign policy making is a highly exclusive affair, for reasons not dissimilar to those which make it so in Western societies. One of these is that foreign policy making and the opportunity it provides for ceremonial display is one of the most prestigious under-takings in government. Thus as political power in South-East Asian states has tended to become concentrated increasingly in fewer hands, those on whom the political system tends to pivot exercise a jealous control over such matters. Not only does this practice insulate foreign policy from domestic influences, but it also makes the process unduly cumbersome and protracted as decisions, often of minimal import, cannot be made by the official foreign ministry hierarchy, but have to await the pleasure of one overburdened individual. One example of this problem has been demonstrated in the functioning of the regional organisation, the Association of South-East Asian Nations (ASEAN), which has set up a myriad of advisory committees over a range of issues of common concern but cannot progress much in regional co-operation. The problem of reaching decisions on a multilateral basis is aggravated when each advisory opinion on common policy has to be ratified by member states whose foreign policy process is heavily overloaded because of its quasi-monarchical nature. This situation may serve to explain other problems of initiative in co-operation among members of ASEAN and, for example, in the case of Indonesia, why foreign policy decisions often emerge as a consequence of crisis situations, when the issue or issues are so sharply defined that a decision is forced on the President in the absence of any opportunity for habitual deferral.

Of course, the states of South-East Asia do operate through the conventional vehicles of foreign ministries organised formally on geographic and functional lines. But very few of these ministries would appear to

33

have developed a sense of professionalism based on recognised methods of training and promotion. In the non-communist countries there is an established practice of using ambassadorial posts either as long service medals for political hacks or as places of temporary exile for political recalcitrants. In addition, the more important of such posts are filled by reliable confidants of the ruling few, in order to provide a direct line of political communication often by-passing bureaucratic networks. And where the military is dominant in government, as in Burma and Indonesia, not only overseas representation but also the formal bureaucratic structure of policy making reflects the subordinate position of the foreign ministry.

South-East Asia has thrown up its share of so-called idiosyncratic leaders whose style of rule has tended to be intensely flamboyant as well as personal. Sihanouk and Sukarno come to mind as leaders who have apparently exercised considerable personal licence in the making of foreign policy decisions in the opinion of some observers without any great sense of consistency. It would be as well to bear in mind, however, the reasoned argument of one scholar that in the case of so-called idiosyncratic aspects of foreign policy, only those idiosyncracies that neither violate dominant attitudes nor radically alter the domestic political configuration are likely to find expression in foreign policy. [3]

It should be stated also that where foreign policy has been identified with a particular leadership and correspondingly with a particular political order, there has not been any significant correlation in South-East Asian experience between change of that leadership and substantive foreign policy change. Indeed even when the change in political order has been of a radical and fundamental kind involving a total replacement of the ruling group, the degree of continuity in foreign policy can be quite remarkable. This feature is exemplified in the recent experience of Cambodia. Although there has been a complete social and political transformation within that once Buddhist Kingdom since April 1975, ideological commitment has not so eradicated the sense of national identity of the new masters of the country as to erase differences of tangible interest with their neighbour Vietnam, which is their traditional antagonist but ideologically akin to them. Thus, while undoubted differences obtain in terms of style and policy between the Cambodia of Prince Sihanouk and the country headed formally by Khieu Samphan, basic similarities exist in terms of the oft-discredited notion of national interest.

The impact of political succession on foreign policy, in circumstances where that policy has been identified closely with a particular leadership, has been generally diverse. One might contrast the foreign policies of Sukarno and Suharto in terms more of style than of substance. [4] Significant continuity stands out in the succession from U Nu to Ne Win in Burma, from Macapagal to Marcos in the Philippines, and from Ho Chi Minh to Le Duan in Vietnam. In these examples continuity of policy is less than remarkable because change of personality was less significant than the attendant persistence of dominant values. A contrasting example of discontinuity of a kind obtained in the succession in Malaysia from Tunku Abdul Rahman to the late Tun Abdul Razak, which was governed by changes in both domestic and environmental circumstances, yet without any corresponding substantial change in political system. In the case of Thailand, where major change did take place in the nature of the political system after the collapse of military government in October 1973, there was an element of undoubted continuity in the direction of the foreign policy of Marshal Thanom (at least from 1969) and that of his three civilian successors as Prime Minister; this was not, however, sustained after the 1976 *coup d'etat.*

The degree of generalisation that is possible from the examples cited above is somewhat limited. Personality, or more to the point personal leadership, is of undoubted importance in the actual making of foreign policy among the states of South-East Asia. But while individual leadership may be expressed in distinctive style, any radical discontinuity of policy would appear to arise primarily from changes in the very nature of domestic political order and from significant alterations in external environment. And even when both of these factors obtain, as we have seen in the case of Cambodia, there may be more than just a tendency for state behaviour to indicate not only a striking measure of continuity but also characteristics of the much discredited billiard ball model of international politics.

In terms of readily available data, only a sparse amount is known about the actual process of foreign policy decision making within the South-East Asian states. Some form of collective decision making of a prerogative kind would seem to be the case in the three socialist states of Indochina, but little is known of the collective leaderships concerned and to what extent decisions are the result of a standard deliberative procedure. A more conventional collective decision making also of a prerogative kind would seem to obtain in both Malaysia and Singapore, where cabinet systems of a conventional kind do operate, although in these cases inner circles and dominating individuals would appear to have the final say. In countries such as Burma, Indonesia and the Philippines, where personal leadership is more apparent irrespective of collective forms, decision making assumes a more Byzantine-like manner with court politics the major and unpredictable element. It is only in Thailand after October 1973 that there emerged a less exclusive process of decision making in which the component elements of the bureaucracy (including the military) and politicians articulated competing interests.

The external environment

The context comprised of the individual states of South-East Asia is much less than uniform. For example, unlike Africa there are no all-embracing regional conventional wisdoms which give rise to a rhetoric of regional identity. Neither the equivalent of Negritude nor white settler regimes provide a common reference point. The most extensive regional organisation − ASEAN, founded in August 1967 − comprises only five states and has not added to its numbers since inauguration. Its region-wide aspirations are denied by its conservative orientation; its members adopt the same attitude if not co-operative practice towards ideological challenge to social and economic order. They cannot tempt the adhesion of isolationist Burma and they cannot expect more than a *modus vivendi* with the revolutionary states of Indochina. Thus, although the ASEAN states adhere to a joint declaration of November 1971 advocating the eventual creation of 'a zone of peace, freedom and neutrality' coterminous with the region, their international economic associations, general political disposition and in some cases military connections make them appear part of a Western alignment.

Although the ASEAN states have been in special association for nearly a decade and have reached a limited consensus on trying to promote regional autonomy on a co-operative basis in order to contain disruptive intrusions, individual differences of interest arising from differences in individual circumstances have obstructed practical co-operation, and modified initial enthusiasm over regional visions. Thus ASEAN, which was established initially as an instrument through which to promote reconciliation after Indonesia's confrontation of Malaysia, and then evolved as a possible alternative vehicle for the management of regional relationships, has now come up against the dual barrier of internal discordance and intra-regional resistance. However, the Indochina states do not represent a solidary alternative regional pole in so far as their individual differences reflected in external associations inter-pose between ideological affinities. [5]

The extra-regional impact on the external setting has undoubtedly changed over the decades since the transfers of power, especially given the revision of American policy whereby South-East Asia — or at least its mainland portion — has been extracted from strategic perspective. External penetration continues throughout the region but no longer in dramatic form. The nature of the economies of the ASEAN states ensures close links with the Western-dominated international economy including Japanese interests, although this relationship does not mean an automatic vulnerability, as exemplified by Indonesia's successful attempt in 1976 to prise additional revenue from the American-owned oil companies. At the same time the socialist states are not completely free of external penetration. Their development priorities alone necessitate economic assistance from friendly patrons.

In retrospect, the experience of the region has been a subordinate one, yet the circumstances of external intervention and the impinging competitive nature of the international system has offered opportunities to overcome such subordination and to exploit such competition. Vietnam, in its resistance to American intervention and utilisation of Sino-Soviet conflict, represents an example of both kinds. Nonetheless the general condition of the states of the region has not changed fundamentally, in that economic and military weakness is the rule rather than the exception. This condition was exemplified by Indonesia, the largest and most populous state of the region and the most influential among the ASEAN states, which annexed the Eastern half of the island of Timor by force in December 1975, though not without exposing fundamental deficiencies in military organisation. Vietnam is, of course, the exception in terms of military capability, but the scale of developmental undertakings will place a heavy burden on national resources for many years to come.

Although tensions between states in South-East Asia manifest themselves recurrently, major threats to territorial integrity *per se* do not appear to be presented either by forces external to them or to the region as a whole. The irredentist claim by the Philippines to Sabah is of diminishing reality, while Indonesia's incorporation of East Timor was at the expense of residual *imperium*. Similarly, any challenge to the separate identity of the once British-protected state of Brunei in North Borneo is not likely to serve as a precedent, given the extent to which it is regarded in a similar light to Portuguese Timor. In general, threats to security which do exist arise not from any external challenge to the integrity of the state but from internal challenge to social and economic order, which may be supported from outside but which often has a regional minority focus. Such challenges direct the attentions of governments inwards and foreign policy priorities are appraised accordingly.

The transformation in the general external setting of South-East Asia arises from the fact that at one time there appeared to exist a close junction between the prospect of the kind of internal political change alluded to above and the politics of global balance. American military intervention was intended to deny such political change, which was regarded as likely to destabilise that balance. In the wake of the Indochina War, with a modified interest on the part of the United States focussing on the maritime states of the region, and with limited opportunity for competitive access for either China or the Soviet Union on a basis equivalent to that once enjoyed by the United States, South-East Asia possesses a reduced global significance. Indeed one way of pointing up its international condition would be to refute the parallel often drawn with the states of South-East Europe at the turn of the century. The states of South-East Asia may still be 'too large for cultural realities or too small for political ones', [6] but they are no longer the Balkans of the Orient in the sense that external powers will regard internal political changes as bearing on the central balance of power and respond accordingly.

South-East Asia extruded into the global system when its conflicts involved the competing interests of major extra-regional powers. These circumstances and these alone provided opportunities for men like Sihanouk and Sukarno to parade their nostrums on the world stage. In circumstances when the region has assumed a lesser significance in global terms, and has ceased to be a major arena for the slaking of competitive lusts, foreign policy has come to centre even more on domestic needs.

Conclusion

Common features arising from domestic social and economic circumstances and their regional expression give some sense of definition to what is otherwise little more than a category of convenience. The features which might be regarded as essentially representative of South-East Asia comprise an intrinsic diversity. This diversity, added to the general characteristics of Third World identity such as economic underdevelopment and limited international standing, governs the emphasis and orientation of foreign policy. Although once a more mixed enterprise involving heroics and stoicism in face of colonial residues and external intervention, the priorities of the late 1970s have become increasingly pragmatic. The animosities of the post-colonial relationships and the great gestures against the windmills of the international system have given way to more mundane yet vital considerations of distribution of international wealth which link states in South-East Asia to other parts of the Third World. Even the revolutionary states have turned their energies inwards at least for the time being, and hold out the prospect of a *modus vivendi* to their conservative neighbours who look increasingly to their domestic bases to prevent political emulation. For states which entered the contemporary international system in embryonic form, the fundamental priority has not changed and in consequence the maxim 'foreign policy begins at home' is no less apposite today than at the time of the transfers of power.

Bibliographic note

In the main, the states of South-East Asia either individually or collectively have not attracted the attention of authors concerned specifically with testing theoretical propositions about foreign policy. The bulk of the literature on foreign policy practice deals with one-country studies or with specific disputes or relationships involving South-East Asian states.

Some consideration of the relationship between state-making and foreign policy can be found in John Badgeley *Asian Development*, Free Press, New York 1971; Michael Leifer, *Dilemmas of Statehood in Southeast Asia*, University of British Columbia Press, Vancouver, and Asian Pacific Press, Singapore 1972; and Richard Butwell, *Southeast Asia: A Political Introduction*, Praeger, New York 1975. State definition is discussed in Robert L. Solomons, 'Boundary Concepts and Practices in Southeast Asia' *World Politics* October 1970; and Alastair Lamb, *Asian Frontiers: Studies in a Continuing Problem*, Praeger, New York 1968, Chs 8–10. The relevance of domestic setting is treated in terms of a particular example in Franklin B. Weinstein, *Indonesia Abandons Confrontation: An Inquiry into the Functions of Indonesian Foreign Policy*, Cornell, Ithaca 1969; and in Jon M. Reinhart, *Foreign Policy and National Integration: The Case of Indonesia*, Yale, New Haven 1971. The sole general account of the apparatus of foreign policy making is Peter J. Boyce, 'The Machinery of Southeast Asian Regional Diplomacy' in Lau Teik Soon (ed.), *New Directions in the International Relations of Southeast Asia: The Great Powers and Southeast Asia*, Singapore University Press, Singapore 1973.

Elitist and idiosyncratic influences are discussed by Werner Levi in *The Challenge of World Politics in South and Southeast Asia*, Prentice-

Hall, New Jersey 1968, Ch. 1; and in Bernard K. Gordon, *The Dimensions of Conflict in Southeast Asia*, Prentice-Hall, New Jersey 1966, Ch. 4, while ideology is examined in Donald E. Weatherbee, *Ideology in Indonesia: Sukarno's Indonesian Revolution*, Yale, New Haven 1966, Ch. 3. Regional environment provides the focus for much of Peter Lyon's *War and Peace in South-East Asia*, Oxford UP, London 1969 and Sudershan Chawla et al. (eds) *Southeast Asia under the New Balance of Power*, Praeger, New York 1974. Franklin B. Weinstein's 'The Uses of Foreign Policy in Indonesia', *World Politics*, April 1972 is the sole example of an attempt to provide a general theory of foreign policy in the light of the experience of a South-East Asian state.

The literature dealing specifically with the foreign policy practice of the South-East Asian states takes the form of both general and individual country studies. The former include Russell H. Fifield, *The Diplomacy of Southeast Asia: 1945–1958*, Harper, New York 1958; Wayne Wilcox et al. (eds), *Asia and the International System*, Winthrop, Cambridge, Mass. 1972, Chs 5–8; and Michael Leifer, *The Foreign Relations of the New States*, Longman, Melbourne 1974. Ralph Pettman in *Small Power Politics and International Relations in South-East Asia*, Sydney 1976, discusses four sets of relations with external powers within a theoretical framework.

Individual country studies include: W. C. Johnstone, *Burma's Foreign Policy*, Cornell, Ithaca 1966; Donald E. Neuchterlein, *Thailand and the Struggle for South-east Asia*, Cornell, Ithaca 1965; Roger Smith, *Cambodia's Foreign Policy*, Cornell, Ithaca 1965; Michael Leifer, *Cambodia: The Search for Security*, Praeger, New York 1967; Peter Boyce, *Malaysia and Singapore in International Diplomacy*, Sydney 1968; Robert O. Tilman, *Malaysian Foreign Policy*, Research Analysis Corporation, McLean, Virginia 1969; Dick Wilson, *The Future Role of Singapore*, Oxford UP/RIIA, London 1972; Ide Anak Agung Gde Agung, *Twenty Years of Indonesian Foreign Policy 1945–1965*, Mouton, The Hague 1973; and Milton W. Meyer, *A Diplomatic History of the Philippine Republic*, University of Hawaii, Honolulu 1965.

Specific disputes and issues relating to the region are dealt with in B. K. Gordon, *The Dimensions of Conflict in Southeast Asia*, Prentice-Hall, New Jersey 1968; Michael Leifer, *The Philippine Claim to Sabah*, Hull University, Hull 1968; J. A. C. Mackie, *Konfrontasi: The Indonesian-Malaysian Dispute 1963–1966*, Oxford UP, Kuala Lumpur 1974; Cyril E. Black et al., *Neutralization and World Politics*, Princeton UP, Princeton 1968; and Dick Wilson, *The Neutralization of Southeast-Asia*, Oxford UP, New York 1975.

Notes

[1] The ten comprise Burma, Thailand, Vietnam, Laos, Cambodia, Malaysia, Singapore, Indonesia, the Philippines, and the minuscule Sultanate of Brunei whose foreign relations are conducted by the government of the United Kingdom.

[2] See R. L. Solomons, 'Boundary Concepts and Practices in Southeast Asia', *World Politics*, vol. 23, no. 1, October 1970, pp.1–23.

[3] F. B. Weinstein, 'The Uses of Foreign Policy in Indonesia: An Approach to the Analysis of Foreign Policy in the Less Developed Countries', *World Politics*, vol. 24, no. 3, April 1972, pp.356–81.

[4] See Michael Leifer, 'Continuity and Change in Indonesian Foreign Policy', *Asian Affairs*, vol. 60, no. 2, June 1973, pp.173–80.

[5] Ellen J. Hammer, 'Indochina: Communist but Nonaligned', *Problems of Communism*, vol. 25, no. 3, May–June 1976, pp.1–17.

[6] Clifford Geertz, 'The Socio-Cultural Context of Policy in Southeast Asia', in William Henderson (ed.), *Southeast Asia: Problems of United States Policy*, MIT Press, Cambridge, Mass. 1963, p.49.

3   The Middle East

A. I. DAWISHA

The Middle East: A conceptual definition

The Middle East is an area of intensive political activity, and is usually
regarded as the most volatile and politically explosive region in the
world. Since the end of the Second World War, the Middle East has under-
gone persistent and chronic political upheavals which have been
primarily due to the high level of inter-state conflict and intra-state
instability. This regional volatility has been made even more acute by the
intrusive activities of the Great Powers in Middle Eastern affairs;
activities which have assumed the form of political, cultural and
economic penetration, as well as outright military intervention. During
these last two decades, however, superpower intrusion into the regional
system has increasingly occurred in the form of massive military aid
accorded to competing and avowedly antipathetic client states in the area.
Due to this combination of indigenous regional instability and great
power penetration, it is not surprising that the states of the Middle East
have been very active in regional and international affairs. The analysis
in this chapter, therefore, will endeavour to identify and examine the
domestic, regional and extra-regional factors which, in their totality,
have determined the nature and substance of foreign policy making in the
Middle East.

Before proceeding any further, however, a basic conceptual question has
first to be answered: what exactly constitutes the Middle East? Unlike
other international regions such as Africa, South America, South-East
Asia or the Caribbean, the Middle East as a geographically based entity is
a rather nebulous term. Indeed, there has been little agreement among
specialists in the field on the accurate geographical designation of the
Middle East. It seems to be an arbitrary term used mainly for purposes of
convenience rather than precision. Like its forerunner, the 'Near East',
which was used by nineteenth-century Europeans, and which usually
included the Balkans, 'the Middle East' is a phrase generally utilised to
describe the area between Europe and the Far East. Even disregarding the
blatant Eurocentrism of the term, there still is no universal agreement on
the delineation of its geographical boundary. At its narrowest, the term

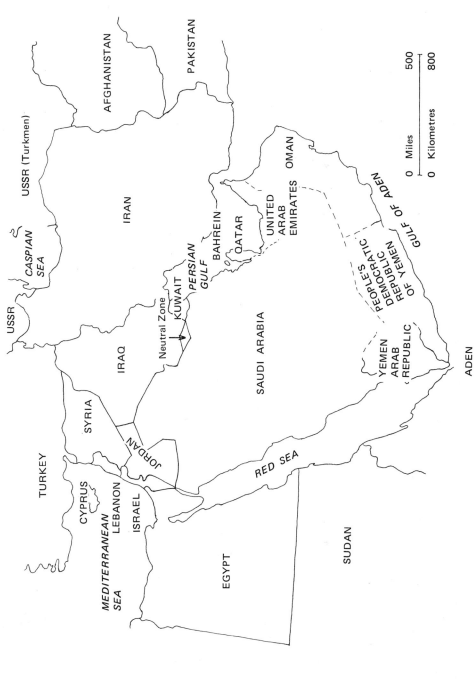

Map 3 The Middle East (for African Middle East States, see map 4)

43

'Middle East' is confined to the area covering South-West Asia and Egypt. At the other extreme, the term is deemed to include, in addition to the aforementioned location, Afghanistan in Asia, the North African states plus Somalia, Ethiopia, Sudan and Mauritania in Africa, and Turkey, Cyprus and Greece in Europe. [1] To eliminate possible confusion, therefore, the Middle East will be defined in this chapter as a region containing twenty-one states which span three continents. In Europe, there is Turkey; in Asia, we find Syria, Lebanon, Jordan, Israel, Iraq, Iran, Saudi Arabia, North Yemen, South Yemen, and the five Gulf states of Kuwait, Bahrain, Qatar, UAE and Oman; and in Africa, there are Egypt, Sudan, Libya, Algeria, Tunisia and Morocco.

The analytical framework

The framework employed in this chapter will follow the pioneering scheme suggested by James Rosenau for the purpose of analysing foreign policy behaviour. [2] Rosenau conceived of foreign policy behaviour as sequences of interaction which span national boundaries and which unfold in three stages: the initiatory, implementive and responsive stages. These stages, according to Rosenau, encompass respectively the independent, intervening, and dependent variables of foreign policy analysis. [3] It must be noted, however, that the dependent variables of foreign policy behaviour lie outside the scope of our analysis because they relate to the external conditions and activities that occur as a result of a foreign policy undertaking. Since the concern of this chapter is to explore the making of foreign policy, the analysis will accordingly be confined to the independent and intervening variables only.

The independent variables include all human and non-human factors and conditions which influence decision makers to follow a specific foreign policy. These variables, sometimes conceptualised as 'policy inputs', can have their origins either in the external environment or in the domestic environment. The former contains all situational and relational conditions and activities existing outside the territorial boundary of the state. These conditions and activities usually operate at two significant levels: the global and the regional. In the domestic environment, the influences on the decision makers emanate from within the territorial boundary of the state. These influences usually include such factors as geography, demography, culture and religion, the economic and military capabilities, and the role of pressure groups and public opinion. It is important to note here that the independent variables, whether located in the external or domestic environments, will be examined according to the conceptual differentiation between the operational and psychological environments. [4] In other words, the analysis will not only be concerned with the objective elements of the independent variables, but also with the way these elements are perceived by the decision making elites.

The intervening variables refer to the processes, procedures and personalities whose task is to convert policy inputs (independent variables) into policy outputs (dependent variables). [5] Thus, in this section we shall deal with the constitutional and institutional structure of the Middle Eastern states, the composition and circulation of the decision making elite, the interactions and relationships that exist among the members of the elite, and the role of 'personality' on foreign policy behaviour.

The external environment

In the immediate post-war period, the global system became polarised into two blocs grouped around two major actors who possessed awesome levels of destructive power and who were separated by extreme ideological antipathy. These two actors were the United States and the Soviet Union. However, during the late 1950s and early 1960s, the global system underwent marked structural and behavioural changes which weakened the polarisation of the system. These changes included (1) the emergence of units such as China, Japan and the infant EEC from their earlier situations of economic and/or military dependence on the superpowers to positions of high status in the system, (2) the decolonisation process which created numerous independent units, many of whom followed the non-conformist policy of non-alignment to either bloc, and (3) the gradual perceptual transformation which occurred at the superpower level and which led both parties to accept the maxim that ideological polarity need not produce military confrontation.

As a result of these changes, the structure of global relations in the Middle East underwent an important modification. Both superpowers tacitly agreed that the pursuit of their conflicting interests in the region need not develop into actual military confrontation. An implicit understanding seems to have been reached that local conflicts would be contained regionally and not allowed to spill over into the global arena. This was manifestly evident from superpower behaviour during the October 1973 war. [6] Nevertheless, apart from this modification, superpower competition and rivalry in the Middle East were vigorously pursued on all levels, especially, and most crucially, through the injection of massive military aid, which included the dispatch of sophisticated military equipment to conflicting states in the region (see Table 3.1).

Table 3.1

Total arms transfers of major suppliers to ten core
Middle Eastern states, 1965–74
(million current dollars)

	United States	Soviet Union	United Kingdom	France	Others	Total
Algeria	3	265	1	8	–	277
Egypt	–	2,425	7	18	181	2,631
Iraq	11	1,033	11	19	159	1,233
Iran	1,718	574	185	–	321	2,798
Israel	3,172	–	26	131	51	3,380
Jordan	324	–	52	6	41	423
Libya	66	200	76	309	98	749
Saudi Arabia	372	–	212	188	48	820
Syria	3	1,573	1	–	117	1,694
Turkey	1,959	–	–	–	260	2,219

Source: United States Arms Control and Disarmament Agency, *World Military Expenditures and Arms Trade, 1965–1974,* Washington DC, 1976, pp.73–6

This intrusive activity of the superpowers has obviously had a profound impact on the foreign policies of the Middle Eastern states. Naturally, because of the dynamics of the patron–client relationship, the superpowers have sometimes constrained the policies and actions of regional states. Thus, for example, the decision by the United States in the spring of 1975 to freeze an Israeli request for $3,000 million in military aid was meant to induce Israel to accept an interim agreement with Egypt. Indeed, Israel duly complied in September 1975, albeit after extracting from the United States better terms, including the promise of supplying Israel with the Pershing surface-to-surface missile. Similarly, the refusal of the Soviet Union to grant President Sadat's repeated request for a long-term moratorium on the repayment of Soviet credits can be interpreted as a 'punishment' of Egypt for its increasing rapport with the United States after the October 1973 war.

While successful in these two instances, in some cases superpower pressure has not achieved the desired results. Because of the competitive nature of the polarised system, client states have sometimes been able to modify, alter or completely sabotage the policies of patron states. Thus, utilising its crucial strategic position on the southern flanks of NATO as a bargaining ploy, Turkey has been successful in rejecting vigorous and repeated American demands to reach a compromise over Cyprus which would satisfy the pro-Greek United States Congress. Similarly, the Soviet Union's adamant refusal to supply President Sadat with offensive weapons with which Egypt could regain the territories occupied by Israel, led to the expulsion of all Soviet advisers from Egypt in July 1972. Sadat's 'electric shock' [7] was so successful that sophisticated Soviet weaponry soon began to flow into Egypt, thus making the October 1973 war possible.

Indeed, because of the region's strategic and economic importance, various Middle Eastern states have been able to overcome the strict limitations traditionally associated with the patron–client dependency relationship. Thus, Egypt's position as the leader of the Arab world in the early 1960s allowed her to extract simultaneously from the two competing superpowers massive economic aid. [8] This happened at a time when President Nasser was virtually following an 'anti-Western' foreign policy and an 'anti-communist' domestic policy. Contemporary Iran is a similar case. Membership of the Central Treaty Organisation and an avowedly pro-Western posture have not constrained Iran's relations with the Soviet Union, which have included diplomatic interactions and representations, multifaceted trade relations and even military agreements. Indeed, in other cases, the flexibility was such that regional–global relations could have been best understood by reference to intra-regional interactions. For example, in recent years, the nature of Libyan–Soviet relations seemed to depend on Libya's posture towards Egypt. When in 1973, Soviet–Egyptian relations were very cordial, Libya's foreign policy orientation was explicitly anti-Soviet, and the Libyan leaders accused the Soviet Union of harbouring imperialist tendencies towards the Middle East generally and Egypt specifically. However, in the wake of the post-1973 Soviet–Egyptian rupture, Libyan relations with the Soviet Union abruptly and dramatically improved to the extent that the Egyptians accused the Libyan leaders of being Soviet agents in the area.

The preceding discussion suggests the existence of a fluid system in the linkages between global and regional actors. As an independent variable, the global system can, in some instances, effectively constrain, and even direct, the foreign policies of local powers. This is especially the case when a particular client state is inexorably linked through cultural, economic and military ties to the patron state. In other instances, however, when local states can succeed in achieving a certain amount of manoeuvrability, primarily through manipulating superpower competition, the global system as an independent variable can be transformed into a capability of the local state's foreign policy.

The next level of interaction in the external environment is the regional system which forms the immediate area of activity of the local states. Their interaction at this level is both intense and multifaceted. These interactions are conducted along two axes. First, there is the Arab—Israeli conflict. The intense hostility existing between the antagonists in this relationship has produced a condition of enduring conflict which has persisted for nearly thirty years and, moreover, shows very little propensity towards being resolved. With its ideological, human, religious and economic bases, the Arab—Israeli conflict must rank as the major focus of activity in the Middle Eastern regional system. The second axis of interaction concerns the other intra-regional relations which have reflected intermittently conditions of both conflict and co-operation. Inter-Arab relations and inter-state activity in the Persian Gulf area are the most salient of these concerns. [9] In both cases, conditions of conflict, varying from the physical (wars and military interventions) to the verbal (propaganda), have tended to dominate state interactions along this axis. However, while overshadowed by the persistence of regional conflict, there have nevertheless been some co-operative conditions and activities in the area. These have usually taken the form of summit conferences attended by regional heads of state, and co-operation in regional organisations such as the League of Arab States and the Organisation of the Petroleum Exporting Countries (OPEC), many of whose members are Middle Eastern states.

Obviously, the multilevel activities on both axes of regional interaction profoundly affect and influence the conduct of the foreign policies of the local powers. Thus, for example, due to the persistence of high-intensity regional conflict, local states have tended to exhibit a clear propensity towards utilising military means for achieving their foreign policy objectives. Indeed, when compared with the other regions of the international system, the Middle East registers a very high frequency in the occurrence of regional violence. Thus, along the axis of Arab—Israeli relations, the Middle East has endured, since the end of the Second World War, four major wars: the first in 1948 involved Israel and all the Arab states; the second in 1956 was confined to Egypt and Israel; and the third and fourth in 1967 and 1973 respectively saw Israel confronting the forces of the Arab world.

Similarly, major eruptions of violence have occurred along the second axis of regional interactions. In the 1960s, there were the war between Egypt and Saudi Arabia over the Yemen which lasted from 1962 to 1967, and the border war between Algeria and Morocco in 1963. Three major military operations have so far occurred in the 1970s: the Iraqi–Iranian war which was intermittently pursued between 1969 and 1975; the Algerian–Moroccan military conflict over the Spanish Sahara during 1975–76; and the Syrian military interventions in Jordan in 1970 and in the Lebanon in 1976.

Cutting across the two axes of conflict interaction lie the activities of the Palestine Liberation Organisation (PLO) as a non-state actor in Middle Eastern politics. There can be no doubt that the operations of the Palestinian guerrillas in the area have considerably intensified the level of inter-state regional conflict. Since 1965, the Palestinians, with varying degrees of success, have waged an obdurate guerrilla campaign against Israel. In addition to the numerous infiltrations and subversive activities inside Israel, the Palestinians, helped by the Jordanian army, engaged the Israeli forces in a major battle at Karemeh in Jordan in 1968. Moreover, guerrilla activity led to a number of Israeli armed interventions in Jordan and Lebanon between 1965 and 1975. Along the other axis of regional interactions, the Palestinian guerrillas were actively engaged in the civil wars in Jordan in 1970 and in Lebanon in 1975–76; and as such they could be regarded as having contributed to the ensuing Syrian military interventions in the two countries.

What is becoming clear from the discussion so far is that the accepted contention, which suggests that physical coercion 'is frequently the last [foreign policy instrument] to be used, because the losses that may be incurred by the use of force may be very high', [10] is not borne out by these examples of conflict activity and behaviour in Middle Eastern politics. On the contrary, it could be persuasively argued that, because of the high level of regional conflict, Middle Eastern states seem to have accepted the use of force as a viable, legitimate and even attractively easy method of achieving foreign policy objectives.

Because of the prominence of high-intensity conflict in the region, co-operative relationships have lacked an independent momentum of their own. Apart from OPEC, in which economic considerations have successfully subsumed political rivalries, efforts at co-operation have tended frequently to be a function of conflict behaviour. For example, the first summit meeting of the Arab heads of state in Cairo in January 1964, which heralded two years of regional tranquillity, was organised in order to respond to Israel's decision to divert the head waters of the river Jordan, and to resolve the Egyptian–Saudi Arabian conflict over the Yemen. Similarly, the purpose behind the Khartoum summit meeting in August 1967 was to evaluate the Arab response to Israel's crushing victory in the June 1967 war. Indeed, the conference produced a militant resolution which reaffirmed the Arab position of 'no peace with Israel, no recognition of Israel, no negotiations with it'. [11] The conferences which followed usually met either to discuss the Arab–Israeli impasse or inter-Arab conflicts, such as the September 1970 meeting in Cairo which was assembled during the Jordanian civil war. Nor is the situation in the League of Arab States much different. In fact, the League has frequently acted as theatre for the various inter-Arab conflicts and rivalries of the time. Arab states have usually used the League as an instrument of their foreign policy, particularly for propaganda purposes, and consequently, contrary to its intended goal, the League has, in various instances, perpetuated and even intensified conflict in the area. For example, the bitter hostility which pervaded the Arab League meeting in Shtoura in Lebanon in August 1962 constituted an indirect input into Egypt's decision to intervene militarily in the Yemen in September 1962.

Conceptually separate from, but acting as a reinforcement to, high-level conflict in the regional system, is the intensely ideological nature of intra-regional activity. Thus, the pervasion of strong nationalist ideology forms the second systemic force operating at the regional level. The four major nationalist ideologies in the Middle East are Arab, Iranian and Turkish nationalisms, and Zionism in the case of Israel. Although contiguous, each boasts an independent identity manifested by a different language and a separate historical and cultural development. Arab nationalism represents the intellectual repository of a great civilisation which lasted for over 700 years, and which, at its height, stretched from China in the east to France in the west. After the disintegration of the Arab Empire in the sixteenth century, the Arabic language and the Islamic faith ensured the perpetuation of Arab nationalism, which flourished again with the political and social awakening of the Arab people during the late nineteenth and early twentieth centuries. The Iranians boast an even older civilisation in the great sixth century BC Achaemenian Empire which extended throughout the contemporary Middle East. Although defeated by Alexander in 330 BC, and later overrun by Arabs, Turks and Mongols, the Iranians successfully maintained their ethnic and linguistic identity until the emergence of a Sovereign Iranian Kingdom in the fifteenth century. Similarly, Turkish nationalism owes its potency to the historical legacy of the vast Ottoman Empire, whose territory, during the sixteenth and seventeenth centuries, stretched from

50

the Arabian Peninsula to Algeria and from Sudan to South Russia. Its final collapse in 1918 only served to heighten the nationalist sentiment, thus making possible the emergence of modern Turkey under the intensely nationalist leadership of Kamal Attaturk. Finally, the establishment and perpetuation of the state of Israel owes much to the nationalist doctrine of Zionism, which advocates the return of the Jewish people to the land of their ancestors. Developed in 1896 by Theodor Herzl, Zionism, like the other three nationalist ideologies, looks back to an historical inspiration, in this case the old Jewish Kingdom in Palestine which lasted from the twelfth century BC until the fall of Jerusalem to the Babylonians in 586 BC. Here again, ethnic identification, religious affinity and linguistic continuity have constituted the major components of Jewish nationalism.

The high ideological content prevalent at the regional level has obviously influenced the conduct and direction of the foreign policies of the local states. Thus, a major underlying determinant of the Arab–Israeli impasse has been the irreconcilable conflict existing between the two opposing ideologies of Arab nationalism and Zionism. Since both ideologies have laid claim to the same piece of territory (Palestine to the Arab nationalist, Israel to the Zionist), each, therefore, has been perceived by the opposing 'camp' as an expansionist doctrine. Moreover, the exclusivist nature of both ideologies has severely restricted communication and as such has increased the level of perceptual hostility and mistrust. This ideological polarity has naturally tended to limit the alternatives open to the decision makers, and consequently, it could be argued that, in the Arab–Israeli case, the ideological factor has acted as an effective systemic constraint on the foreign policies of the Arab states and Israel.

While not so prominent as the Arab–Israeli conflict, political and territorial disputes among other Middle Eastern states have also been conducted along ideological lines. For example, since 1939, when France consented to cede to Turkey the Sanjaq of Alexandretta (Iskenderun) in Northern Syria, the Syrians and the Turks have persistently invoked the nationalist contention that the disputed territory has always fallen within the historical boundaries of their respective motherland. Similarly, Iran's claim to sovereignty over Bahrain throughout the 1950s and 1960s was based primarily on the nationalist claim that prior to 1783 Bahrain had formed an 'indivisible' part of the Persian Empire. Indeed, until its formal independence in 1970, Bahrain constituted a major point of tension between Arab and Iranian nationalisms.

In conclusion, therefore, influences emanating from the external environment have constituted important determinants of the foreign policies of local states. Because the Middle East is a highly penetrated region, inputs from the global system, especially from the superpowers, have acted either as constraints on, or capabilities of, the foreign policies of regional states. Similarly, the existence of systemic influences at the regional level, particularly in the form of high-intensity regional conflict and high-level ideological content have played an important role in shaping and directing the foreign policies of local states.

The domestic environment

Some international relations analysts have argued that a state's geography is the most central and permanent of all the domestic independent variables. [12] While such a claim is probably exaggerated, nevertheless, the geographic factor does constitute an important determinant of foreign policy. This is particularly true of the Middle East, whose importance as a region throughout the centuries could be related primarily to its location as the bridge between the West and the East. Indeed, its strategic disposition constituted one important reason for the extreme interest shown by the European imperialist powers in the area during the nineteenth and twentieth centuries.

The general withdrawal of the European powers from the Middle East between 1920 and 1970 left in its wake a number of states created by the departing imperialist powers. These states were on the whole artificial creations whose legitimacy was based not on any geographic, ethnic, or religious rationale, but on purely political criteria designed to serve the interests of the European powers. Because of the consequent fluidity in the designation of state boundaries, Middle Eastern countries have become preoccupied with territorial issues; and as such, their foreign policies, particularly at the regional level, have been greatly influenced by the geographic factor. Thus, for example, immediately after Britain had granted independence to Kuwait in 1961, General Kassem of Iraq laid claim to the neighbouring and newly-independent country, arguing that Kuwait formed an integral part of the historical boundary of Iraq, and that its separation from 'the mother country' was a ploy of British 'imperialist' policy. [13] The ensuing crisis necessitated the re-entry of British troops into Kuwait, and subsequently the dispatch of a joint Arab military force to the country to safeguard its newly-won independence. Since then, Iraq has transmitted several muted, yet clear, signals to Kuwait and other regional and international actors that its concern over the boundary issue is still alive. Similarly, due to the ambiguous status of the Spanish Sahara, the departure of the colonial power in 1975 precipitated an immediate triangular conflict between the neighbouring states of Morocco, Algeria and Mauritania over the ownership of the territory. Indeed, this was the second territorial clash between Morocco and Algeria; the first, which occurred in the wake of the French withdrawal from Algeria in 1963, concerned disagreements over the precise designation of the boundary between the two former French colonies. In addition to these two cases, the last three decades have witnessed a number of territorial disputes occurring between neighbouring countries in the Middle East, such as those involving Turkey and Syria, Saudi Arabia and Iraq, Qatar and Bahrain, North and South Yemen, and Iran's territorial disputes with Iraq, Bahrain and the UAE. Naturally, these local feuds and disagreements have in no small measure contributed to the general instability of the area.

Of all the Middle Eastern states, however, Israel has been the one most concerned with territorial issues. Apart from the controversy surrounding the nature and location of Israel's borders, which ranges from the maximalist conception of Eretz Israel to the minimalist view of the country returning to its pre-1967 borders, Israel's preoccupation with its geography also relates to matters of strategy and security. For a small country which, for almost thirty years, has been surrounded by antagonistic neighbours, Israel's geographic situation, particularly before the June 1967 war, was a strategist's nightmare. As such, Israeli citizens and decision makers alike have tended to develop something akin to a security complex, which has propelled the issue of defensible borders to the forefront of Israel's foreign policy, [14] an issue which has significantly contributed to the inflexibility of the Israeli position regarding a possible settlement in the Middle East conflict.

The conduct of foreign policy is also influenced by demographic factors. The size, composition and characteristics of a country's population are important determinants of the nature and direction of the state's external relations. A large population can be a tremendous capability since it can be utilised as a reservoir for industrial expansion and military might. In addition to this objective dimension, a large population can enhance the power and influence of a state in its international activity by affecting the perceptions of other states in the international system. This is certainly one important reason why Egypt has always occupied a central and leading position in the Arab world, since Egypt's population alone constitutes nearly 30 per cent of the total population of the Arab world. [15] Similarly, Iran and Turkey owe their positions of influence in the regional system, if not wholly then partially, to their comparatively large populations. Conversely the immensely wealthy yet sparsely populated micro-states of the Persian Gulf have very rarely been able to translate their considerable economic power into effective political influence.

Yet, this is a partial picture. The size of a population should not be analysed in isolation, but must be related to the resources of the country in order to attain a more comprehensive assessment of the influence of demographic factors. Thus, while constituting a capability for the reasons discussed above, Egypt's large population has increased to such proportions that it has also tended to limit Egypt's foreign policy, primarily in the way it has caused the political leadership to divert resources from the external to the domestic sector. Indeed, the necessity to support a large population is a major reason for Egypt's seeming withdrawal from the Middle East conflict. Accordingly, it seems that of all the contemporary Middle Eastern states, only Iran, which possesses the manpower and the resources, has the capability to attain great power status.

Ethnic affiliation is another element of the demographic factor. It is obvious that heterogenous ethnic groupings can weaken the unity of a country and consequently can constitute a distinct limitation on the achievement of foreign policy goals. More ominously, fragmentation of society can lead to outside intervention. Thus, the civil war in Iraq between the Arabs and the Kurds in 1968–74 facilitated the military intervention of Iran. Similarly, the civil war in Jordan between the Jordanian army and the Palestinian guerrillas in 1970 precipitated Syrian military entry into the war, which, in turn, nearly led to Israeli, and even American, intervention. Furthermore, in both cases, the civil wars adversely affected the conduct of the states' foreign policies. In the October 1973 war, the Iraqis had to await a promise of a truce from the Kurds and the Iranians before they could commit their troops to the hard pressed Syrian front. The Jordanian leadership were even more constrained in their external relations during the years of domestic disintegration which spanned 1968–70. The complete preoccupation with the domestic situation imposed a general paralysis on Jordan's international activity to the extent that a coherent foreign policy was almost non-existent. Finally, while lying dormant for many years, ethnic divisions in Israel have recently become more apparent and more acute. The increasing domestic turmoil in Israel in recent years related in no small measure to the ever widening schisms existing between the Ashkenasi (European) Jews, the Sephardi (Oriental) Jews, and the Israeli Arabs. Indeed, it is probable that in years to come these divisions will prove a far greater threat to Israel's existence than the hostility of neighbouring Arab states.

Another potent influence on the foreign policies of Middle Eastern states is the religious factor. The majority of the populations of the Middle Eastern states, except for Israel, are adherents of the Islamic faith. Indeed, many of these populations' values and norms emanate from the inspiration and moral teachings of Islam. Consequently, Islam can be effectively utilised as an instrument for deriving public support from the traditionally devout and conservative Middle Eastern Moslem populations. In this respect, the religious factor can prove a distinct capability for the decision making elite. For example, during his bitter conflict with Saudi Arabia over the Yemen in the 1960s, President Nasser of Egypt frequently used the influence wielded by Cairo's al-Azhar (Islam's oldest intellectual institution) in the Moslem Arab world to counteract the undoubted religious advantages the Saudi leaders possessed as the guardians of Islam's holiest shrine, the Kaaba. Thus, when the Saudi leaders equated Nasser's socialism with anti-Islamic atheism, the Sheikh of al-Azhar took it upon himself not only to sanction socialism as an intrinsic component of Islam, but also to present it as a crucial element in the system of values which characterised a new and vigorous Arab and Islamic revival under the leadership of President Nasser. [16]

However, given the existence of various sects within Islam, an over-emphasis on the religious variable can prove counter-productive. Although the Sunnis constitute the major sect of Islam, an undue concentration on religion can alienate the other Islamic sects such as the ruling Shiis of Iran and Wahabis of Saudi Arabia, and the influential Allawis of Syria, Shiis of Iraq, Zaidis of Yemen and Druzes of Syria and Lebanon. Moreover, an extreme utilisation of Islam can antagonise the economically influential Christian minorities of the Arab world. Indeed, there can be no doubt that the hostility of the Lebanese Christians towards Arab nationalism and Arab unity stems from their almost pathological fear of a Moslem domination of Lebanon. Another example can be found in the effect of Islamic sectarianism on Iraqi–Iranian relations. Membership of the same sect has contributed to a strong fraternal bond between the Iranians and the Shiis of Iraq who form the majority of the population. In recent years, the Iraqi Baathist leadership, most of whose members belong to the minority Sunni sect, have frequently accused the Iranian leaders of trying to exacerbate religious divisions in Iraq for purely irridentist purposes. Accordingly, the religious factor was a potent determinant of the antagonistic relations which existed between Iraq and Iran in the years 1969 to 1975.

In Israel, too, the religious factor constitutes a primary force. While it is true that Zionism is a political and secular doctrine, which is based on the attachment of world Jewry to Zion over the last two thousand years, it is, nevertheless, argued 'that this attachment was overwhelmingly based on the religious vision'. [17] As such, the political and religious dimensions of Jewish nationalism tend to overlap considerably. For example, in present day Israel, it is only through strict rabbinical exegesis that a Jewish national can be defined. Thus, according to Michael Brecher, Israel's Jewishness 'pervades thought, feeling, belief and behaviour in the political realm'. [18] It is thus obvious that the Jewish faith provides a highly integrative societal force, and as such acts as a powerful capability for Israel's decision making elite in their pursuit of foreign policy goals. Indeed, the preservation of Israel's Jewish character has been the primary value of Israel's foreign policy over the last thirty years, as well as constituting a major determinant of Israel's foreign policy behaviour towards its Arab neighbours.

The next component of the domestic environment which influences foreign policy making is the economic factor. Since decision makers formulate and execute policy objectives according to the images they have of the relative power of their state in comparison with other states, the economy of the country becomes an important determinant of foreign policy behaviour. Thus, a healthy economy can raise capital internally as well as invest and grant economic aid externally. Such activities will naturally increase the bargaining power of the decision makers in their pursuit of foreign policy goals. Conversely, a weak economy which is vulnerable to externally generated forces can severely limit the decision makers' freedom of manoeuvrability, and as such can become a potent constraint on the achievement of foreign policy goals.

The primary source of wealth in the Middle East is oil. The region contains more than two-thirds of the proven oil reserves in the world. Europe and Japan are almost entirely dependent on Middle Eastern oil, and it is estimated that by 1985 nearly 35 per cent of United States oil consumption may have to come from the Middle East. [19] This condition of dependence has encouraged the oil-producing countries to utilise their precious commodity as an effective instrument of foreign policy. Thus, when the 1973 October war erupted, the Arab oil ministers met in Kuwait and decided to use the oil weapon for the Arab cause. Consequently, they reduced their exports by 10 per cent as compared with the average September output and followed this reduction with a further cut of 25 per cent in November. The Arab ministers made it clear that these cuts would be directed only at unfriendly countries. This induced an immediate response from the consumer countries. At a meeting in Brussels, the European Economic Community (EEC) issued a declaration which was clearly sympathetic to the Arab cause, and this was promptly followed by a similar pronouncement from the Tanaka government in Japan. [20] In this case, the oil weapon was dramatically successful in achieving the foreign policy goals of the Arab countries, but whether it can be utilised again with the same effectiveness is open to conjecture.

It must be noted, however, that not all of the Middle Eastern countries are blessed with oil, and as such the phenomenon of a healthy economy is not universal in the Middle East. Indeed, some of the Middle Eastern states are characterised by very weak economic structures. A good indicator of the relative strength of a country's economy is the state of its trade balance, since it is usually the surplus states which tend to invest in, and grant economic aid to, foreign countries. On the other hand, countries with a relatively large trade balance deficit tend to become dependent on foreign aid for internal capital investment and balance of payments rectification. In the Middle East, examples of both the above economic characteristics abound. As Table 3.2 shows, the economic strength of the ten core Middle Eastern countries can vary from Saudi Arabia which in 1974 boasted a trade balance surplus of 27,615 million dollars to Israel which suffered a deficit of 2,405 million dollars in the same year.

Table 3.2

Trade balance of ten core Middle Eastern states, 1974
(million dollars)

Country	Exports	Imports	Balance
Algeria	4,259	4,035	+ 224
Egypt	1,516	2,348	− 832
Iraq	7,278	2,273	+ 5,005
Iran	21,554	5,672	+ 15,882
Israel	1,734	4,139	− 2,405
Jordan	155	488	− 333
Libya	8,261	2,762	+ 5,499
Saudi Arabia	31,088	3,473	+ 27,615
Syria	784	1,230	− 446
Turkey	1,532	3,720	− 2,188

Source: United Nations, *Monthly Bulletin of Statistics,*
May 1976, pp.114—15

Given its vast economic wealth, Saudi Arabia has been able to use foreign aid effectively as an instrument of its foreign policy. Thus between 1967 and 1975, Saudi Arabia extended aid to Egypt totalling $2,600 million. This aid was made conditional on Egypt's commitment not to interfere in the affairs of the Arabian Peninsula. Similarly, Iran's decision to grant Egypt $500 million in credit in 1974 could be interpreted as a reward for President Sadat's friendly posture towards Iran after the long years of Egyptian–Iranian hostility which existed during Nasser's presidency. Conversely, Saudi Arabia's threat to freeze its annual $600 million aid to Syria in the spring of 1976 was undoubtedly meant to check the gradual escalation of Syria's intervention in the Lebanon and its uncompromising anti-Egyptian posture. Indeed, the Egyptian–Syrian reconciliation of June 1976 would not have occurred had it not been for the efforts of the Saudi and Kuwaiti paymasters. All these examples illustrate the potency of the economic factor in its capacity to act as a capability of a state's foreign policy.

On the other hand, a structurally weak economy can adversely affect the conduct of foreign policy, particularly if it makes the country dependent on foreign aid. In this respect, Egypt and Israel have been the most obvious sufferers. In January 1976, President Sadat disclosed that Egyptian debts to the Soviet Union amounted to $7,000 million. In Israel's case, it is generally accepted that the massive American aid has been the primary contributor to the solvency of an economy whose foreign currency obligations reached the staggering figure of $8,000 million in 1974. [21] Both superpowers have used their aid to induce a specific reorientation in the foreign policies of the two Middle Eastern recipient states. Thus, in the wake of the increasing rapport between Egypt and the United States in 1974, the Soviet leaders adamantly refused to grant President Sadat's request for a long-term moratorium on the repayment of Soviet credits. Similarly, as mentioned before, the decision by the United States administration in the spring of 1975 to freeze an Israeli request for $3,000 million in aid contributed crucially to Israel's later acceptance of the interim agreement with Egypt in September 1975. The two illustrations, especially the latter case, clearly show the limitations imposed by foreign aid on the recipient's foreign policy.

In addition to the economic situation of the country, its military power is a further influence on the country's foreign policy. Ideally, the military factor should be analysed in qualitative as well as quantitative terms. However, due to the highly subjective nature of evaluating precisely such intangible factors as the motivations, attitudes, courage and morale of a whole army, the analysis will be restricted to the examination of the defence expenditures of various Middle Eastern countries. This will facilitate objective comparisons within the regional system and with extra-regional states, and as such, can provide a good indicator of a country's ranking in terms of military power. [22]

The data for the defence expenditures of ten core Middle Eastern states are provided in Table 3.3. Two points are immediately discernible.

Table 3.3

Defence expenditures of ten core Middle Eastern states in 1974
(billion dollars)

	Gross national product	Defence expenditure	Defence as % of GNP
Algeria	8·80	0·40	5
Egypt	17·90	3·12	18
Iraq	5·60	0·80	14
Iran	35·60	3·23	9
Israel	11·70	3·69	31
Jordan	1·00	0·14	14
Libya	5·90	0·40	7
Saudi Arabia	12·00	1·81	15
Syria	2·90	0·46	16
Turkey	31·90	1·00	3

Source: International Institute for Strategic Studies, London,
The Military Balance, 1974–1975, pp.31–40; *1975–1976,* pp.31–9

First, defence expenditure seems generally to claim a high percentage of the gross national product of Middle Eastern states. The mean for the ten states is a very high 13.2 per cent. Indeed, in the case of Israel it runs to an almost crippling 31 per cent. The strain of the defence burden on the Middle Eastern states can be clearly appreciated when compared with Britain and the USA, whose defence expenditures in 1974 amounted to 5 and 6 per cent of their GNPs respectively. The high priority given to defence by the states of the Middle East can probably be attributed to the pervasiveness of high-level conflict in the regional system which imposes on member states a disproportionate preoccupation with security and defence. This naturally contributes to the predominance of the defence establishment in the decision making process of almost all the

Middle Eastern states, which in turn leads to the centrality of defence in public expenditure.

The second interesting point about Table 3.3 is the primacy of Egypt, Israel and Iran in terms of their actual expenditure on defence. In Egypt's case especially, this primacy has substantially contributed to its centrality in, and leadership of, the Arab world. Table 3.3 shows that Egypt's defence expenditure was almost equivalent to the total combined expenditures of Syria, Iraq, Saudi Arabia and Jordan, the next four Arab states in military ranking. Thus, in its impact on Arab perceptions, the quantity of Egypt's military hardware has constituted a potent capability for Egypt. Arab public and leaders alike have consistently regarded Egypt's armed forces as the backbone of the Arab struggle against Israel, and this has been effectively used by Egypt in the pursuit of its foreign policy goals in the Middle East. Indeed, this perception is shared by Israel, which explains why Israel's primary objective in the Arab–Israeli con- flict is the neutralisation of Egypt. Similarly, the respect accorded to Israel and Iran by their regional neighbours relates in no small measure to the relative military ascendency of these states. Thus, the operational manifestation of the Arab's hostility towards Israel has been effectively constrained by their perception of Israel's military capability. The same can be said of Iran's behaviour in the Persian Gulf regions in which foreign policy goals have been achieved by the utilisation of the country's military capability. Thus in 1971, mainly for reasons of security, Iran forcibly wrested the Gulf islands of Tanbs and Abu Musa from the ownership of the Sheikhdoms of Ras al-Khayma and Sharja respectively. And in 1975, by placing the full weight of its military power behind the Kurdish insurrection, Iran was able to extract from Iraq an extremely favourable agreement regarding the territorial disputes which had existed between the two countries. In all the above cases, therefore, the military factor constituted an important determinant of foreign policy.

The final factor which affects the conduct of foreign policy relates to the influence of pressure groups and public opinion. Pressure groups are defined as sectional groups, clusters or organisations bound by vocational and/or associational interests who seek to influence policies. Groups who participate in the decision making process, such as political parties, parliaments and the defence establishments, do not fall within this par- ticular conceptualisation. The influence of a pressure group will vary according to the nature of the political system and the group's accessibility to the leadership. Since most Middle Eastern states are authoritarian, the influence of pressure groups and public opinion on foreign policy tends to be minimal. Foreign policy decisions in most

Middle Eastern states are reached in the light of discussions and debates which occur at the very top of the decision making process, and these are then communicated downward to the public. In these countries, therefore, pressure groups and public opinion influence foreign policy only in the sense that leaderships are aware of the prevalent value systems of their respective countries which tend to set broad parameters for what is possible in the formulation of their policies. It can thus be argued that the weakening of President Asaad's domestic position in the summer of 1976 occurred because he ventured beyond acceptable limits when intervening on the side of the Lebanese Christians against the Palestinians and their Moslem allies.

Only in Israel do pressure groups and public opinion constitute effective determinants of foreign policy. Due to the pluralist characteristics of its political system, and to the conflictual nature of its international position, Israel possesses a number of active and competing pressure groups who concentrate their activities on the issue of Arab–Israeli relations. They range from the right wing Gush Emunim group, who regard the occupied territories as part of the historic borders of Israel, and who advocate their retention at all costs, to the Siah and other peace groups who recommend complete and unconditional withdrawal. Such pressure groups, and indeed public opinion in general, are extremely effective in Israel since successive Israeli governments have been traditionally weak coalitions with a diffuse and uncertain public support. It has thus proved extremely difficult for Israeli governments to pursue unpopular policies for fear of undermining their already tenuous public support. For example, in the wake of the West Bank uprising in the spring of 1976, Prime Minister Rabin was obliged to make statements which suggested that the Israeli government did not contemplate relinquishing the West Bank in the foreseeable future. While winning him domestic support, these statements did not improve Israel's tarnished image abroad, nor did they advance Israel's precarious relations with the United States. Similarly, the intransigence of the Israeli government throughout the negotiations for an interim agreement with Egypt during 1975 was due in no small measure to the sensitivity of the weak coalition government to a vociferous and clearly hostile public.

The preceding analysis has treated the independent variables as actual or perceived influences on, and determinants of, the formulation and implementation of foreign policy. These variables, whether emanating from the domestic or external environments, tend to consititute either a positive impetus for, or a negative limitation on, the pursuit of foreign policy. Their impact is directed at the intervening variables which encompass the processes, procedures and personalities whose role is to convert policy inputs into policy outputs — i.e. the decision making process.

The decision making process

This category refers to the process by which policy inputs are converted into policy outputs. The ensuing analysis, therefore will be concerned with identifying those individuals, groups and institutions who constitute the decision making elite, [23] and explaining their roles and activities in the process of policy formulation and implementation. Thus, the composition and the roles of the Middle Eastern decision making elites will be analysed according to three subcategories classified in a scale of descending importance in terms of the power and influence they possess, and the frequency with which they exercise this influence. These subcategories are: the principal decision maker, the ruling elite and the political elite.

As an analytical category, the principal decision maker is far more important in the analysis of developing political systems than in developed western democracies. The category refers to the hegemony over the decision making structure of one person, who, in some cases, can exercise profound normative influence on the population as a whole. The phenomenon of the principal decision maker is widely prevalent in the Middle East because of two factors relating to the region's political culture. First, the tribe and the village had for centuries formed the core units of society in the Middle East; and in both cases authority had been traditionally bestowed on one person. Even the accelerating urbanisation process of the last two decades has had little influence on the structure of political relationship embodied in the traditional pattern of authority. Secondly, Islam, which dominates the political culture of the region, prescribes the concentration of religious and political power in the hands of one man. This man is referred to as the Caliph, that is, the successor of the Prophet Mohammed. While the Caliph as an institution has been politically extinct since the collapse of the Ottoman Empire in 1918, the idea of an identifiable and personalised authority is still embodied in the normative orientations of Middle Eastern Moslem societies.

The phenomenon of the principal decision maker predominates in all Middle Eastern states except for Israel and Turkey — Israel, because it is the one Middle Eastern country which possesses a political culture vastly different from the rest of the local powers, and Turkey, because since

Attaturk's efforts in the 1920s to westernise the country the Turkish elite have 'gone out of their way to express their identification with Europe and the West and to turn their backs on their traditional Islamic heritage'. [24] In the rest of the region, the institutionalised structure, particularly as it relates to the domain of foreign policy, tends to be dominated by a strong and central figure. It could thus be persuasively argued that a better understanding of Middle Eastern foreign policy making can be facilitated through analysing leaders' personalities, perceptions, values and needs than by examining organisational procedures or bureaucratic competition. [25]

The predominance of personalised leaderships in Middle Eastern societies has had positive and negative effects on the conduct of foreign policy. On the positive side, strong leaders have been able to formulate and implement major decisions swiftly and decisively. The nationalisation of the Suez Canal Company in 1956, the proclamation of the United Arab Republic in 1958, the Egyptian intervention in the Yemen in 1962, the Iranian takeover of the three Gulf islands in 1971, Egypt's expulsion of its Soviet advisers in 1972, the Egyptian and Syrian execution of the 1973 October war, Egypt's dramatic and abrupt abandonment of its long-standing pro-Soviet stance in 1974, and Syria's military intervention in the Lebanon in 1976 were all major decisions taken by powerful leaders operating under minimal constraints from organisational, bureaucratic and/or parliamentary interference. On the other hand, strong personal animosities existing between authoritarian leaders have tended to be reflected in the relations between their respective countries in a way which would very rarely have happened in countries with active and established organisational infra-structures. Thus, President Nasser's immense dislike of Iraq's General Kassem contributed in no small measure to the bitter antagonisms which characterised the relations between the two countries during the period 1958–63. Similarly, the present impasse in Egyptian–Libyan relations can be almost wholly attributed to the intense personal hostility existing between Presidents Sadat and Qadhafi.

A further salient feature of personalised foreign policy is its lack of continuity. Sudden changes in leadership can radically alter the foreign policy of a state; and in a region characterised by the frequency of its *coups d'etat*, complete reversals of policies are regular occurrences. The advent of Colonel Nasser in Egypt in 1952, Brigadier Kassem in Iraq in 1958, Brigadier Sallal in Yemen in 1962, Brigadier Hafaz in Syria in 1963, and Colonel Qadhafi in Libya in 1969, led to abrupt and radical changes in the foreign policies of their respective countries. Even

President Sadat, who was perceived as the most faithful and obsequious of Nasser's lieutenants, needed no more than three years to reverse his predecessor's foreign policy completely. Indeed, as is the case with Libyan foreign policy under President Qadhafi, frequent, and sometimes even startling, policy reversals can occur during the leadership of one person.

The category of the ruling elite refers to a small group of people who are either independent individuals or representatives of institutions, and who are regularly consulted by the principal decision maker and could influence his decisions on various issues. They are also occasionally allocated powers to make formal decisions. In the case of Israel and Turkey, where no principal decision maker exists, this group becomes the highest level of authority and the ultimate arbiter of power in the land. This category, therefore, will usually comprise the members of the Cabinet and the representatives of the defence establishment.

When a political system is characterised by the predominance of a principal decision maker, the cabinet wields far less influence in foreign policy than is the case with pluralist societies. Thus, while individual members of the cabinet can influence the leader on issues relating to their own specific departments, collectively they are less effective in influencing broad policy matters. Foreign policy decisions are usually taken by the leader himself, and it is left entirely to his discretion to bring the matter to the cabinet. For example, at the height of the 1967 crisis, the Egyptian cabinet had collectively discussed the explosive situation only once in the middle of May after the return of the Prime Minister from the Golan Heights. [26] Similarly, the Egyptian and Syrian cabinets seem to have been as surprised as the rest of the world by the news of the Egyptian–Syrian attack on Israel on 6 October 1973. Indeed, even in countries lacking a principal decision maker, such as Turkey, the cabinet has been persistently constrained by other organs, particularly the defence establishment.

A further factor which has contributed to the relative weakness of the Cabinet is the tendency of Middle Eastern authoritarian regimes to create parallel institutions to the Cabinet. These institutions have been allowed to share executive authority with the principal decision maker, and in many cases have wielded far greater power than the Cabinet. Thus, President Qadhafi has been far more responsive to the wishes and demands of Libya's Revolutionary Command Council than his Cabinet, especially in the issue-area of Libyan–Egyptian relations. In a similar vein, the regional commands of the Baath party in Syria and Iraq have been far more influential than the cabinets of these two states in matters of foreign policy. It is interesting, for example, that during the Egyptian–

Syrian break in 1975–76, the Egyptian propaganda machine very rarely mentioned President Asaad or his cabinet, but confined its verbal attacks almost exclusively to the regional command of Syria's Baath party.

Only in Israel does the Cabinet play a powerful role in the formulation and implementation of foreign policy. As the highest institutional organ in the Israeli decision making process, the Cabinet is actively involved in all major foreign policy decisions. Thus, after a long six-hour meeting, it was the cabinet who took one of Israel's most fateful decisions on 4 June 1967 to launch the surprise military attack on Egypt. This decision came only a week after the same institution had delayed military action by becoming deadlocked over the issue of a military response to Egypt's closure of the Straits of Tiran. Moreover, the traditional power of the Israeli cabinet was reflected in November 1955 when it categorically rejected a recommendation by Prime Minister Ben Gurion (the nearest Israel had got to producing a charismatic leader) to use force against Nasser's blockade of the Port of Eilat. Indeed, when, on two occasions in the late 1950s, major decisions regarding arms deals with Germany were taken without a cabinet vote, the government, in each instance, immediately fell. [27]

One characteristic which binds all Middle Eastern states is the influence of the defence establishment in the decision making process. The ascendency of the military in Middle Eastern politics is illustrated by the fact that in 1976 seven out of the twenty-one regional states were headed by a man with military credentials. Even such a high percentage disguises the profuse and pervasive influence of the military over the decision making processes of all Middle Eastern countries. This primacy is generally prevalent in most developing countries, where the armed forces are accorded great esteem as the guardians of the newly-acquired national integrity, and as the primary agents of the modernisation process. These favourable attributes are compounded in the Middle East by the traditional culture of the region which 'rests upon a religion that accords great prestige and legitimacy to the military'. [28] As such, the defence minister, as the representative of the armed forces, has always constituted a most powerful figure. Thus, at the height of President Nasser's charismatic authority in Egypt, Marshal Abd al-Hakim Amer, the defence minister and the spokesman for the armed forces, was able to question, and even reverse, Nasser's foreign policy decisions. [29] Similarly, pressure from the Turkish military as conveyed by the defence minister and the army chiefs constituted an important input into the Cabinet's decision to invade Cyprus in the summer of 1974. Indeed, it is highly unusual that major foreign policy decisions are taken in the

Middle East without consultations with the representatives of the military establishment.

In the case of Israel, the centrality of the defence establishment in the decision making process results not so much from the country's cultural traditions, but from the situation of perpetual external conflict in which Israel has found itself since its inception. Since the security issue has persisted in permeating Israeli life at all levels, the military have continued to exert profound influence in Israel's decision making process. Thus, Israel's policy of massive retaliation adopted in the early 1950s resulted from the advocacy of General Dayan and the entire hierarchy of Israel's armed forces. More directly, members of the General Staff in at least two stormy sessions demanded clear-cut action from Prime Minister Eshkol in response to the perceived Egyptian threat in May 1967. [30] There is no doubt that unequivocal demands from the military significantly contributed to Eshkol's grudging acceptance of Dayan's assumption of the defence portfolio. Indeed, since 1967, its administrative duties in the occupied territories have perceptibly increased the power and influence of the defence establishment in Israel's decision making process.

The category of the political elite refers to those individuals and institutions who participate in the decision making process without necessarily being allocated any powers to make formal decisions. They exercise intermittent and diffuse influence primarily through their role as a gauge of public opinion. Accordingly, political parties and parliaments constitute the primary membership of this category.

In the authoritarian systems of the Middle East, the influence of political parties and parliaments on foreign policy making is generally minimal, although variations between states certainly do exist. Thus prestigious parties which were instrumental in creating their respective states (e.g. Baath party in Syria and Iraq, FLN in Algeria, Neo-Destour in Tunisia) tend to be more influential than parties which were established after the state was formed (e.g. Arab Socialist Union in Egypt and Syria). Thus, there can be no doubt that the Baath's hostility to Egypt's interim agreement with Israel in September 1975 contributed to the ensuing break in Syrian–Egyptian relations. It can also be argued that the bitterness which has pervaded Iraqi–Syrian relations during this decade has resulted from the doctrinal differences existing between the two factions of the Baath party. However, apart from such isolated examples, political parties on the whole tend to serve mobilisational and legitimising functions for the leadership. The same can be said about the role of parliaments. Where they exist, they act merely as rubber stamps for executive decisions. Their function is confined to providing the leadership with a semblance of constitutional legitimacy, and their role in foreign policy is almost negligible.

The multiparty system of Israel, however, allows political parties and the parliament greater scope in influencing foreign policy. Because it is perceived as representing the demands of the population, the Knesset (the Israeli parliament) exercises some influence on foreign policy by operating as a platform for discussing and debating important issues. Particularly significant is the role of the Knesset Committee on Foreign Affairs and Security which is accorded broad administrative and legislative powers and which hears ministerial testimonies on foreign policy issues. Political parties too can sometimes influence the conduct of foreign policy in Israel. The broad support needed to ensure the survival of the weak coalition governments gives the Israeli parties strong bargaining positions which they can utilise in order to advocate or sabotage particular foreign policy undertakings. Thus the persistent threats by the National Religious Party to withdraw from the Rabin government in the case of any compromises over the occupied territories, particularly the West Bank, have certainly constrained the Israeli government from pursuing a more conciliatory policy with regards to the Palestinian problem.

Analysis of the decision making process in Middle Eastern societies as it relates to foreign policy, therefore, depends on the type of political system under question. Obviously, in authoritarian systems, the exercise of power is the domain of the highest level of the decision making elite, whereas in pluralist societies, power tends to be more diffuse. It must be noted, however, that the difference is marginal, since, unlike domestic policy, foreign policy generally is an elitist activity, and as such the external relations of all Middle Eastern states tend to be conducted by a small group of people at the ruling elite level.

Conclusions

The preceding analysis has clearly shown that various aspects of foreign policy making in the Middle East exhibit common features which result from the influence of underlying regional factors. However, the analysis has also illustrated that this similarity does not preclude the existence of certain variations between states in the conduct of foreign policy which relate to specific idiosyncratic national factors. Indeed, the utility of the analytical framework is in its ability to highlight the similarities, as well as the differences, between Middle Eastern states in order to compare and contrast systematically their foreign policies.

As a highly penetrated area, the region as a whole is influenced by the behaviour of the global system, particularly as it is manifested by the superpowers. The Middle Eastern states have, thus, become actively involved in frequent and wide-ranging global interactions transcending regional boundaries – an unusual occurrence for an underdeveloped region. This global–regional interpenetration, in which most Middle Eastern states are active participants, is an important common feature of foreign policy in the Middle East.

At the regional level, the pervasiveness of high level conflict in the Middle Eastern system, which is reinforced by the intensely ideological nature of intra-regional activities, has imposed various constraints on the conduct of the foreign policies of local states. This is particularly evident in the preoccupation of Middle Eastern states with defence and security – a preoccupation which has resulted in the acceptance of the use of force as an attractive instrument of foreign policy. Therefore, systemic influences at the regional level have, on the whole, tended to impose on local states a common mode of behaviour in relation to the external environment of these states.

At the domestic level, the independent variables have had varied influences on the domestic policies of Middle Eastern states. Thus, the geographic, religious and military factors have all been crucial policy determinants which in their own issue-areas, have contributed substantially to the uniformity in foreign policy outputs, such as the overriding concern of most Middle Eastern states with territorial issues, with defence and security, and with the preservation of cultural and religious continuity. On the other hand, while no less important policy determinants, the economic and demographic factors have, in a number of cases, highlighted the different features existing among the foreign policies of the various Middle Eastern states. Thus, in certain instances, these two factors have constituted effective capabilities of foreign policy (e.g. the economic factor in the case of Saudi Arabia and the demographic factor in the case of Iran), whereas in other examples they have severely limited the formulation and implementation of foreign policy (e.g. the demographic factor in the case of Lebanon and the economic factor in the cases of Egypt and Israel). Naturally, different inputs into the foreign policy system produce variance in foreign policy outputs.

The similarities and differences in foreign policy behaviour result also from the influence of the intervening variables. Since the vast majority of Middle Eastern states are authoritarian systems with a propensity towards personalised leadership, they tend to exhibit similar traits in their foreign policy behaviour, particularly in the swiftness and decisiveness which characterise the formulation and implementation of foreign policy decisions. As has been pointed out earlier on in this chapter, many momentous and consequential foreign policy decisions were executed with a swiftness that would not have been possible in western liberal democracies hampered by organisational, bureaucratic and parliamentary constraints. The only variant from this general rule is Israel, which boasts the only pluralist system in the Middle East. The weak coalition governments have tended to be over-sensitive to the demands of the Israeli public, and this has sometimes adversely affected the conduct of foreign policy, particularly in the issue-area of Arab–Israeli relations. However, because of its conflictual international situation, Israel has not lacked decisiveness or swiftness in matters of security and defence. In this particular area, Israel's foreign policy behaviour exhibits similar characteristics to the rest of the Middle Eastern states.

A further common feature relates to the predominance of the military in the decision making processes of the Middle Eastern states. Whether for social, cultural, or security reasons, the defence establishment constitutes a crucial component of the Middle Eastern decision making elite. This centrality is reinforced by the degree of high level conflict in the Middle Eastern regional system, and consequently many important foreign policy decisions have occurred as a result of direct advocacy by the representatives of the armed forces. Naturally therefore, because of the military's dominance in the decision making process of Middle Eastern states, foreign policy behaviour, particularly as it is manifested in the outputs of policy, tends to exhibit common characteristics. As has already been discussed, the general propensity to use military force as a convenient instrument of foreign policy is a common feature of foreign policy behaviour in the Middle East.

The operationalisation of the analytical framework elucidated at the beginning of this chapter was meant to provide a conceptional as well as an empirical analysis of foreign policy behaviour in the regional system of the Middle East. The approach has aimed to highlight an overall pattern of the similarities, as well as the differences existing in the influences on, and the conduct of, Middle Eastern foreign policies. Such a treatment should form the basis for rigorous comparative analysis not only within the boundaries of the Middle East, but also, and perhaps more importantly, with the other regions of the global system.

Selected bibliography

The systematic analysis of foreign policy in the Middle East is an under-developed area of study. Only in the last few years have academics under-taken foreign policy studies of Middle Eastern states. The vast majority of scholarly works dealing with the region have been primarily concerned with the domestic politics of the Middle Eastern states, and many of these have been essentially biographical essays of the various leaders of these countries. Therefore, only some of the books and articles which appear in the following bibliographical list are foreign policy studies. The rest of the list includes works which are cited because they deal with aspects of the states' external relations, and/or because they contain material that should aid the reader in understanding the foreign policies of the Middle Eastern countries.

General area studies

P. Y. Hammond and S. S. Alexander (eds), *Political Dynamics in the Middle East,* Elsevier Publishing Company, New York 1972.
Tareq Y. Ismael, *The Middle East in World Politics: A Study in Contemporary International Relations,* Syracuse University Press, Syracuse, New York 1974.
George Lenczowski (ed.), *Political Elites in the Middle East,* American Enterprise Institute for Public Policy Research, Washington, DC 1975.
Majid Khadduri, *Political Trends in the Arab World: The Role of Ideas and Ideals in Politics,* John Hopkins Press, London 1970.
Malcolm H. Kerr (ed.), *The Elusive Peace in the Middle East,* New York University Press, New York 1975.
Maxime Rodinson, *Israel and the Arabs,* Penguin Books, Harmonds-worth, Middlesex 1968.
J. C. Hurewitz (ed.), *Soviet – American Rivalry in the Middle East,* Fredrick A. Praeger, New York 1969.
Yair Evron, *The Middle East: Nations, Super-powers and Wars,* Elek Books, London 1973.

Country studies

R. Hrair Dekmejian, *Egypt Under Nasser: A Study in Political Dynamics,* University of London Press, London 1972.
Robert Stephens, *Nasser: A Political Biography,* Allen Lane, Penguin, London 1971.

A. I. Dawisha, *Egypt in the Arab World: The Elements of Foreign Policy*, Macmillan, London 1976.

Malcolm H. Kerr, *The Arab Cold War: Gamal Abd al-Nasir and His Rivals, 1958 – 1970*, 3rd ed., Oxford University Press, London 1971.

Mohammed Heikal, *The Road to Ramadan*, Collins, London 1975.

Michael Brecher, *The Foreign Policy System of Israel: Setting, Images and Processes*, Oxford University Press, London 1972

Michael Brecher, *Decisions in Israel's Foreign Policy*, Oxford University Press, London 1974.

Rouhollah Ramazani, *Iran's Foreign Policy, 1941 – 1973: A Study of Foreign Policy in Modernizing Nations*, University Press of Virginia, Charlottesville 1975.

Shahram Chubin and Sepehr Zabih, *The Foreign Relations of Iran: A Developing State in a Zone of Great Power Conflict*, University of California Press, London 1975.

R. M. Burrell, 'Iranian Foreign Policy: Strategic Location, Economic Ambition, and Dynastic Determination,' *Journal of International Affairs*, vol. 29, no. 2, Autumn 1975, pp.129–38.

George S. Harris, *Troubled Alliance: Turkish – American Problems in Historical Perspective, 1945 – 1971*, American Enterprise Institute for Public Policy Research, Washington, DC 1972.

F. Tachau and M. D. Good, 'The Anatomy of Political and Social Change: Turkish Parties, Parliaments, and Elections', *Comparative Politics*, vol. 5, no. 4, July 1973, pp.551–73.

M. Tamkoc, 'Stable Instability of the Turkish Polity', *Middle East Journal*, vol. 27, no. 3 summer 1973, pp.319–41.

A. I. Dawisha, 'The Transnational Party in Regional Politics: The Arab Baath Party', *Asian Affairs*, vol. 61, no. 1, February 1974.

Majid Khadduri, *Republican Iraq: A Study in Iraqi Politics Since the Revolution of 1958*, Oxford University Press, London 1969.

Itamar Rabinovich, *Syria Under the Baath, 1963 – 1966: The Army – Party Symbiosis*, Israel Universities Press, Jerusalem 1972.

Derek Hopwood (ed.), *The Arabian Peninsula: Society and Politics*, Allen and Unwin, London 1972.

Muhammed T. Sadik and William P. Snavely, *Bahrain, Qatar, and the Arab Emirates*, Lexington Books, Lexington 1972.

Edgar O'Ballance, *The War in the Yemen*, Faber and Faber, London 1971.

Michael Brett (ed.), *Northern Africa: Islam and Modernization*, Frank Cass, London 1973.

Alaal al-Fasi, *The Independence Movements in Arab North Africa*, Octagon Books, New York 1970.

71

Ruth First, *Libya: The Elusive Revolution,* Penguin Books, Harmondsworth, Middlesex 1974.

Notes

[1] See, for example, the different designations of the Middle East offered by the following books: H. B. Sharabi, *Governments and Politics of the Middle East in the Twentieth Century,* D. Van Nostrand Company, London 1962, p. 5; Michael Brecher, *The Foreign Policy System of Israel: Setting, Images, Processes,* Oxford University Press, London 1972, p.49; Louis J. Cantori and Steven Spiegel, *The International Politics of Regions: A Comparative Approach,* Prentice Hall, Englewood Cliffs, New Jersey 1970, p.8.

[2] 'Comparative Foreign Policy: Fad, Fantasy or Field?' in James Rosenau, *The Scientific Study of Foreign Policy,* The Free Press, New York, 1971, pp.67–94.

[3] Ibid., pp.80–1.

[4] The terms were first introduced into the literature of International Relations by Harold and Margaret Sprout in their article, 'Environmental Factors in the Study of International Politics', *Journal of Conflict Resolution,* vol. 1, no. 4, December 1957, pp.309–28.

[5] See James Rosenau, 'The Study of Foreign Policy' in James Rosenau, Kenneth W. Thompson and Gavin Boyd, *World Politics: An Introduction,* The Free Press, New York 1976, pp.15–35.

[6] See Coral Bell, 'The October Middle East War: A Case Study in Crisis Management during Detente', *International Affairs,* vol. 50, no. 4, October 1974, pp.531–43.

[7] Mohammed Heikal, *The Road to Ramadan,* Collins, London, 1975, p.174.

[8] See Peter Mansfield, *Nasser's Egypt,* Penguin, Harmondsworth, Middlesex, 1969, pp.184–5.

[9] For more elaborate discussions of the Middle East as a regional system, see Yair Evron, *The Middle East: Nations, Superpowers and Wars,* Elek, London 1973, pp.192–207; Brecher, op. cit., pp.47–64; Leonard Binder, *The Ideological Revolution in the Middle East,* Wiley, London, 1964, pp.254–78.

[10] P. A. Reynolds, *An Introduction to International Relations,* Longman, London 1971, p.147.

[11] See A. I. Dawisha, *Egypt in the Arab World: The Elements of Foreign Policy,* Macmillan, London 1976, p.53.

[12]   See for example, Roy C. Macrides, *Foreign Policy in World Politics,* 3rd ed, Prentice-Hall, Englewood Cliffs, New Jersey 1967, pp.4–7.

[13   British Broadcasting Corporation, *Summary of World Broadcasts,* part IV: *The Middle East,* 27 June, 1961, ME/675/A/1-3.

[14]   See for example, Yigal Allon's statement in Brecher, op. cit., p.349.

[15]   Dawisha, op. cit., p.80 and p.183.

[16]   See *Majallat al-Azhar* (the al-Azhar Magazine), vol. 34, no. 6, January 1963, p.574; also quoted in Dawisha, op. cit., p.90.

[17]   Ronald Segal, *Whose Jerusalem?: The Conflicts of Israel,* Penguin, Harmondsworth, Middlesex 1975, p.118.

[18]   Brecher, op. cit., p.229.

[19]   See Tareq Y. Ismael, *The Middle East in World Politics: A Study in Contemporary International Relations,* Syracuse, University Press, Syracuse, New York 1974, p.231; see also Mason Willrich, 'Energy Independence for America', *International Affairs,* vol. 52, no. 1, January 1976, p.55.

[20]   The entire issue of *Daedalus,* vol. 104, no. 4, autumn 1975 was devoted to an analysis of the oil crisis.

[21]   For a fuller account of Israel's economic plight, see Peter Kellner's excellent article in *The Sunday Times,* 7 December, 1975, p.60.

[22]   For the importance of military expenditure on the ranking of a particular state in the international system, see David O. Wilkinson, *Comparative Foreign Relations: Framework and Methods,* Dickinson Publishing Company, Belmont, California 1969, pp.53–61.

[23]   For a definition of the term 'elite' see Gaetano Mosca, *The Ruling Class,* trans. H. Kahn, ed. A. Livingstone, McGraw-Hill, New York, 1939, p.50; also Robert A. Dahl, 'A Critique of the Ruling Elite Model', *American Political Science Review,* vol. 52, no. 2, June 1958, pp.463–75.

[24]   N. R. Keddie, 'Is there a Middle East?', *International Journal of Middle Eastern Studies,* vol. 4, 1974, p.255.

[25]   See Graham T. Allison, *Essence of Decision: Explaining the Cuban Missile Crisis,* Little, Brown and Co., Boston 1971; also Graham T. Allison and Morton H. Halperin, 'Bureaucratic Politics: A Paradigm and Some Policy Implications', in Raymond Tanter and Richard H. Ullman (eds), *Theory and Policy in International Relations,* Princeton University Press, Princeton, New Jersey 1972, pp.40–79.

[26]   Anthony Nutting, *Nasser,* Constable, London 1972, p.410.

[27]   See Brecher, op.cit., pp.415–26.

[28]   D. A. Rostow, 'The Military in Middle Eastern Society and Politics' in Sidney N. Fisher (ed.), *The Military in the Middle East,* Ohio State University Press, Columbus, Ohio 1963, p.9.

[29] See Dawisha, op.cit., pp.115–17.
[30] See Brecher, op.cit., pp.134–7.

4   Sub-Saharan Africa

CHRISTOPHER CLAPHAM

The African setting

For the states of sub-Saharan Africa, [1] foreign policy is a re-export. African states, with few exceptions, were created by the superimposition on indigenous societies of forces external to the continent which involved them in an international system which they had little if any part in establishing. Independence, which for most of the states with which this chapter is concerned, took place between 1956 and 1965, gave them the opportunity to participate formally in international exchanges, but left unfinished the task of achieving some synthesis between the indigenous and the external elements in their make-up. This task is central to their domestic politics, but, because external involvement affects every aspect of their political life, it inevitably involves a re-definition of their relationship with the outside. At the centre of almost every concern and every controversy in African foreign policy is the legacy of some previous foreign incursion into the continent. To understand how and why African foreign policies are made, and to find a structure within which to compare them, it is therefore necessary to go back to their beginnings.

The common origins of almost all African states lie in colonialism. [2] In the whole region, only Ethiopia and Liberia were not created by the partition of the continent into territories administered by the various colonial powers. Much of the colonial experience, of course, is common to the whole of the third world. What is distinctive about its impact on tropical Africa is the juxtaposition of the territorial structures which colonial rule created, and the indigenous societies on which these structures were imposed. The colonial rulers did not shape the entire society which they governed, as happened in the West Indies and parts of Latin America. Nor did they shape their colonies to existing societies, as happened in those parts of mainland South-East Asia where colonial boundaries largely coincided with those of the main pre-colonial river valley civilisations. Instead, the continent was divided between colonies in a way which bore almost no relationship to the existing divisions between peoples, who were gathered together haphazardly under the control

Map 4 Africa

76

of one or another colonial power. The only exceptions were microcolonies such as Swaziland or Burundi, derived from pre-colonial African monarchies. The gap between social identities and administrative structures, between the potential nation and the potential state, was therefore exceptionally wide.

The colonial administrations themselves did something to bridge this gap, by associating Africans with government, and hence with the territory-wide hierarchy through which government operated. The time scale was not a long one. In most non-coastal areas, a period of only sixty to seventy years separated the establishment of effective colonial administration from independence, very much less than in India or the West Indies. Penetration was correspondingly uneven. Some areas of the territory and sections of the society were drastically affected by colonial government, while others were scarcely touched. It varied in scope and intensity, too, with the policies of the colonial regime: British policies of indirect rule and French ones of assimilation, though the impact of both is easily exaggerated, created varying interests each of which had some effect on post-independence foreign policies. But the overall tendencies were fairly uniform: by spreading the colonial language, building roads, establishing a cash economy, educating Africans and recruiting them into the army and civil administration, the colonial rulers created groups for whom the colonial territory was a major level of social and economic, and ultimately political, activity. From the viewpoint of future foreign policy, what is especially significant about this process is the way in which each step increased linkages with the outside world, and especially with the metropolitan power. Foreign languages, education, travel, cultural assimilation, technical skills, association with the monetary – and hence the international – economy, all illustrate the same theme. Those individuals who acquired the skills necessary for the management of an independent state, and who consequently came to constitute the governing elite, were correspondingly those who had been most exposed to external influence.

The economic aspect of this process merits special attention. In economic as in other ways, the African colonies were very unevenly penetrated by colonialism. In none, for example, was the penetration so complete as that of the sugar colonies of the Caribbean. In many areas, subsistence cultivation remained the dominant mode of production throughout and beyond the colonial era. Where economic penetration took place, however, it invariably involved the incorporation of the colonial economy into an exchange relationship primarily with the metropolitan country and secondarily with other industrial powers. The colony exported primary produce in the form of tropical crops or minerals, and imported manufactured goods and other metropolitan products. The particular primary product depended partly on the natural endowments of the territory, partly on a source of demand in the industrial world, and partly on the colonial administration's need to create an economic base from which to sustain itself. Individual territories easily became extremely dependent on a single product: the Gold Coast (Ghana) on cocoa, Sierra Leone on diamonds, Northern Rhodesia (Zambia) on copper. Productive groupings developed accordingly. Mineral production generally necessitated large scale operations, with integrated mining, processing and marketing arrangements, organised by a company based in the metropolitan state. Agricultural production was often − especially in West Africa − organised at the local level by indigenous farmers and at the national level by government marketing monopolies, though some areas were subject to European settlement. Trade was carried out at the top through metropolitan banks and import−export houses, and at a lower level very often by alien entrepreneurs such as Indians or Lebanese. One consequence of penetration was thus the presence within the colonial territory of expatriate economic groups with special skills or privileges in the management of cross-national transactions. After independence, their presence was bound to give rise to domestic tensions which in turn affected foreign relations. Another consequence was that communications with the industrial world assumed an importance which made them a critical element in the foreign relations especially of land-locked states. Thus economically, too, development was coterminous with external linkages.

From the colonial viewpoint, all of these linkages formed part of a coherent set of social, political and economic relationships centred on the home country. From the viewpoint of the indigenous governments which took over at independence, their impact was much more ambivalent. The leaders of the anti-colonial movements tended on the one hand to identify themselves strongly with the indigenous peoples, while on the other hand they tended also, as has been seen, to have been most strongly exposed to outside influences. The level of political identity and activity represented by the colonial territory might easily clash with identities at the local level with indigenous ethnic groupings, and at the continental level with feelings of Pan-Africanism and racial solidarity. The transfer of power which gave them control over the local administrative structure did not of itself enable them to control even the local manifestations of cross-national economic linkages, much less the overall economic system within which these linkages were set. Their own governments depended on outside connections in that by far the greater part of their revenues derived from customs duties, royalties and other levies on production for the international market and imports from it. In some cases, independence was made possible only by continuing dependence on the colonial power for financial aid, technical skills, and military support. At the same time, though external linkages were as great as ever, these had to adapt themselves to the presence of African governments which had interests of their own, and some opportunities to further these interests through governmental action within the state and diplomatic initiatives outside it. Foreign policy became possible in a sense in which it had not previously been so.

In essence, this policy turns on the brokerage role of the governing elites, who stand at the point of intersection of domestic society and external linkages, and need to manage as best they can the tensions which arise between them. The first goal of such elites is, of course, to maintain themselves, both as states operating in the international arena and, more narrowly, as governments consisting of particular groups of men. This goal pushes governments, with greater or lesser success depending on their skill and circumstances, into varying twists of policy determined by the immediate predicaments in which they find themselves. Over and above this, however, it is possible to discern the general goal and interest of all such elites in increasing the integrity of their own base. On the one hand, this calls for an increase in national unity and identity, to be achieved partly by specifically nationalist appeals, but partly also by more general racial and anti-colonial ones which promote a sense of identity against the most easily perceived threats to national integrity. On the other hand, it calls for an increase in the extractive and regulatory capabilities of the state, and thus its brokerage capacity. In pursuing this goal, governing elites must labour under the constraints created by poverty, disunity, domestic expectations and external penetration, but they also have resources created by their ability to combine domestic control with access to the international system. The following sections will indicate some of the ways in which these constraints and resources have operated in practice.

The domestic environment

Though foreign policy by definition concerns relationships with actors external to the domestic political system, it is inevitably strongly influenced by policy makers' domestic predicaments: the structure and situation of the state which they control, the nature of their control over it, and the goals which they pursue and, more immediately, the requirements for the maintenance of their own regimes. For the newly-independent African states, these domestic preoccupations were intensified by all the problems of trying to create a viable political structure under very unpromising circumstances, from an artificial unit, created and maintained by outside force, often with deep internal divisions and with very slender economic and administrative resources. Though the rhetoric of foreign policy was often outward-looking, expressing such themes as positive neutralism or the liberation of remaining colonial enclaves, its effective springs were overwhelmingly internal.

The most basic foreign policy issue confronting the new governments concerned the identity of the state itself. The artificiality of the colonial boundaries might well have been expected to lead either to fragmentation or to African unification once independence was achieved and the external force which had created them was withdrawn. In fact, this did not happen. For one thing, the colonial powers had built up within each territory an administrative hierarchy which, Africanised but in other respects not essentially altered, continued in most cases to provide a unifying core for the newly independent state. Secondly, the African nationalist leaders who from the 1940s onwards sought independence had perforce to do so by confronting' the colonial administration. They had therefore to organise their anti-colonial parties within the boundaries of the colonial state; and even when, as often happened, rival leaders mobilised ethnic groups into competing parties, these parties competed for control over the state as a whole. Once they obtained it, they had a very strong vested interest in maintaining it, and hence in combating secessionist tendencies. In no case did independence lead to partition, though in one case — Somalia — it led to the unification of adjoining colonies, and in another — Cameroon — it was accompanied by a transfer of territory from one state to another. Thirdly, there was effectively no alternative base for nationhood. At the continental level, Pan-Africanism, though it generated a common rhetoric and a sense of continental identity, was quite incapable of transcending territorial differences to create a united African state. At the local level, few indigenous political structures could be adapted to support the kind of modernising nation-state to which educated African leaders aspired; most were too small anyhow, and the disruption involved in substituting them for the colonial structure was too great to contemplate. So the colony became the new state, and acquired in the eyes of its rulers a legitimacy denied to the divisive tribalism of pre-colonial identities. When it was threatened, by the Biafran secession from Nigeria in 1967–70, for example, the threat was legitimised by claims to nationhood on behalf of another colonial creation, and was countered by the support which the existing state was able to call on from other actors in the African and international state system. The one exception is Somalia, which has from the start based its claim to nationhood on the unity of the Somali peoples, regardless of the territories to which they were allocated by artificial frontiers, and this is the principal reason why Somali foreign policy has been so very different from that of other African states.

In practice, the territorial integrity of most African states has not been seriously challenged. Their weakness in terms of any index of state effectiveness or performance has not resulted in any very obvious threat of conquest or dismemberment. The reasons for this must be looked for partly in the interests of established elites, and partly in the support brought to the existing state structure by both regional and international actors. This will be examined later. Where there is a threat to the integrity of the state, however, it takes a dominant role in determining the foreign policy of the regime. The most obvious case is the Nigerian civil war, when the Nigerian government looked for any state which would provide it with arms and moral support to pursue the struggle against Biafra; the Soviet Union thus gained influence and popularity by supplying sophisticated weapons which the United Kingdom, responsive to domestic sympathies to Biafra, was reluctant to hand over. The legacies of the civil war have been very evident in subsequent Nigerian foreign policy, for example, in reluctance to recognise the Bangladesh secession from Pakistan, or in support for the MPLA in Angola against rivals supported by many of the same actors as had favoured the Biafrans. [3] Another example, less salient but more enduring, is that of Ethiopia, which although not set up by colonialism has acquired many of the same interests as the ex-colonial states in protecting itself against dismember- ment. This has been the overriding preoccupation both of Haile-Selassie's government and of the radical military regime which took over in 1974, and explains why, despite sharp differences in domestic policy, many of the foreign policy stances of the two regimes have been similar. While Nigeria, by far the largest and richest state in the West African region, was safe against intervention by its neighbours during the civil war, Ethiopia has no such immunity, since it is on the edge of the Middle East conflict zone and the main threats to its integrity, the Somalis and the Eritrean Liberation Front, have strong links with the Arabs and the Soviet Union. [4] In other cases, notably in the military agreements between France and many of her former colonies, African states have sought to protect themselves by continuing dependence on the colonial power. The Chad government in this way called on French military assistance against rebels in the northern part of the country in 1969–72.

Even when there has been no such direct threat to the state's survival, foreign policy has often depended critically on its domestic political problems, and especially on its government's concern for domestic security and control. At independence, the predicaments facing the new state were neatly embodied in its nationalist movement, which needed on the one hand to relate the existing collection of ethnic groups to the national level of political action, and on the other to relate indigenous anti-colonialism and demands for independence to the continued importance of linkages with the former colonial power. During the decolonisation period and the immediate aftermath of independence, the nationalist movements were – at any rate by comparison with their later decay – reasonably well organised to link societal demands to government activity. This was a period during which African politicians needed to gain indigenous support in order to confront the colonial regimes and establish their claims to the succession. This obliged them to mobilise demands, some of which fed through into the foreign policy field. In particular, there is an obvious connection between the nature of the groups in the colonial society on which the successful nationalist party mainly relied, and the relations ·between the new state and the ex-metropole after independence. The relationship with the former metropole in turn set the tone for other areas of foreign policy. The clearest example is the contrast in their relationships with France between Guinea and the Ivory Coast. In Guinea, Sekou Toure's Parti Démocratique de Guinée (PDG) rested at independence on the support of a radicalised peasantry whose allegiance Sekou Toure had gained through anti-colonialism and perhaps especially the abolition of the chieftaincy system which acted as an agency of French colonial rule. The PDG consequently gained an overwhelming majority for immediate independence in the 1958 referendum which offered a choice between that and continued association with France. The French abruptly withdrew, in a way which not only left a legacy of lasting bitterness, but also compelled Guinea to seek compensating relationships and aid from Ghana, eastern bloc countries, and the United States. [5] In Ivory Coast, by contrast, Houphouet Boigny's Parti Démocratique de la Côte d'Ivoire (PDCI) was formed from a conglomerate of interests, many of which – especially the planters and businessmen – were closely associated with the French. Independence came in 1960, with none of the traumas which accompanied it in Guinea, and the relationship with France has since formed the bedrock of Ivory Coast foreign policy. A similar though less extreme contrast can be drawn between Sierra Leone, where the governing Sierra Leone People's Party (SLPP) relied on Paramount Chiefs and members of the educated elite who had favoured collaboration with the colonial power, and Ghana, where Nkrumah's Convention People's Party (CPP) found its support in lower, more anti-colonial, strata of the population.

Where the nationalist movement was divided into competing parties at independence, this also affected foreign policy. Though party support was generally differentiated on ethnic and regional, rather than class or ideological, grounds, very often the experiences of the different groups would incline them towards a more or less strongly anti-colonial stance. In Nigeria, the close alliance between the colonial administration and the northern emirs associated with the Northern People's Congress (NPC) led to friendlier relations between Britain and the NPC government after independence than would have been likely had the government been drawn from the more highly developed and anti-colonial regions of the South. [6] Some of the same processes applied to relations between African states: for example, the experience of the African miners in the Copperbelt who provided much of the support for the United National Independence Party (UNIP) in Zambia can be related to the Zambian government's hostility to the white settler regimes in Rhodesia and South Africa. The perceptions acquired during the decolonisation period may also colour reactions to events in other African states. Ghana's role in the Congo crisis of 1960–61 has been very plausibly illuminated by suggesting that Ghanaian leaders drew a false analogy between their own predicament in 1956–57 and that of the Congolese; thus Lumumba and his Mouvement National Congolais (MNC) were regarded as nationalists similar to Nkrumah and the CPP, while the other Congolese parties were likened to the regionalist oppositions which sprang up in Ashanti, Togoland, and northern Ghana. [7]

After independence, governments tried to establish themselves in power by dismantling the electoral arrangements which had bound them too closely to popular demands. The resulting decay of the nationalist parties has removed an important source of influence on foreign policy, and connections between foreign policy and domestic pressures have tended to become less specific and less clearly organised. Reaction to domestic pressure has become a matter more of following or anticipating general attitudes, often xenophobic ones, which may be articulated by groups such as students or trades unions. Hence, when Colonel Acheampong repudiated the Nkrumah debts in Ghana, and General Amin expelled the Asians from Uganda, each was making a vote-catching gesture to gain popularity for an uncertain and newly-established regime, which had repercussions on foreign policy. Similarly, the highly strained period in Anglo-Nigerian relations which followed the assassination of General Murtala Mohammed in 1976 reflected widespread suspicion of Britain — itself an indication of post-colonial tensions — among many groups in Nigeria. Ruling groups may share and sympathise with popular demands, even if they are under no direct electoral pressure to respond to them.

One underlying feature of African states which has become increasingly clear with the decay of the nationalist movements is the state-centredness of their domestic political systems. One of the few clear points to have emerged from the confusion of single-party states and military regimes in post-colonial Africa has been the overwhelming superiority of those who control the central state apparatus over any other organised source of power within the political community. Hence oppositions are easily suppressed, and governments are generally overthrown by a quick *putsch* to seize the levers of state power rather than by any general mobilisation of support in the country as a whole. The weakness of regular and organised channels of communication through which both pressures and supports can be brought to bear on government has the paradoxical effect of making governments both powerful and unstable. It is not surprising then, either that foreign policies should sometimes be capricious, or that they should be one of the instruments through which governments try to strengthen their precarious hold on power. The use of foreign policy issues by both Acheampong and Amin to gain domestic support has already been referred to. More generally, African leaders may take part in public displays of foreign policy activity in order to demonstrate their acceptability to international actors and hence increase their authority at home. State visits, exchanges of communiques, and participation in high-level international conferences may all be used in this way. This aspect of foreign policy, of course, is by no means restricted to African states: the attempts of the later Nixon administration in the United States to use its foreign policy prestige to bolster its declining domestic authority were essentially similar. It is likely to be especially marked, however, when regimes feel themselves to be threatened. There are few African regimes which do not regard their foreign policy as integral to their own survival, and opposition to that policy, correspondingly, as treasonable. This has been particularly marked in Zambia, the black African state most critically placed in the whole Southern African complex, where Kaunda's UNIP government had first to beat off challenges from the opposition African National Congress (ANC), which favoured a

greater measure of accommodation with the white South, and subsequently to deal with domestic opposition to its tacit support for the
Unita/FNLA side in the Angolan civil war. As a land-locked state with
intractable communications problems in an area of international conflict,
Zambia's foreign policy choices are inevitably linked with domestic
politics and hence with the stability of the regime. [8] Much the same goes
for Malawi, where Dr Banda's policy of co-operation with South Africa
and the Portuguese colonial regime in Mozambique was established in
the wake of a cabinet crisis immediately after independence in which
Banda broke with the group of Malawi Congress Party (MCP) leaders who
favoured a more radical line, in foreign as in domestic policy. Banda's
foreign policy was connected with his reliance on expatriate civil
servants and security officials to counter any internal threat to the regime,
and his reliance on South African aid to build a new capital at Lilongwe
in Central Malawi, the region of his greatest support; more generally, it
was intended to foster economic expansion and so to create a prosperous
rural middle class with an interest in maintaining the government. [9]
Occasionally, but only occasionally, the links between foreign policy and
regime security have been so close that foreign troops have been brought
in to maintain the government in power, as in the French intervention
in Gabon to support President Mba in 1964, and President Stevens' introduction of Guinean troops to Sierra Leone to guard vital installations
after an army mutiny in 1971. [10]

When governments resort to foreign connections to stay in power,
opposition groups can of course do likewise in order to oust them, though
their very much smaller capacity to make official contact with external
actors is likely to count against them. Governments whose own foreign
policies are closely geared to domestic security are quick to denounce
their opponents as lackeys of outside powers, a good example being Dr
Banda's denunciation of Malawian opponents who took refuge in
Tanzania. Domestic opponents may also take up foreign policy issues as a
cover for more general disaffection with the regime, as in demonstrations
by students against Senghor's government in Senegal, and against Haile-
Selassie's in Ethiopia; the regime's riposte is invariably to dismiss the
demonstrators as the dupes of foreign ideologies.

Domestic and foreign policy making are particularly closely connected
in the field of economic management, since any attempt to alter the
structure of economic relationships inherited at independence is bound
to affect the external linkages through which these relationships operate. It
is worth emphasising that the impetus for altering these relationships,
from the viewpoint of African states, has been practical rather than

85

ideological. Certainly, African states have varied appreciably in their rhetorical approaches to questions of economic development, in the extent to which they have attempted to follow strategies labelled as socialist on the one hand or capitalist on the other, and in the closeness of their corresponding affiliations with states in the western or socialist blocs (in so far, indeed, as such blocs can be said to exist). However, all of them come up against basic facts of economic and political existence which set the scene within which such policy alternatives must operate. The first is that no African economy has been in any position to seek development through a policy of autarchy, by cutting itself off from the world economy in the way that Russia and China did during critical periods of development, or that Burma and Cambodia appear to have done or be doing at present. All except possibly Nigeria and Zaire are in any case too small, and all without exception have existing productive structures so tied in with world markets that a 'go it alone' strategy would cause immense disruption. [11] The government's dependence on external trade for its own income is one mark of this. Development has, therefore, been sought in ways which called for further international involvement: by expanding primary production, for which new markets had to be found; by seeking to maintain international prices, through agreements with primary produce consumers or alliances with fellow producers; by attracting capital, through private investment or foreign governmental aid; by bringing in expatriate experts and planners; and in many other ways which lead back to the international system.

The second basic fact is that African governments have had to meet constantly increasing demands on government resources from fluctuating and uncertain sources of revenue. The greatest of these demands is for employment, either directly by government or through job opportunities created by government action. This has placed on all governments an overwhelming need to increase the range of economic transactions which come under their control, and the proportion of pay-offs from international trade which accrue directly to them. This can be done in various ways. Foreign companies may be nationalised, either wholly or through some partnership arrangement; royalty agreements may be renegotiated; debts may be repudiated; exchange control regulations may be imposed to prevent the export of capital; jobs and entrepreneurial opportunities may be reserved for local citizens, either by some form of restrictive legislation or simply by ejecting the foreigners who occupy them. All of these have been resorted to, and all are likely to upset interests which, having been established during the colonial period, are overwhelmingly western. The decline of Britain's relations with Uganda provides a case in point.

This started with the move to the left which followed President Obote's consolidation of power after his internal coup against the Kabaka of Buganda in 1966; it went a step further with the 'Common Man's Charter' of 1969 which resulted in the nationalisation of British companies; and, after a brief respite following General Amin's coup against Obote in 1971, it culminated in Amin's expulsion of Ugandan Asians, who, with their fellows elsewhere in East Africa, provide the classic example of a group which, having established itself under colonial protection, found itself dangerously exposed once that protection was withdrawn. [12] There is nothing particularly exceptional in the Ugandan situation, except that in most countries rulers have valued or needed continued western linkages enough to be more circumspect and conciliatory in the actions they have taken. But even Liberia, one of the most self-confessedly capitalist of all African states, has taken measures to increase royalty and customs payments by foreign companies, and to reserve business opportunities to Liberian citizens. [13] Examples could be multiplied almost indefinitely.

The decision making process

The state-centredness of African political systems is carried a stage further in the distribution of power within the government, which is generally personalised in the hands of a single leader who is not subject to appreciable constraints from his colleagues. The immediate decision making setting of foreign policy is as a result highly personalised. To African leaders, as to Renaissance monarchs, foreign policy is an attribute of sovereignty which remains in their hands even when important tasks in the domestic political system are delegated. This is, therefore, an area in which the gratifications of individual policy makers can play an important part. The trappings of international relations, after all − state visits, heads of state conferences, meetings with world leaders, policy declarations in international crises − confer pleasures of a kind scarcely to be gained from governing small poor states with intractable domestic problems. International relations offer the chance of an escape into the big time world of global politics, which must be justified rhetorically in terms of world peace or third world development, but in which the activity itself is to a large extent its own reward. This extends beyond the head of state to other members of the government; ministers of finance, trade, health, posts, agriculture or information, as well as foreign affairs, take part in a round of visits and conferences which are certainly linked to their ministerial responsibilities, but

87

which can scarcely repay in other than personal terms the amount of time spent on them.

Since foreign policy making is a field in which powers were until the moment of independence reserved to the colonial government, which acted through its own foreign ministry rather than through institutions within the colonial territory, foreign ministries — except in Liberia and Ethiopia — had to be established from scratch at independence, and were late to develop a cadre of experienced African civil servants. [14] Missions abroad could sometimes be built up from commercial and consular offices dating from the colonial period, but indigenous personalities with the standing to serve as ambassadors were hard to come by. Such missions were also extremely expensive. Some of the larger states, such as Zaire and Ethiopia, built up extensive networks, but smaller ones often had to make do with embassies to their immediate neighbours and the former colonial power with perhaps a continental listening post in a capital such as Lagos or Addis Ababa, and a global one at the United Nations. By contrast with more developed industrial states, the communication and information networks at the disposal of African policy makers are often extremely slight. The Minister of Foreign Affairs, as the head of state's principal foreign policy assistant, may often possess a measure of personal influence, but foreign ministries and missions abroad have rarely acquired either interests or procedures through which to process foreign policy options, except for those personal interests which derive from their position in a prestigious part of the state apparatus. Studies of the foreign ministries of Malawi, Nigeria and Uganda show them all as providing negligible inputs to the policy making process. [15] This may partly be due to their smallness and newness, and the nature of individual political leadership in some of these states. A more basic problem, however, is in my view the structure of African governments as a whole, which are poorly adapted to respond to institutionalised pressures and procedures whether these arise within or outside the governmental apparatus. The difficulties are especially great in the foreign policy field, because the scope for individual judgement and opportunities for personal intervention are much greater there than in at any rate the more technical areas of domestic administration. This is an area, then, in which bureaucratic approaches to decision making derived from more institutionalised political systems clearly fail to apply. In looking at the foreign policy making process in Malawi, one is effectively looking at President Banda; in Nkrumah's Ghana, at Nkrumah himself and a group of presidential advisers who by-passed the formal machinery of the Ministry of Foreign Affairs. [16] There is not much point in looking further.

Although the military have played a prominent part in the domestic politics of African states — to the extent that just over half the states of sub-Saharan Africa are ruled by men with military credentials — it would generally be a mistake to ascribe to the military as such any particular influence in foreign policy making. Since the norms for dispute settling between African states are (except in the Horn) overwhelmingly peaceful, armies are not generally used as an extension of diplomatic influence, and so — in striking contrast to the Middle East, for instance — do not acquire specific foreign policy interests. Nor, as in Latin America, do they come to function as the guardians of an established social order with implicit foreign linkages, since such an order barely exists. Because of the generational structure of the army, early coups were often led by men who had risen from the ranks within the colonial forces, and thus had personal linkages with the colonial power. Later military regimes led by younger officers have tended to be more radical, nationalist and neutralist in out-look, though it may be questioned whether this is due to their military background, or whether it is more because the army has been over-whelmingly the most important route by which a younger generation of Africans have acceded to political power. A similar pattern applies to the readiness of military leaders to seek civil service advice in foreign policy matters. The early generation, represented for example by General Abboud in the Sudan or General Ankrah in Ghana, was more uncertain of its role and consequently more ready to defer to bureaucratic guidance, whereas their successors, Colonels Numeiry and Acheampong, have been quicker to scorn such advice and take a personal lead. The institutional structure of African societies as a whole, and not just of the military, is still in most cases so fluid that it can scarcely be looked to for any enduring influence on the foreign policy making process.

This means that the personalities of individual leaders may be an important influence on foreign policy, especially in the areas of declaratory policy and formal diplomatic postures which are much more directly subject to the leader's control than economic flows. Even these, however, may to some extent be affected. A good example is the contrast between Presidents Kaunda of Zambia and Banda of Malawi. Each came to power at the head of relatively radical (though by no means revolu-tionary) nationalist parties, dedicated to smashing the Central African Federation which effectively subjected their two territories to a settler-dominated government in Southern Rhodesia. Each had to reckon with the fact of strong economic linkages with the white-ruled territories of Southern Africa which severely curtailed their freedom of action. Kaunda reacted to this situation by joining the mainstream of African nationalist opinion opposed to the South African, Rhodesian and Portuguese regimes, and by trying so far as possible to limit Zambia's dependence on them. The great symbol of this policy was the Tanzam railway, built with Chinese aid, which would give Zambia a friendly outlet to the sea at Dar-es-Salaam. Banda, on the other hand, went out of his way to flaunt his differences with most other African states, encouraging the southern connection and establishing diplomatic relations with Portugal and South Africa. The new rail outlet which he sought went not to Dar-es-Salaam but to Nacala in what was at the time Portuguese Mozambique. Certainly, Kaunda was subject to important domestic pressures which helped account for his policy, but then so too was Banda, whose foreign policy was by no means popular, especially with the younger educated sections of Malawi society. A major factor in any explanation must be the simple fact that Kaunda opted one way whereas Banda opted the other. Foreign policies may thus change abruptly with changes in leadership, as happened in Ghana in 1966 after Nkrumah was ousted by a group of army officers who had close links with Britain, or even while the same leader remains in power, as has happened with Uganda's foreign policy under General Amin. The continuity derived in more developed states from institutional persistence or shared assumptions among leadership groups may thus fail to operate, though the greater the degree of shared national identity, the greater also will be the continuity in foreign policy postures derived from it. It would be hard for any Somali leader, for example, to abandon the ultimate goal of Somali unification, just as it would be very difficult for any regime in Addis Ababa to contemplate the loss of Ethiopian territory which Somali unification would entail.

The external environment

The external setting of African foreign policy making falls into two fairly distinct spheres. On the one hand, there is the sphere of equals, comprising other African states and on some occasions states elsewhere in the underdeveloped world. On the other hand, there is the sphere of outsiders, comprising especially the world superpowers and the former colonial powers, with their associates in Eastern and Western Europe and elsewhere. The relations between African states and states in each of these two categories, and the influence which these have on the foreign policy of the state concerned, are different enough to make them worth considering separately.

For most African states, the other African states taken as a whole constitute an important reference group for the determination of their own foreign policy. Much of the rhetoric of foreign policy making is couched in terms not of the individual country's interests but of the continent as a whole, a trait which is especially marked over issues such as policy towards the white-ruled states of southern Africa. This reference group behaviour is institutionalised in the Organisation of African Unity, and the African group at the United Nations. The OAU was founded at the conference of independent African states in Addis Ababa in May 1963, following earlier conferences in Accra, Lagos and elsewhere, and its annual meetings have attracted attendance by a high proportion of African heads of state. Despite its name, it has never been actively concerned for the unification of African states under a continental government; its main function, rather, has been to serve as a forum for discussion of continental issues between states, and especially for the formulation of common policies for the liberation of the remaining colonial territories and the white-ruled states of southern Africa. Its success has varied. Its nadir followed the Rhodesian UDI, when the Council of Ministers, composed of the foreign ministers of member states, threatened to break off diplomatic relations with the United Kingdom unless the Rhodesian rebellion was crushed within a month, a decision which only a quarter of the thirty-six members subsequently implemented. [17] The meeting over Angola in January 1976 saw the organisation deadlocked 22–22 between the supporters of the MPLA and those of a coalition between the three nationalist movements, a deadlock broken by the subsequent military victory of the MPLA. As against that, the OAU has provided an effective means for channelling support for liberation movements and for co-ordinating African responses to proposals such as the policy of dialogue with South Africa put forward by the Ivory Coast. It has also, over issues like the Nigerian and Angolan civil wars, provided an indication of African opinion which, to some extent, guided the reactions of outside powers. More important than its conclusions on any particular policy, it has kept alive the convention that the foreign policies of individual African states over continental issues are matters of legitimate concern to African states as a whole, with the result that leaders seeking to establish a role for themselves in continental diplomacy have had to adapt themselves carefully to it. The most striking example is perhaps that of policy towards the Middle East, which until 1971 was regarded as a matter of special concern to some African states, but not to the organisation as a whole. In 1971 the OAU appointed a mediatory committee on the Middle East, the failure of which was ascribed to Israeli intransigence. This was followed by the breaking of diplomatic links with Israel by almost all OAU states during 1973, even conservative states with strong Israeli links such as Liberia and Ethiopia being obliged to follow suit in order to maintain their status in the organisation. The one conspicuous maverick state is Malawi, whose policy of diplomatic co-operation with South Africa and the Portuguese colonial regime in Mozambique was accompanied by denunciations of the OAU and a refusal to send any Malawian delegation to its meetings.

Smaller groupings of a few African states, based either on ideological affinities or on common geographical or historical linkages, have had only a limited influence on one another's foreign policies. In the early years of continental diplomacy, the Monrovia, Casablanca and Brazzaville groups gathered together states with more or less radical approaches to the contemporary issues of anti-colonialism, positive neutralism, and continental union, but these groups were all dissolved into the OAU in 1963. Since then, the existence of the OAU has inhibited the formation of formalised blocs on ideological lines, but other groupings have remained. The largest have been the group of eighteen states, former colonies of the original six members of the EEC, which was formed to negotiate the Yaoundé Conventions with the EEC in 1963 and 1970, [18] and the much larger group of forty-six African, Caribbean and Pacific states involved in the Lomé Convention of 1975. In this case, of course, unity of decision making was imposed by the requirements of the EEC rather than springing from any particular solidarity among the African states themselves. The same goes for the Arusha agreements between the EEC and the three states of the East African Community, Kenya, Tanzania and Uganda, which in other respects have had divergent foreign policies. [19] Other groupings, formal or informal, have on the whole had little effect in promoting common foreign policies. The Council of the Entente, for example, links five francophone West African states under the effective leadership of the Ivory Coast; yet none of the other members followed the Ivory Coast's lead in recognising the Biafran secession from Nigeria. Even one of the closest personal links in African diplomacy, that between Presidents Nyerere of Tanzania and Kaunda of Zambia, failed to result in any common approach to the Angolan issue in 1975–76; Tanzania was a steadfast supporter of the MPLA government, which Zambia refused to recognise until some weeks after its military victory in the civil war.

This comparative inability of individual African states to influence the foreign policies of their fellows goes back to a number of general features of African regimes – their overall weakness, the weakness of transactional linkages between them, the state-centredness of their domestic political structures – all of which have the effect of insulating each state from its neighbours. This insulation is reflected in the twin conventions which have developed to regulate relations between African states: acceptance of the boundaries inherited from colonialism, and acceptance of whatever government has gained power in any other state. The first of these conventions, implicit in the OAU Charter of 1963, was explicitly reaffirmed at its Cairo Conference the following year. Though a few states have made territorial claims on their neighbours, these have generally been little more than reflections of existing bad relations between the governments concerned, and have been abandoned when relations improved. They have been based, almost invariably, on disputes over the correct location of the colonial boundary, rather than on any rejection of the colonial frontiers themselves. [20] The exception here is Somalia, whose claims on territory in Ethiopia, Kenya and the Afar and Issa Territory are the result of a longstanding desire for Somali unification which – whatever the tactics adopted by successive Somali governments – can never be entirely abandoned. While Malawi is a maverick because of the policies of its leader, Somalia is one because of the aspirations of its people. It has received no encouragement from the OAU for ambitions which go directly against OAU policy, and this is doubtless one reason why it has oriented its major foreign policy linkages towards the north, through membership of the Arab League and strong military connections with the USSR. The only other important infringement of the boundary convention has been the recognition by four African states – Gabon, Ivory Coast, Tanzania and Zambia – of the Biafran secession from Nigeria. For the first two of these states, the reasons may most plausibly be seen in the desire of two of the wealthiest and most francophile states in the region, with tacit support from de Gaulle's government in Paris, to weaken a potentially rich and powerful anglophone neighbour: an incursion into Africa of European rivalries. For the second two, the reasons seem to have been entirely humanitarian reactions by the two African leaders, Nyerere and Kaunda, most prone to take a moral approach to international problems. The convention was, however, strengthened by the reluctance of any other African state to take a step which could impair its relations with Nigeria, create domestic problems, or both. Senegal provides an example: despite Senghor's close relations with Paris, recognition of Biafra was ruled out by the importance in domestic Senegalese politics of Moslem brotherhoods, especially the Tijaniyya, who had close links with their fellows in northern Nigeria. [21]

The second convention, acceptance of whatever government is in power in other African states, has taken longer to establish, since especially for the more radical states it has involved the abandonment of the belief that they could legitimately seek to oust any government which did not live up to their conception of Pan-Africanist principles. Bad relations between African states have consistently sprung from the belief that such principles entitled states to become involved in the internal politics of their fellows. President Nkrumah, who regarded himself as leader not merely of Ghana but of Africa, thus became embroiled with most of his immediate neighbours, and good relations were not restored until after his overthrow in 1966. His overthrow in turn led to bad relations between Ghana and Guinea, which were only normalised with the ousting of the Busia government – led by Nkrumah's greatest opponent – in 1972. The Tshombe government in the Congo (Zaire) in 1964–65, led by a man whom many African leaders regarded as the embodiment of neo-colonialism, equally prompted hostility from the more radical African states. The convention of non-involvement may partly reflect the common insecurity of all African governments, and has been strengthened by the OAU's practice of accepting the delegation of whatever government is in power in a member state, including even Tshombe and the post-coup government of 1966 in Ghana. It also reflects the incapacity of any African government to change any neighbouring regime. There is no evidence that any of the numerous *coups d'état* in Africa have been substantially influenced by neighbouring states. Attempts by groups of exiles based in Tanzania to invade Malawi against President Banda, and Uganda against General Amin, both ended in pathetic failure, and President Nyerere subsequently came to accept the Banda and Amin regimes, and cease public criticism of them. Outbursts by Sekou Toure of Guinea at various times over the last fifteen years against Presidents Senghor in Senegal and Houphouet-Boigny in Ivory Coast have been equally ineffectual. The sheer ineffectiveness of an aggressive foreign policy to achieve its goals in neighbouring states has thus forced a greater realism in the uses of foreign policy, and in the process prompted a decline in conflicts between African states. [22] It is by no means clear, though, that this trend is permanent. The scale and success of Cuban involvement in the Angolan civil war of 1975–76 aroused fears of invasion among the governments of neighbouring states, notably Zaire. It is also possible – though it has not so far happened – that the military strength of a large state such as Nigeria might be used to impose friendly regimes on its neighbours.

Policies towards extra-continental powers have been governed by a different set of conventions, and in particular by the need to strike some balance between a formal ideal of independence and non-alignment, and the practical limitations imposed by economic and military weakness. Non-alignment is in a sense the natural expression in global affairs of the general interest of governing elites in increasing the integrity of their own base. It offers an increase in their bargaining power in international politics, at the same time as reaffirming the opposition to outside domination which in domestic politics was the mainspring of the nationalist movements and the attainment of independence. Non-alignment is not a universal ideal. Some leaders, such as Houphouet-Boigny of the Ivory Coast, place their countries firmly and explicitly in the western camp. Others, identifying western Europe and the United States with colonialism, capitalism and the maintenance of exploitation, see their natural allies in the Soviet bloc or the Chinese. But non-alignment may be seen as a mean from which states may diverge in one direction or the other. Such a mean is practicable, at least in formal diplomatic terms, because of a comparatively low level of great power involvement. It is an area neither of major confrontation, like the Middle East or South-East Asia, nor of great power hegemony like Eastern Europe or Latin America. In some measure, this is the freedom of weakness. Many African states are simply not important enough for the great powers to lose much sleep over them. But at least it means that if African states wish to establish close diplomatic relations with one or another bloc, there is not very much to stop them. In 1973, for example, six African states (Chad, Congo, Guinea, Mali, Somalia and Uganda) had more resident missions from communist than from western bloc countries.

In practice, non-alignment is inevitably compromised, occasionally and directly by the military requirements of African states, pervasively and indirectly by their economic ones. The most spectacular case of military dependence was the massive Soviet/Cuban intervention on the side of the MPLA in Angola, but other cases are not hard to find. Many former French colonies retained military links with France after independence, and such links led, for example, to French involvement in the Chad civil war. Nigeria's need for sophisticated weaponry to pursue the civil war against Biafra provided an entrée for the USSR, which, unlike either Britain or the USA, was willing to supply it. Soviet–Nigerian ties have remained close, even though there has been no question of the USSR attaining a position strong enough to dictate Nigerian foreign policy. The Somali government's expansionist aims led it to seek a larger army than any of the western powers were prepared to fund, and hence to a military agreement with the Soviet Union in 1964.

Since then, with a Soviet-supported coup in 1969 and the expansion of Soviet advisers and military facilities, Somalia has come more closely under Soviet influence than any other black African state. The Ethiopian regime has equally had to avoid steps which would compromise arms supplies from the United States, a point rubbed home by the interruption of arms shipments following political executions in Ethiopia in November 1974. [23]

The influence of economic linkages on foreign policy is much more difficult to assess. Malawi relied on direct budgetary aid from the former colonial power for several years after independence, and some of the poorer former French west African states, such as Upper Volta, still do. This obviously makes them very vulnerable to pressure. The francophone states as a whole, with a few marked exceptions such as Guinea, have retained close relations with France which offer them advantages but exact a corresponding price in dependence. Membership of the franc zone, for example, enables them to use an internationally accepted currency which they would not be able to sustain on their own, but denies them any freedom of action in international monetary affairs. Escape from one dependence, moreover, may be achieved only by falling into another, a point illustrated by Guinea's search for alternative sources of support to replace the French connection. The aid relationship as a whole exchanges benefits on the one hand for dependence on the other, and the dependence is compounded by the constantly increasing burden of debt which most African states have suffered. Debts, like trading linkages, are overwhelmingly with western industrial states. Even when these do not affect the formal foreign relations of the state, they very considerably limit the area within which an effective foreign policy can be undertaken. Educational and cultural linkages increase the element of dependence, especially when, as already discussed, the governing groups at independence come from sections of the society which have enjoyed close relations with the colonial regime.

As African governments have become established, however, it has become clear that the relationship of dependence is by no means one way. The economic linkages between metropole and former colony provide hostages for the latter as well as levers for the former. Britain's relations with Nigeria are a case in point. British economic interests in Nigeria at the time of the civil war were such that Britain was scarcely in a position to refuse Nigerian requests for arms; at the same time Britain's equivocal response to these requests, refusing the more sophisticated weapons and concealing the scale of other supplies in order not to offend the Biafran lobby at home, severely reduced the goodwill that arms supplies might otherwise have gained from the recipient. The post-war oil boom further increased the importance of the Nigerian market for Britain, while the Nigerians for their part could afford to shop around for alternative suppliers. Finally, popular resentments against Britain, almost inevitable in a post-colonial relationship and fuelled by a number of minor incidents, further increased the bargaining power of the Nigerian government. Indeed, Nigerian influence on British foreign policy, especially over the Rhodesian issue, is more evident than any British influence over Nigeria.

Viewed as a whole, then, the international system is not only a source of pressure on African foreign policy makers; it is also a resource which they can use to increase their own options and strengthen their bargaining positions. Nigeria again provides an apt illustration, in that the critical element which enabled the federal side to win the civil war was the access to the international system which it enjoyed as an established independent state. Arms could be openly supplied to Nigeria by foreign governments, while the Biafrans had to move in the shady world of mercenaries and arms dealers. The OAU provided valuable support, and outside powers could to some extent be neutralised by balancing them against one another. Even a state as poor and weak as Botswana is enabled, by the mere fact of independence, to gain access to alternative sources of aid and moral support which offset, to some extent, its previously total reliance on South Africa. [24]

It is also worth noting that the state-centredness of African political systems does in some ways insulate them from external penetration. The rivalries between political parties which to some extent provided levers for external involvement in the immediate post-independence period − in Kenya and Zambia, for example − have now disappeared. Only in an extreme case such as the Nigerian civil war can foreign interests openly attach themselves to opponents of the central government. For the most part, foreign governments have to work with whoever is in power; and if the African ruler is intractable, then there is often extraordinarily little that the foreign government can do about it. The most obvious case here is the complete inability of the British government either to influence or to displace General Amin in Uganda, whatever actions he may take against British citizens or economic interests. It is equally unable to do much about the repudiation of British debts by the Ghanaian government, or the nationalisation of British firms in both Ghana and Nigeria. Although most African states are weak, it does not follow that their foreign policies can be 'teleguided' by external forces.

The foreign policy preoccupations of African states have, however, been overwhelmingly domestic and continental ones. Not surprisingly, in view of their weakness by any global standard, few of them have attempted to play any very active role in the international system which is not directly related to their own predicaments, even though these predicaments may call for action on an extra-continental scale, as for instance in participation in non-aligned conferences or the United Nations Conference on Trade and Development. Similarly, participation in the United Nations has been heavily concerned with issues such as South Africa, Rhodesia and Portuguese colonialism, which African states have been very successful in maintaining in the front of global diplomatic awareness. Participation in other issues has been heavily coloured by analogies with themes such as imperialism or racial discrimination derived from their own experience, and, not being central to their own concerns, has allowed personal or rhetorical themes to play an important part, subject to the usual mechanisms of arm-twisting, log-rolling and covert influences in institutions such as the United Nations. Perhaps the cruellest reflection on the inability of individual African states or leaders to influence major world crises is the ousting of President Nkrumah by a coup in Ghana while he was in Peking trying to mediate a solution to the Viet-Nam war. [25]

Conclusion

The states of sub-Saharan Africa have enough in common to make comparative treatment of their foreign policy making processes a matter of more than simple geographical convenience. Though their place in the international stratification system and particularly their economic underdevelopment make them very much part of the third world, with the general foreign policy consequences which that implies, they possess in addition features which are distinctly African. Almost all of them derive their existence not merely from colonialism, but from a particular form of colonialism which was imposed and withdrawn throughout the continent at much the same time, and — despite individual variations — stood in much the same relationship to indigenous societies. Despite a variety of formal constitutional arrangements, they have too a similarity of domestic political structures, marked by what I have termed the state-centredness of political power, and the weakness of institutions capable of converting social — or even bureaucratic — inputs into regular government policies. In the international system, the relationship with, and frequent dependence on, the former colonial power assumes a

98

particular importance, with tensions of its own. A sense of continental solidarity is created by these similarities of background and by a common racial consciousness unmarred, for the most part, by historic national enmities: territorial nationalism has been concerned more with creating a sense of unity among the peoples within the arbitrary ex-colonial state, than with rivalries between the state and its neighbours. Nor has the sense of regional solidarity been challenged by revolutionary states with radically different self-perceptions, like Cuba in the Caribbean or North Vietnam in South-East Asia.

There are exceptions, especially among the states of north-east Africa, which, for one reason or another, have special circumstances attached to them which distinguish them from the majority. Sudan has much closer links with the Arab Middle East than with black Africa, though division between north and south within the country keeps the conduct of its foreign relations uneasily balanced between the two areas. Ethiopia is set apart not only by its long history as an independent state, but even more by the nature of the Ethiopian state itself and the conflicts, both internal and external, to which this gives rise. Somalia is distinct in its definition of nationhood and its consequent reluctance to abide by the conventions established by differently constituted states. None of these states, either, has important metropolitan linkages, Ethiopia because it was not colonised, the others because their colonial inheritance is in different ways peculiar, Sudan being the result of a condominium, Somalia of a merger between two former colonies. All of them as a result stand outside the mainstream of post-colonial successor states. Another important source of variation remains the difference between the former colonies of each colonial power, and especially that between anglophone and francophone states, which affects not only language but educational systems, economic flows, and personal contacts between leadership groups.

But for the most part, the similarities between their predicaments on the one hand, and their interests and goals on the other, place before African states a very similar set of choices. These choices, which essentially are set by the tension between the societies and state structures which governing groups control, and the cross-national economic and other linkages on which they necessarily depend, range over many issues between extremes of heroism and pragmatism. Heroism points to the implementation in foreign policy of moral themes which reflect the natural aspirations of African peoples for independence, against colonialism, racial discrimination, or too subordinate-seeming a relationship with the former colonial powers. It is expressed in the Guinean vote for No in the 1958 referendum, the breaking of diplomatic relations with Britain over Rhodesian independence in 1965, the expulsion of aliens by Amin in Uganda, or the building of the Tanzam railway to relieve Zambian dependence on Portugal and Rhodesia. Pragmatism points to the maintenance of relationships, however unheroic, which have already been established, which seem necessary for the maintenance and expansion of the economy, and which it would be expensive and potentially disruptive to change. The dilemma between the two is frequently overcome by adopting a dual foreign policy: a rhetorical one, which is pursued by means of resolutions and declarations against colonialism or international capitalism and in favour of continental liberation; and a transactional one which consists in maintaining, and possibly even encouraging, the linkages with the international economy on which in practice the government depends. Perhaps the extreme examples are to be found in Nkrumah's Ghana, where sweeping condemnations of neo-colonialism were accompanied by a liberal foreign investment code and a widespread use of suppliers' credits, but a similar combination has been noted in Obote's Uganda and elsewhere. [26] It is in effect a response at two levels to foreign policy requirements which arise at different levels and can to a fair extent be kept apart. However, as some of the cases cited above indicate, some African leaders have carried 'heroic' responses to foreign policy issues from the rhetorical over into the transactional sphere, by taking decisions which appreciably affected economic flows; while in one case, Malawi, Dr Banda has sought to justify a foreign policy founded on maintaining transactional linkages with the white south, and in doing so has taken a rhetorical line which is all his own.

There are, however, important differences in the constraints on African states and the capabilities which they can employ, which in turn affect the degree of independent action open to them. One variable is the size of the state and its consequent scope for diplomatic activity, reflecting the great range among African states from microstates like Burundi or The Gambia to ones of at least medium size on a global scale. After a period during which the date of a country's independence or the personality of its leader played a large part in determining its international prominence, the scope of diplomatic activity has now settled on a scale which can be fairly closely related to its wealth and population. A list of the number of resident diplomatic missions from other states in each African capital, for example, places Nigeria first with 68, followed by Ethiopia with 62, Zaire (58), Senegal (51), Sudan (50), and Kenya (48); at the bottom come The Gambia (6), Botswana and Swaziland (5 each), and Lesotho (3). [27] These figures reflect, more probably than they influence, the different opportunities open to states such as Zaire and Nigeria, which can at least attempt a global foreign policy, and ones which are effectively restricted to their own immediate region.

The figures for diplomatic missions in each African state reflect the importance which other powers accord it, and are broadly correlated to its size and wealth as expressed by population and gross domestic product. Landlocked states such as Uganda, Upper Volta and Malawi generally receive a much smaller number of missions than these indicators would entitle them to, whereas a well-placed state such as Senegal, which can act as a centre from which to cover the whole of francophone West Africa, receives proportionately more. Figures for missions maintained by African states, on the other hand, are less well correlated with GDP and population, and reflect the scale of the diplomatic effort which the state wishes to make. Some states, such as Kenya and to a lesser degree Tanzania, maintain a very small diplomatic presence in relation to their resources. Others, such as Liberia, Gabon, and the Central African Empire, have a disproportionately large one, though in none of these cases are any very obvious national benefits to be gained; presumably the reasons are to be found either in the pretensions of the head of state (as perhaps with CAE), or in the opportunities for patronage (as perhaps with the other two). It is different with Somalia, which maintains a very high diplomatic presence in support of an active expansionist foreign policy. The total figures reveal African states as net receivers of embassies (with 866 in them agains 663 by them), while of those that they send out, 283 (43 per cent) go to other African states, 195 (30 per cent) to 'Western' countries, 101 (15 per cent) to 'communist' ones, and only 84 (13 per cent) to other third world states.

A more important variable is the nature of the economy, with its resulting degree of external dependence. At one extreme, there are states such as Swaziland or Lesotho which are so closely tied to South Africa that they are scarcely in a position to have a foreign policy at all, whereas Malawi or Zambia, whatever their dependence on their communications with the sea, do nonetheless have some choice open to them between alternative policies. Again, in some cases (such as Kenya) colonialism left behind it sizeable alien commercial or landowning groups, whereas in others (such as Ghana) it did not. While in general terms every African economy depends on the export of primary products to industrialised states, it makes a considerable difference whether these are produced by indigenous farmers (as with Ghanaian cocoa) or expatriate corporations (as with Zambian copper); whether the prices received for them can be kept constant or increasing (as with Nigerian oil) or whether they are

Table 4.1

Population, gross domestic product, and diplomatic representation of Sub-Saharan African states

Name	Population		Gross domestic product				Diplomatic representation in African state, 1974						Diplomatic representation by African state, 1974					
	1973	rank	1970 total	rank	per capita 1970	rank	Africa	Third world	Western	Communist	Total	rank	Africa	Third world	Western	Communist	Total	rank
(1)	(2)	(3)	(4)	(5)	(6)	(7)	(8)	(9)	(10)	(11)	(12)	(13)	(14)	(15)	(16)	(17)	(18)	(19)
Nigeria	59·6m	1	7,978m	1	145	12	24	17	18	9	68	1	26(+ 5)	8(+ 9)	11(+ 6)	6(+4)	51(+24)	2
Ethiopia	26·1m	2	1,777m	5	72	29	22	16	15	9	62	2	12(+ 8)	6(+ 4)	8(+ 7)	3(+5)	29(+24)	5
Zaire	23·6m	3	1,926m	3	89	22=	26	7	15	10	58	3	26(+ 8)	8(+ 3)	15(+ 4)	6(+1)	55(+ 9)	1
Sudan	16·9m	4	1,832m	4	117	18	13(+ 1)	15	12	10	50(+ 1)	5	13(+ 8)	11(+ 7)	7(+11)	7(+3)	38(+29)	4
Tanzania	14·4m	5	1,284m	7	100	20	10(+ 5)	6(+3)	15(+ 2)	13	44(+10)	5	6(+ 6)	2(+ 2)	8(+ 8)	4(+4)	20(+20)	15
Kenya	12·5m	6	1,611m	6	143	13=	13(+10)	9(+3)	17(+ 2)	7(+1)	46(+16)	4	7(+ 7)	1(+ 4)	5(+11)	2(+4)	15(+21)	21
Uganda	10·8m	7	1,323m	9	135	15	9(+15)	5(+4)	6(+12)	7(+1)	27(+32)	13	6(+ 3)	3(+ 1)	5(+ 6)	3(+1)	17(+11)	18
Ghana	9·4m	8	2,214m	2	256	6	14(+ 7)	8(+8)	12(+ 4)	8(+1)	42(+20)	6	19(+ 9)	6(+ 8)	10(+ 7)	4(+5)	39(+29)	3
Cameroon	6·2m	9	1,082m	11	185	9	9(+ 8)	2(+5)	13(+ 4)	3(+1)	27(+18)	14	8(+ 8)	1(+ 2)	7(+ 7)	2(+1)	18(+18)	16
Upper Volta	5·7m	10	320m	18=	59	31	2(+10)	0(+7)	3(+10)	3(+4)	8(+31)	29	5	0(+ 4)	5(+ 6)	2(+1)	12(+ 7)	25
Mali	5·4m	11	267m	22	53	33	9(+ 2)	4(+6)	3(+ 8)	9(+4)	25(+20)	17	8(+ 8)	1(+ 2)	4(+10)	2(+1)	11(+35)	26
Malawi	4·8m	12	326m	17	73	28	2(+ 2)	3(+4)	4(+11)	0	9(+17)	28	4	0(+ 1)	4(+ 9)	3(+8)	8(+10)	29
Zambia	4·6m	13	1,495m	8	347	3	15(+ 2)	7(+4)	14(+ 4)	0(+1)	36(+11)	9	10(+ 4)	3(+ 2)	10(+ 7)	0	23(+13)	13
Ivory Coast	4·6m	14	1,761m	6	421	2	8(+12)	4(+7)	11(+ 6)	6(+4)	29(+29)	12	12(+10)	0(+ 6)	7(+ 9)	5(+2)	24(+27)	11
Niger	4·3m	15	363m	14	90	21	5(+10)	0(+8)	4(+ 9)	1(+3)	10(+30)	26	6(+ 4)	1	5(+12)	1(+1)	13(+17)	23
Senegal	4·2m	16	852m	12	217	8	17(+ 1)	11(+3)	13(+ 3)	11	52(+ 7)	4	11(+13)	5(+ 7)	6(+11)	4(+6)	26(+36)	8
Guinea	4·2m	17	320m	18=	82	24=	8(+ 2)	6(+2)	4(+ 2)	13	31(+ 6)	10	11(+13)	3(+12)	2(+10)	8(+5)	24(+40)	10
Rwanda	4·0m	18	211m	27	57	32	3(+10)	0(+3)	6(+ 7)	2(+5)	11(+25)	23=	6(+ 0)	4(+ 2)	5(+ 4)	2(+3)	13(+13)	24
Chad	3·9m	19	270m	21	74	26=	6(+ 4)	0(+6)	2(+ 7)	3(+1)	11(+18)	25	7(+ 5)	0	4(+12)	2(+1)	18(+12)	17
Burundi	3·6m	20	230m	25	71	30	6(+ 5)	0(+4)	5(+ 7)	5(+3)	16(+19)	20	6(+ 2)	0	7(+ 9)	4	14(+14)	22
Somalia	3·0m	21	249m	24	89	22=	4(+ 1)	7	6	7	24(+ 1)	18	11(+ 1)	8(+ 4)	5(+11)	3(+2)	29(+16)	6
Dahomey	2·9m	22	221m	26	82	24=	4(+ 9)	1(+7)	4(+ 9)	3(+5)	12(+30)	22	2	0	4(+ 8)	4(+5)	9(+11)	27=
Sierra Leone	2·7m	23	426m	13	167	10	7(+ 6)	1(+4)	4(+ 5)	3(+6)	15(+21)	21	8(+ 5)	0	4(+11)	4(+5)	16(+18)	19
Togo	2·1m	24	264m	23	134	16	4(+ 5)	0(+8)	4(+ 7)	3(+5)	11(+25)	23=	3	0	4(+11)	3(+5)	9(+11)	27=
CAE	2·0m	25	205m	28	127	17	10(+ 4)	5(+2)	6(+ 6)	5	26(+12)	16	12(+ 1)	2(+ 1)	7(+ 7)	3(+4)	24(+14)	12
Liberia	1·7m	26	354m	15	233	7	10	7	11(+ 6)	3	31	11	12(+ 6)	2(+ 3)	11(+ 6)	2(+1)	27(+16)	7
Mauritania	1·3m	27	180m	27	155	11	7(+ 4)	3(+3)	4(+ 8)	3(+5)	17(+20)	19	8(+10)	0(+ 1)	5(+10)	3(+4)	22(+25)	14
Congo	1·0m	28	283m	20	301	4	10(+ 6)	0(+2)	5(+ 6)	12(+1)	27(+15)	15	5	0(+ 1)	3(+ 9)	8(+2)	16(+12)	20
Lesotho	1·0m	29	69m	32	74	26=	0(+ 4)	1(+5)	2(+10)	0	3(+19)	33	2(+ 4)	0	2(+ 9)	0	5(+13)	31
Botswana	0·6m	30	83m	31	143	13=	2(+ 2)	0(+2)	3(+ 9)	0(+5)	5(+18)	31	1(+ 3)	0	2(+ 9)	0	3(+10)	32
Gabon	0·5m	31	335m	16	670	1	4(+ 5)	0(+3)	6(+ 7)	0(+3)	10(+15)	27	11(+ 5)	3(+ 2)	8(+ 8)	4	26(+15)	9
Gambia	0·5m	32	46m	33	107	19	3(+10)	1(+7)	2(+10)	0(+4)	6(+31)	30	1(+ 3)	0	2(+ 7)	2	6(+ 7)	30
Swaziland	0·5m	33	112m	30	274	5	0(+ 1)	2(+4)	3(+ 8)	0	5(+13)	32	1(+ 2)	0	2(+ 5)	2	3(+ 7)	33

Notes to Table 4.1

(1) Angola, Equatorial Guinea, Guiné, Madagascar, Mauritius and Mozambique are excluded; the three former Portuguese colonies had not established diplomatic networks at the date concerned; the two islands lie outside the scope of this chapter; and no adequate data were available for Equatorial Guinea.

(2) Population figures, rounded to the nearest hundred thousand, are mid-year estimates for 1973 from *United Nations Statistical Yearbook 1974*.

(4) and (6) Gross domestic product figures (total, Col.4, per capita, Col.6) are 1970 estimates in US dollars from *United Nations Yearbook of National Accounts Statistics 1974*, vol. 3.

(8) − (12) These columns refer to diplomatic missions maintained by other states in the African state referred to, and thus indicate the weight attached by other states to the African state concerned.

(14) − (18) These columns refer to diplomatic missions maintained by the African state referred to in foreign states, and thus indicate the scale of the African state's diplomatic effort.

(8) − (18) Figures not in parentheses refer only to permanent missions involving the maintenance of an Embassy or High Commission in the capital of the country concerned; figures in parentheses refer to additional cases in which, though an Ambassador or High Commissioner is formally accredited, there is no permanent mission. Both African states, and other states in Africa, frequently maintain a permanent mission in one capital, and in addition accredit their ambassador to one or several neighbouring states.

(8) − (18) Information on permanent and other missions is taken from the Europa Handbooks, *Africa South of the Sahara 1975, Middle East and North Africa 1975–1976, World Survey 1976*, vol. 1, and *World Survey 1975*, vol. 2.

(8) and (14) 'Africa' includes all states on the African continent, covering northern and southern Africa as well as sub-Saharan Black Africa.

(9) and (15) 'Third World' includes South and Central America, and all states in Asia and Oceania not covered in any of the other categories.

(10) and (16) 'Western' includes North America, Australia, and all European states except those classed as 'communist'.

(11) and (17) 'Communist' includes all the Soviet bloc states of Eastern Europe, as well as China, Cuba, North Korea, North Vietnam, and the Provisional Revolutionary Government of South Vietnam.

liable to fluctuate (as with both cocoa and copper); whether the economy depends heavily on a single crop (like Ghanaian cocoa again) or on several (like Ivory Coast cocoa, coffee and timber). The size of the domestic market, and the degree of dependence on external aid, are other factors in the same equation. Even though they may have very little effect on the rhetorical foreign policies, these variations strongly influence the extent to which states can actually use foreign policy to bring pressure on other states or achieve internal goals.

A third variable is the structure of domestic politics, its penetrability to external influence, and the nature both of decision making groups and of the societal demands of which they must take some account. The variations arising from differences between nationalist movements have already been discussed. Another possible source of difference, that between civilian and military regimes, has had no discernible general effects. There have certainly been cases where a military government sought closer relations with the former colonial power than did its civilian predecessor, most noticeably the Ghanaian NLC ousting Nkrumah in 1966; but the Ghanaian coup of 1972, which ousted the Busia government, had just the opposite effect. The critical difference is not that between civilian and military, so much as that between leadership groups which have, and have not, had close personal and cultural links with the former metropole. An uneven process of generational change is causing those with such links to die away, though individuals for whom they are important, such as Senghor in Senegal and Houphouet-Boigny in the Ivory Coast, still at the time of writing remain in office.

A recent study of Tanzanian foreign policy has characterised it as a process of 'adaptive response'. [28] The phrase might be applied to the foreign policy of any country at any time, encapsulating as it does the tension implicit in the foreign policy making process between the decision making machinery of the state and an environment which it can never totally control. In the states of sub-Saharan Africa, these tensions have been particularly great. For some purposes, insulated by their domestic political systems and the comparative absence of great power conflict or hegemony, foreign policy making elites in African states have the opportunity to express aspirations which are common not only to Africa but to much of the third world. They have thus had far greater freedom than Latin America or Caribbean states, or even Middle Eastern or South-East Asian ones, to establish close diplomatic relations with any of the major world blocs and take an independent line in forums such as the United Nations. But this freedom of action has always had to be tempered, for practical purposes, by their brokerage role between the demands of their fragmented domestic societies and the requirements of the international economic system on which they depend for their revenues. Liberty in one respect is constantly tempered by impotence in the other.

Critical bibliography

General studies: The three available general studies of African foreign policies were all published over ten years ago. Doudou Thiam, *The Foreign Policy of African States* (Dent, London 1965), deals largely with the ideological and rhetorical background to foreign policy, and scarcely at all with its domestic dynamics or the way in which it is made; it was first published in 1963, and is inevitably rather dated. Vernon McKay (ed.), *African Diplomacy – Studies in the Determinants of Foreign Policy* (Praeger, New York 1966), is a useful collection of papers on ideological, economic, military, cultural, domestic, political, and external influences on foreign policy. Undoubtedly the best of the trio is I. W. Zartman, *International Relations in the New Africa* (Prentice-Hall, Englewood Cliffs 1966), even though this confines itself to the states of north and west Africa. It displays a sensitive awareness of both domestic and external sources of foreign policy behaviour, and remains the best general introduction to the subject.

Pan-Africanism and non-alignment: As the dominant rhetorical themes of African diplomacy, Pan-Africanism and non-alignment have attracted a good deal of attention. C. Legum's early study, *Pan-Africanism* (Pall Mall, London 1962) is a useful introduction which, however, antedates the formation of the OAU. V. B. Thompson, *Africa and Unity* (Longman, London 1969), is also largely concerned with the pre-1963 period. I. Wallerstein's *Africa: The Politics of Unity* (Random House, New York 1969), gives a rather more coherent account of the movement up to the end of 1965; C. E. Welch, *Dream of Unity* (Cornell, Ithaca 1966), covers the scene in West Africa over much the same period. *The Organisation of African Unity and its Charter* (Praeger, New York 1969) by Z. Cervenka is a historical and institutional study, dealing with events up to the end of 1968; it is updated by the same author's *The Unfinished Quest for African Unity* (Hurst, London 1976). The best study of non-alignment in the African context is G. W. Shepherd, *Nonaligned Black Africa* (D. C. Heath, Lexington 1970), which includes case studies of several crises in

African diplomacy. *Africa and International Organization* (Nijhoff, The Hague 1974), edited by Y. El-Ayouty and H. C. Brooks, includes useful papers by Cowan, Wallerstein, and others.

Conflict and integration: A. Hazlewood, *African Integration and Disintegration* (Oxford University Press, London 1967), is the only book available on its subject, and is especially strong on economic integration. T. M. Shaw's two articles, 'Discontinuities and Inequalities in African International Politics', and 'Regional Cooperation and Conflict in Africa', *International Journal*, vols 29 and 30, 1974 and 1975, respectively, are worth noting in this field. R. W. Copson, 'Foreign Policy Conflict among African States, 1964–1969', *Sage International Yearbook of Foreign Policy Studies*, vol. 1, 1973, presents an interesting statistical analysis of conflicts over this period, and assesses reasons for them. S. Touval, *The Boundary Politics of Independent Africa* (Harvard, Cambridge, Mass. 1972), is an exhaustive study of a problem area which has proved rather less important than might have been expected. Relationships between internal and external conflicts are discussed in Adelphi Paper 93, *Conflicts in Africa* (IISS, London 1972).

Economic factors: I. W. Zartman, *The Politics of Trade Negotiations between Africa and the European Economic Community* (Princeton University Press, Princeton 1971), is the only study of African foreign policy making in a specifically economic sphere. This is not the place to go into the literature on economic development, but one book which pulls together economic, political and international aspects, though heavily programmatic in approach, is R. H. Green and A. Seidman, *Unity or Poverty? The Economics of Pan-Africanism* (Penguin, London 1968).

Policy making: Very little is available on foreign policy making institutions, in part no doubt because they are not very important. A. H. M. Kirk-Greene, 'Diplomacy and diplomats: the formation of foreign service cadres in black Africa', in Ingham (ed.), *Foreign relations of African states*, is a useful preliminary study. M. A. East, 'Foreign policy making in small states: some theoretic observations based on a study of the Uganda Ministry of Foreign Affairs', *Policy Sciences,* vol. 4, 1973, is also interesting. For the pattern of African diplomatic relationships, see D. H. Johns, 'Diplomatic activity, power and integration in Africa', *Sage International Yearbook of Foreign Policy Studies*, vol. 3, 1975, and P. J. McGowan, 'The pattern of African diplomacy', *Journal of Asian and African Studies*, vol. 4, 1969.

Regional studies: Several studies exist of interactions within regions of the continent, outstanding among them K. W. Grundy, *Confrontation and Accommodation in Southern Africa* (California, Berkeley 1973); for the same region, see also S. C. Nolutshungu, *South Africa in Africa: a study of ideology and foreign policy* (Manchester University Press 1975), and L. Bowman, 'The subordinate state system of southern Africa', *International Studies Quarterly*, vol. 12, no. 3, 1968. Another important conflict zone, the Horn, is examined in C. Hoskyns, *Case Studies in African Diplomacy: The Ethiopia–Somalia–Kenya Dispute 1960–1967* (Dar-es-Salaam, 1969), and M. Abir, 'The contentious Horn of Africa', *Conflict Studies*, no. 24, 1972.

Source materials: Two useful collections of readings and documents are I. Brownlie, *Basic Documents on African Affairs* (Oxford University Press, London 1971), and Y. Tandon, *Readings in African International Relations* (Nairobi, 1972); only one volume of the latter, dealing mostly with the colonial period, so far appears to be available. For background material on African states, the best source is *Africa South of the Sahara* (Europa, London 1975). The best annual summary of events, with a particular emphasis on international relations, is C. Legum, *Africa Contemporary Record* (London, annual since 1968).

Country studies: Two collections of articles on the foreign policies of individual states are O. Aluko (ed.), *The Foreign Policies of African States* (Hodder, London 1976), with studies of Ethiopia, Guinea, Ivory Coast, Kenya, Tanzania, Zaire and Zambia; and K. Ingham, *Foreign Relations of African States* (Butterworth, London 1974), with studies of Guinea, Tanzania, and Uganda.

Other studies include, in alphabetical order of countries:

W. Henderson, 'Independent Botswana: a reappraisal of foreign policy options', *African Affairs*, vol. 73, no. 290, 1974.

M. D. Anang, *The Administration of Ghana's Foreign Relations, 1957–1965*, Athlone, London 1975.

S. Lindquist, *Linkages between domestic and foreign policy: the record of Ghana 1957–1966*, Lund, 1974.

W. S. Thompson, *Ghana's Foreign Policy, 1957–1966*, Princeton University Press, Princeton 1969.

J. Howell, 'An analysis of Kenyan foreign policy', *Journal of Modern African Studies*, vol. 6, no. 1, 1968.

J. E. Spence, *Lesotho: the politics of dependence*, Oxford University Press, London 1968.

C. McMaster, *Malawi: foreign policy and development*, Friedmann, London 1974.

A. B. Akinyemi, *Foreign Policy and Federalism*, Ibadan University Press, 1974.

O. Aluko, 'The civil war and Nigerian foreign policy', *Political Quarterly*, vol. 42, no. 2, 1971.

G. J. Idang, *Nigeria: internal politics and foreign policy 1960–1966*, Ibadan University Press, 1974.

O. Ogunbadejo, 'Nigeria and the great powers', *African Affairs*, vol. 75, no. 298, 1976.

W. A. E. Skurnik, *The Foreign Policy of Senegal*, Northwestern University Press, Evanston 1972.

J. Pettman, *Zambia: security and conflict*, Friedmann, London 1974.

T. M. Shaw, *Dependence and Underdevelopment: the development and foreign policies of Zambia*, Athens, Ohio 1976.

Notes

Abbreviated references are given for works cited in the bibliography.

[1]   Sub-Saharan Africa, for the purposes of this chapter, encompasses all independent African states except for those of the Mediterranean litoral and the white-ruled states of Southern Africa.

[2]   There is a vast literature on European colonialism in Africa; for a clear though controversial survey, see L. H. Gann and P. Duignan, *Burden of Empire*, Hoover Institute, Stanford 1967.

[3]   See O. Aluko, 'The civil war and Nigerian foreign policy', and O. Ogunbadejo, 'Nigeria and the great powers'.

[4]   See C. Clapham, 'Ethiopia and Somalia', and M. Abir, 'Red Sea Politics', in *Conflicts in Africa*, Adelphi Papers.

[5]   See J. Suret-Canale, 'Les relations internationales de la République de Guinée'.

[6]   See for example, G. J. Idang, *Nigeria: Internal Politics and Foreign Policy 1960–1966*, particularly chs. 4 and 5.

[7]   J. Mohan, 'Ghana, the Congo and the United Nations', *Journal of Modern African Studies*, vol. 7, no. 3, 1969.

[8]   See J. Pettman, *Zambia: Security and Conflict*.

[9]   C. McMaster, *Malawi: Foreign Policy and Development*, p.170.

[10]   For Gabon, see *Keesings Contemporary Archives*, 1964, pp.20024–5, and 'France's new role in Africa', *The World Today*, vol. 20, September 1964, pp.382–4; for Sierra Leone, C. Clapham, 'Sierra Leone: civilian rule and the new Republic', *The World Today*, vol. 28, February 1972, pp.82–91; the French intervention in Chad in 1969–71 is

examined in C. R. Mitchell, 'External involvement in civil strife: the case of Chad', *The Yearbook of World Affairs, 1972*, Stevens, London 1972, pp.152–86.

[11] See I. Wallerstein, 'The Range of Choice: constraints on the policies of governments of contemporary African independent states', in M. F. Lofchie (ed.), *The State of the Nations*, University of California, Berkeley 1971.

[12] See Y. Tandon, 'An analysis of the foreign policy of African states: a case study of Uganda'.

[13] See C. Clapham, *Liberia and Sierra Leone: an essay in comparative politics*, CUP, Cambridge 1976, ch. 7.

[14] See A. H. M. Kirk-Greene, 'Diplomacy and diplomats: the formation of foreign service cadres in black Africa'.

[15] McMaster, op.cit., pp.3–4; Idang, op.cit., pp.113–14; M. A. East, 'Foreign policy making in small states'.

[16] McMaster, op.cit., pp.3–4 and 169; W. S. Thompson, *Ghana's Foreign Policy 1957–1966*, especially pp.414–37.

[17] Z. Cervenka, 'Major policy shifts in the Organization of African Unity', p.331.

[18] See I. W. Zartmann, *The Politics of Trade Negotiations between Africa and the European Economic Community*, pp.24–76.

[19] Ibid., pp.93–107.

[20] See S. Touval, *The boundary politics of independent Africa*.

[21] See J. N. Paden, *Religion and Political Culture in Kano*, University of California, Berkeley 1973, chs 2 and 3.

[22] See R. W. Copson, 'Foreign policy conflict among African states, 1964–69'.

[23] *The Annual Register of World Events, 1974*, Longmans, London 1975, p.239.

[24] W. Henderson, 'Independent Botswana: a reappraisal of foreign policy options'.

[25] The best study of the gap between aspirations and achievement in the impact of individual African states on world affairs remains Thompson, *Ghana's Foreign Policy*.

[26] Y. Tandon, loc.cit.

[27] See Table 4.1.

[28] T. M. Shaw, 'African states and international stratification: the adaptive foreign policy of Tanzania'.

5 The Commonwealth Caribbean

VAUGHAN A. LEWIS

The Caribbean setting

The Caribbean as a geographical entity may be said to consist at its widest of those countries whose territorial boundaries are washed by the Caribbean Sea, including Venezuela, Colombia and the states of Central America (except El Salvador), as well as the archipelago of the Greater and Lesser Antilles. This geographical definition, however, fails to square with the historical criteria, derived from colonial penetration, which continue to be important determinants of the regional subsystem. As well as including several Latin American states, it excludes Guyana, which is identified traditionally (that is, in imperial terms) as well as culturally (by language and its plantation economy experience) as part of the Caribbean. The same might in broad measure be said for the Bahama Islands

This question of the *political* definition of the region is a controversial one which has, as we shall see, given rise to much discussion in the area itself, as each of the governments of newly-independent states has sought to elaborate regional and extra-regional foreign policies specifically for itself, without concern for the imperial aims and interests by which the region has traditionally been defined. For our purposes, it is nonetheless still most convenient to restrict our area of concern to those countries, formerly under British colonial rule, which claim membership of the Caribbean Common Market and Community which came into existence under the Treaty of Chaguaramas of 1973. Within this grouping, the independent states are Jamaica (independent 1962), Trinidad and Tobago (1962), Barbados (1965), Guyana (1966), Bahamas (1973) and Grenada (1974). Many of the smaller island territories, which currently have the status of West Indies Associated States, now claim that they wish to attain full sovereignty in the near future.

The place which the newly-independent Caribbean states saw themselves as occupying in the international system was conditioned by a number of factors, both longstanding and immediate. The first of these was the structural character of their economies, historically plantation

110

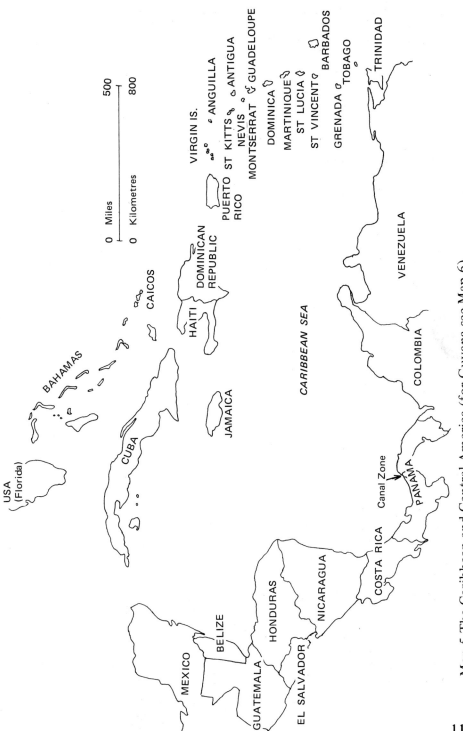

Map 5 The Caribbean and Central America (for Guyana see Map 6)

111

economies, which had been, as one economist put it, 'passively not actively incorporated into the international economy'. [1] They have tended to provide staples for whichever of the metropolitan countries dominated international trade and production at any point of historical time, and in turn the monetary returns from provision of such staples have always constituted the major portion of their national incomes. The metropolitan ownership of the production systems relating to these staples reinforced the resulting penetration and dependency. The economic systems of the Caribbean states are virtually *creations* of the metropolitan systems; they can in no way be said to have had a history of autonomous growth and development.

The second important factor is psychological in nature, though it must be said to constitute a social fact. This is that, given structural dependency and geo-political location, there has existed in the area a strong and widespread awareness of *small size,* leading to perceptions of insignificance in the global political and economic systems. [2] The policy implication of factors such as these for the political elite was a tendency to follow the trends and processes of international relations, rather than any inclination to believe that these could be affected, influenced, or controlled. Passive incorporation into the international economy was therefore reflected in passive rather than active diplomacy in official international institutions, and towards private institutions such as multinational corporations.

These perceptions were reinforced by specific features of the international system at the time of independence. The year 1962, when Jamaica, and Trinidad and Tobago became independent, was also the year of the Cuban Missile Crisis which, following closely on the Bay of Pigs invasion of Cuba in 1961, served to demonstrate the American capacity for unilateral action in the region, and thus to indicate the limits of foreign policy manoeuvres and alliance flexibility. Whatever the global effects of this crisis, as a precursor to US–Soviet detente, it cannot but have left a forceful impression on the newly-independent Caribbean states. Much the same can be said of the American intervention in the Dominican Republic in 1965.

Commonwealth Caribbean states were also more directly affected. The final phase of the movement towards independence in the then British Guiana (1963–66) is marked by controversy about the role of the United States in determining the membership and ideological orientation of the government. And this was a country which as a colony had recently seen its constitutionally elected government removed by the authorities, on the grounds that that government was adopting the ideology of communism.

The Bahamas, which became independent in the 1970s, had an almost integral strategic and economic relationship with the United States. [3] The dominating impression of the time on the political elite of these states must have been the prime significance of the United States in the 'ordering' of the global system, and particularly of Western Hemisphere international relations. It must have been awareness of this that led the Prime Minister of Jamaica to assert in 1962 the 'irrevocable decision that Jamaica stands with the West and the United States'. [4]

In sum, the response of the Caribbean states to the international and regional environment of the time was, for the most part, to stress their allegiance to the norms and values of the American-dominated hemispheric system, and their antagonism towards the communist international system and to the policies, domestic and external, of the Republic of Cuba in particular. Such political and economic relationships, for example, as Guyana had established with Cuba and other socialist countries in the pre-independence period were rapidly dismantled as that country moved towards independence under a new regime.

Another aspect of the regional environment on assuming independence was the question of territorial integrity. Some states, such as Jamaica and Barbados, were island territories for which no boundary problems arose. For others, like Guyana and Trinidad, such problems preceded and followed the assumption of full sovereignty. Before independence, the global significance of the colonial authority, the United Kingdom, had induced a certain subordination of territorial claims by Brazil and Venezuela in the case of Guyana, and Venezuela in the case of Trinidad. The prospect of independence for these colonies, however, led to an immediate revival of these claims, and even to claims by the Government of Surinam, then theoretically a fully autonomous part of the Kingdom of the Netherlands.

The foreign policy significance of this is that, having cast off the diplomatic protection of the colonial authority, both Trinidad and Guyana, but particularly Guyana, were forced to undertake a process of active diplomacy with the objective of warding off claims by their more powerful, and in their eyes predatory, neighbours. This active diplomacy was both regional and international, and, again particularly in the case of Guyana, had spillover effects in other issue-areas in which they were concerned in the global system. A parallel, and apparently more severe, example of this phenomenon can be seen in the case of the colony of Belize, whose independence is being delayed because of territorial claims from Guatemala. Belize, though still a colony, has had to undertake a form of active diplomacy, preparatory to its assumption of independence. This has been made even more necessary by the declining international status of its global protector, the United Kingdom, and a certain historical interest in this territorial integrity problem on the part of the United States.

A contrast may be made here with similar boundary and territorial integrity problems in Africa. There, the regional institution, the Organisation of African Unity, has attempted to settle such problems by adopting the stance that the boundaries existing at independence should be accepted as legal. The Organisation of American States, on the other hand, has been unable or unwilling to proceed in this way. By refusing to accept as a member any new state having territorial disputes with existing members, the OAS may indeed be said to have allowed such disputes to fester, regardless of the validity of the claims. The Cold War and American–Soviet global competition has exacerbated the situation, for the United States, in its search for firm allies, has been unwilling to adopt the definitive stance which might have been expected of a dominant hemispheric and global power.

In summary, then, we can say that neither the regional nor the international environments were seen by the newly-independent Commonwealth Caribbean countries as providing them with much security. Their existence has been perceived by the political elites as fragile, in the sense of exhibiting extreme dependence on circumstances and relationships subject to sudden change, and over which little control could be effected. In the first years of independence, these perceptions were reinforced by the fact that the relevant environment was seen as being predominantly the western international order, which had historically been the base of the countries' insecurity.

The institutional environment

Even before formal independence, there had developed, in Commonwealth Caribbean states, a limited experience of conducting international relations. This derived partly from negotiation with the imperial power, partly as a consequence of new demands, especially in the economic sphere, placed upon political leaderships by the masses through the mechanism of universal suffrage, and partly from the various political unification attempts within the Caribbean region itself. As a result, almost every territory had a small administrative cadre with some experience of negotiation with other countries; a system of Trade Commissionerships was already in existence during the Federal period

(1958–61). Such experience arose from dealing with a limited set of issues concerning constitutionalism on the one hand, and the maintenance of economic privileges on the other. The decision of colonies like Trinidad and Jamaica to undertake programmes of 'industrialisation by invitation' also led to some negotiating experience with private foreign enterprises. At the same time, there also came into existence a political leadership with some, largely intuitive, negotiating experience. This may have been in some sense damaging, since the small political leadership tended to arrogate to itself not only the decision making aspects of external relations (which might be considered its rightful role), but also the rationalisation of decision making, often to the frustration of the administrative cadre. This, however, is an experience common to many countries.

The new states were thus not bereft of some diplomatic experience, though the bureaucratic infrastructure for effecting diplomacy was minimal. This was however limited by the nature of the colonial constitutional relationship itself, and took place within the framework of 'colonial community'. Its restricted character meant that the political elite did not deem it necessary to develop a foreign policy orientation *per se*. Diplomatic positions assumed were of an *ad hoc* and pragmatic character. Examples of this mode of behaviour can still be found in the region, in the conduct of the non-independent West Indies Associated States.

We should also note that, in the first years of independence, the Caribbean countries tended to accept as valid the institutional modes of foreign policy representation characteristic of the United Kingdom, even though that country (like other major states) had developed its institutional paraphernalia in order to protect and advance its own extensive overseas interests. It is only at a later stage of independence that cognisance has begun to be taken of the fact that not only is the prime element of Caribbean external relations the *economic,* but that the resources to be protected exist *within* the territories, though subject not to national but to foreign ownership. A necessary re-organisation of the mechanisms for foreign policy representation has begun to take place, interpreting foreign policy in a manner wider than the traditional sense. [5]

A further problem for the Caribbean states arose from the need for some mechanism to regulate political and economic relations between themselves. Despite the uncertain atmosphere that followed the demise of the West Indies Federation (1958–61), it was quickly realised that some degree of cohesion would be necessary. Dr Eric Williams, Prime Minister of Trinidad, in proposing his country's independence, argued simultaneously the case for a Caribbean Economic Community as the now preferred route towards Caribbean integration. [6] Jamaica, too, despite its hostile attitude to the federal experience, has frequently reiterated the official policy of pursuing all forms of integration with the Caribbean, except political integration. The political–racial dispute within British Guiana in 1963–64 attracted the combined mediatory efforts of the Prime Ministers of Trinidad and Tobago and Jamaica, indicating an awareness both of the need for intra-regional settlement of disputes, and of the possible effect of disturbances in one territory on the image of the region as a whole.

The Federation period is therefore followed by recognition that some new form of regional relations would have to be constructed, especially to negate the effects of small size both for national markets and for bargaining capacity in international economic forums. Hence arose the early attempts in 1965 (between Guyana, Antigua and Barbados) to organise a free trade area, and the formal initiation of the Caribbean Free Trade Area (CARIFTA) among the Commonwealth Caribbean countries (except the Bahamas) in 1968. These attempts were particularly influenced, as Dr Williams remarked in 1962, by the British application for entry to the European Economic Community. We shall explore later some of the considerations influencing countries in their regional behaviour.

The domestic environment

It is increasingly acknowledged in the literature that foreign policy must be seen as partly reflective of domestic social structure and political systems. The traditional literature, which has tended to treat the domestic system as relatively unimportant (deriving from the tradition treating states as autocratic systems, or the external requirements of major powers as overriding the requirements of the domestic system) is clearly now regarded as inadequate. [7]

The Caribbean countries under consideration differ in the make-up of their social structures, in spite of their common plantation economy experiences. Almost immediately after the assumption of independence, these differences had institutional implications for foreign policy making. Thus, for example, the existence of substantial proportions of the descendants of both Indians and Africans in Guyana and Trinidad induced the governments of both these countries to establish ambassadorial representation in India and in specific countries on the continent of Africa (Zambia in the case of Guyana, and Ethiopia, and later Nigeria, in the case of Trinidad and Tobago). On the other hand, rising black and African consciousness among broad strata of the

Jamaican population in the 1960s induced the Government of Jamaica also to establish ambassadorial representation in Ethiopia. It is fair to say that these areas of diplomatic representation were established with little expectation of material gain deriving from them at the time. The substantial rationale was the reinforcing of cultural linkages for populations separated in both time and space from their original homelands.

Countries with somewhat more homogenous populations, like Barbados and the Bahamas, have refrained from such diplomatic endeavours, and have retained the more traditional areas of representation. But again, with the increasing numbers of Caribbean peoples in the American and Canadian metropoles in the 1960s, the rationale for representation in these countries acquired an additional dimension to the traditional one. As we shall see, significant interest in representation for the purpose of protection and advancement of economic interests occurs some years after the attainment of independence, in response to the vagaries of international economic relations in the Western World.

We can proceed now to discuss the, more direct, influence of the political system. Most of the Commonwealth Caribbean countries possess at the minimum two-party political systems based on the principle of universal suffrage. Both internal and external policy, therefore, has had to give perhaps greater deference to the demands of mass populations than is the case in many other Third World countries. The People's National Party in Jamaica, for example, having lost a referendum on the question of regional political integration in 1961 (and having then lost the 1962 General Election), has tended to be extremely conscious of the significance of external policy orientations for domestic politics. Similarly the other dominant party in Jamaica, the Jamaica Labour Party, has consistently attempted to raise the themes of political integration (federation) and relations with Socialist countries (communism) as political and electioneering slogans against the PNP. [8] Such considerations also apply in the case of the attitudes of private enterprise groups, which have tended to see the opening of diplomatic, cultural and economic relations with the countries of the Socialist bloc as implying the destruction of the mixed-economy but private-enterprise-dominant system prevalent in Jamaica. [9]

The case of Guyana is one in which political allegiances and ethnic affiliations coincide. Here the People's Progressive Party, espousing the ideology of Marxism–Leninism and a policy of cohesive relations with the Socialist bloc, and having been virtually forcibly removed from the administration of the country on two occasions, has consistently held the allegiance in electoral terms of the Indian population of Guyana. (The PPP split after the 1953 debacle, the offshoot being the People's National Congress led by Forbes Burnham, holding the allegiance of the African population.) Mainly as a consequence of the solidarity of the PPP support and the prevalence of Marxist ideology in the country, the PNC Government has been induced or constrained to move consistently leftwards in both internal and external policy. [10]

These two examples (Jamaica and Guyana) give an indication of the close relationship between the dynamics of party politics and external policy. There is, however, a general analytical point which needs consideration in a discussion of the connection between the domestic setting and foreign policy.

As was indicated at the beginning of this chapter, stress must be placed on the character of Caribbean countries as creations and objects of metropolitan (international) economy. [11] The important implication of this is their existence as open economies and open systems in general. In large measure they have to be considered, analytically, as subsystems of metropolitan economy, and, in that sense, as somewhat more than simply dependent. The point here is that it is difficult to say *a priori* that such sovereign units have in fact any substantial degree of systemic discreteness or capability for producing internal homogeneity, and thus for producing an autonomous policy. This is, of course, a condition increasingly characteristic of many other countries in the international system, and commonly termed interdependence. It is necessary, however, in the case of the Caribbean countries to see this, for analytical purposes, not as a deviation from the general conception of state and society, but as the normal and historical condition of the Caribbean state.

The analytical and policy implication of this is that, given the open character of these systems and their inter-connection with the metropolitan systems, domestic politics is international politics: any major change of domestic systems involves, and is, an immediate intervention in international (often hegemonic international) systems. The corollary is that external intervention in the countries almost naturally derives from this condition. This must be the basis of any analytical model of Caribbean foreign policy. [12]

The regional environment

In discussing the international environment of the Caribbean states, we need to discuss two broad areas: the regional environment and the wider international environment. Given our theoretical suppositions, it should

118

be clear that the two areas are inter-related. But in both a policy and an analytical sense they merit separate discussion.

The period of West Indian Federation had already indicated that all the states did not share a common view as to the future political character of the region. As early as at the point of declaration of the independence of Trinidad, Dr Williams had proceeded to indicate a preference for a Caribbean Economic Community which, as an economic and negotiating unit, would encompass an area wider than the countries which had come under British suzerainty. [13] This orientation was taken on two grounds. The first was the pragmatic one that, in any case, Trinidad and Tobago had, by virtue of its trading arrangements, 'an economic stake in the non-British territories' in the Caribbean; and the second was that the character of international economic relations required an entity of some reasonable economic size, for the protection of Caribbean interests.

This has been a constant theme in speeches and writings of the Caribbean political elite from thom the early 1960s. And Williams in 1973, at the inauguration of the Caribbean Common Market and Community, gives a reasonable summation of its rationale: 'The harsh reality of the international economy has taught us in practice, if we were unwilling to absorb the theory, the imperative of cooperation in negotiations with the outside world.' He adds that, in the learning of this lesson, 'the accession of the United Kingdom to the European Economic Community has been decisive'. [14]

Nevertheless, among the political leadership of the Commonwealth Caribbean there has been some degree of disagreement as to what should constitute the relevant co-operation and negotiating unit. The relevant definition of the unit has, in addition, been seen as having implications for its degree of diplomatic and political coherence.

If we examine the discussions on Caribbean integration as they have evolved at least since the early 1960s, we can isolate at least three main political conceptions that have served to guide both official and academic thinking about the future of the English-speaking Caribbean. [15]

The first is that which insists on the necessity for the creation of a single West Indian State, composed of the Anglophone islands of the archipelago and Guyana (and perhaps Belize), as the most effective political mechanism for solving the problems of cultural and political identity and material betterment for the mass of the peoples constituting this grouping. This state, following traditional categorisations, could be unitary or federal in character, the emphasis being on the existence of a single central government with effective powers of policy making and implementation. Students of the period of West Indian Federation will recall that there was much debate about the relative efficiencies of the federal, as against the unitary, state mechanisms, as evidenced in the competing conceptions of the Governments of Trinidad and Jamaica of that time.

The Government of Trinidad argued that the loose federal (even confederal) arrangement agreed to by the territories at the Lancaster House Conference in London and supported by the Government of Jamaica was too much of the traditional colonial law-and-order type. It ranged against this the formula of the *Economics of Nationhood* (a Government position paper), in which a tight federation or a unitary state would concern itself with the development of instruments of regional economic planning and growth. The Jamaican Government, on the other hand, argued the case for national (island) initiative at the level of economic policy, at least for some initial period. This corresponded with the Jamaican economic policy of industrialisation under highly protective tariff barriers.

The second conception is that which might be referred to as that of many states within the nation. This view at its widest posits the legitimacy of each territory being a separate sovereign state, continuing the tradition of national independence of the Spanish and French-speaking Caribbean countries of the nineteenth century. While it attributes a certain significance to the cultural unity of the English-speaking peoples, it sees this group as existing within a wider Caribbean area, encompassing the continental countries on the rim of the Caribbean Sea. (The anglophone Caribbean history of migration to this area establishes a certain material and sentimental connection.) This view attributes a degree of cultural–political specificity to each territory (in particular the larger ones) such that political unification is perceived as difficult, if not impossible.

A general characterisation of this view can be seen in a work by the Prime Minister of Jamaica, Michael Manley. While asserting that 'it is vital to Jamaica's future that we should play our part in the creation of a Caribbean Common Market', he argues that:

'...in the broadest sweep of history, economic regionalism must be seen as extending to include all the countries of Central Latin America which embrace the Caribbean. Guyana and Belize represent geographical outposts and are historical pioneers of this concept. Belize, Guatemala, Honduras, El Salvador, Nicaragua, Costa Rica, Panama, Colombia, Venezuela, Guyana, Surinam, French Guiana and Brazil all form a natural economic region bounded by Barbados to the east and stretching up through Cuba, the Bahamas to Bermuda to the north'. [16]

It is predominantly the geographical location of Jamaica that, for Manley, has determined this conception of regional relationships. While asserting a primary commitment to the Caribbean Community, he has argued of Jamaica that 'We are a small island partially surrounded by a continent of Latin American peoples. We cannot begin to contemplate the future of Jamaica without reference to our relation with the nations of the Spanish-speaking Caribbean, and South and Central America.' [17]

This conception of regionalism does not make political unity, even as an objective of economic integration, a primary focus. It sees the countries on the rim of the Caribbean as an integral part of any optimal economic and political co-operation arrangements of the region, and denies in turn that these countries can impose colonialist objectives on the island states of the Caribbean Sea. It must be argued that such a conception implies a Caribbean, widely defined, as an identifiable diplomatic community, based on the national independence of each territorial unit, with rules of behaviour specific to the community *vis-a-vis* the wider international environment – a loosely co-operative system, involving a network of economic agreements, for sustaining the sovereignty of each constituent unit.

The third political conception can be called the CARICOM Conception, and involves the institutions and arrangements proposed in the Treaty of Chaguaramas. It is, in effect, a half-way house between the two other conceptions, and can be said to be the reigning conception of the contemporary era. It substitutes functional integration – integration in terms of specific tasks requiring to be performed, which the policy instruments of the national state are presumed to be incapable of performing – for a unitary state conception of economic and institutional planning. It is, as with other experiments in the Third World, an attempt to apply the main theses of the European Community experience to the Caribbean. In Williams' words, it 'represents in practical terms – a very valuable understanding of the realities of the Caribbean in political terms – a remarkable accommodation between different points of view in the area'. [18]

The acceptance and implementation of the CARICOM conception by the anglophone Caribbean countries has the virtue of subordinating what are assumed to be the more extreme orientations of the other two conceptions to the requirements of necessary co-operative relationships between the states. The CARICOM conception is held to by all the countries, in spite of what appear to be developing differences at the level of political ideology, in terms of the socialist as against the broadly mixed-economy approaches to economic development. But whatever the growing relevance of ideology (a circumstance that has also characterised the development of the East African Community for example) as an input in policy making, a perhaps more important aspect making for differences between the countries is the relationship between the varying impulses of domestic politics and policy.

Specifically, as we have hinted above, the Caribbean countries have only now begun to transform electoral support attuned to competitive politics and free market systems into a base of legitimacy for popularly oriented domestic policies. The necessity for this arises from the growing populations and growing unemployment, both of which, in the system of universal suffrage, have perceptible effects on political parties. The volatility of domestic politics engendered by this attempted transformation is what makes national policy with respect to regional integration unpredictable and shifting. In turn, it makes national leaders unsure about what it is possible to commit governments to.

Another aspect of the regional environment which needs to be considered is the implication for different types of regional conceptions of the geopolitical locations of different countries. We can take some examples of this: although the Government of Guyana has, in recent years, propagated not only the CARICOM conception, but also a unitary state conception of integration among the anglophone countries, it has been constrained to organise relatively coherent relationships with both Brazil and Venezuela, mainly for the purpose of maintaining its territorial integrity. [19] We have alluded to this above. A similar line of policy has been followed by Trinidad in respect of Venezuela. The general institutional formula has tended to be the Mixed Commission. In the case of Trinidad, such institutional arrangements have been attempted in spite of the Prime Minister's verbalised fears of the possibility of an era of Venezuelan colonialism in the Caribbean archipelago. [20]

The wider international environment

The Treaty of Chaguaramas, institutionalising the Caribbean Community and Common Market, implies a certain measure of coherence in the enunciation of foreign policies by the Commonwealth Caribbean states. The requisite institution within the Treaty is the Standing Committee of Foreign Ministers. In spite of the relatively small geographical area encompassing the states, however, specific geopolitical locations and domestic structures have tended to suggest identifications of national interests which do not always coincide with each other. This writer has previously attempted to argue the case for the partial utility of the concept of national interest, in the context of linking it with the notion of issue-area as developed by Rosenau. [21] We have already suggested above how foreign policy relationships with Africa and India developed, in the first phase of independence, out of concern for the social structure make-up of particular countries. [22]

It can further be demonstrated that, in the case of Guyana, for example, the necessity to search for diplomatic support over the global system as a means of maintaining territorial integrity in the face of predatory neighbours directed that country more and more towards the ideology of non-alignment, and towards active subsequent participation in the propagation of economic programmes concerned with strengthening the autonomy of Third World countries as a group. [23] Here also, as we have suggested, the ideological context in which the competitive party system operated in Guyana was an input into the enunciation of policy.

Guyana, Trinidad and Jamaica all assert policies directed at substantial participation in the Third World system. The Foreign Minister of Guyana asserted his Government's view in 1974 that the 'community of Latin American States of which the Caribbean is a sub-region' should be 'a Latin America that confirms and strengthens its identification with the Third World, rejecting an image of the Western Hemisphere as a monolithic unit ... [It is] an identification of Latin American interests with the interests of the developing countries generally, whether its pre-occupation was with economic or with political issues'. [24]

Similarly, the Prime Minister of Trinidad and Tobago has stated that 'Trinidad and Tobago is part of the Third World... The P.N.M. [the ruling party] has envisaged this contact with the Third World ever since it came out with the *People's Charter* of 1956 in support of the Bandung Conference.' The Prime Minister of Jamaica has in the same vein remarked that 'We Jamaicans are part of the Third World...' [25] In the case of Jamaica, the emphasis by the People's National Party Government on relations with the Third World has met with a certain resistance from dominant economic sectors who perceive little immediate material gain to be derived from this, and who would prefer to strengthen traditional links with the metropolitan economies.

But the decision within the context of the CARICOM Treaty to attempt the harmonisation of the foreign policies of the separate states came at a persuasive period, when not only had the international economic crisis (following the world inflation of commodities) indicated that the formation of economic blocs might become the order of the day, but also when, with the decision of the United Kingdom to enter the European Economic Community, it was clear that co-ordination and cohesion at the regional level was the optimal strategy that might form the basis of Third World negotiation with the European countries towards the rearrangement of their then existing preferential arrangements. [26]

This connection between regional cohesion and international action has been re-emphasised in the context of the Caribbean in the case of the decision of Jamaica not only to exact greater financial returns from the multinational corporations producing bauxite, but (with the support of Guyana) to establish an international organisation for the protection and advancement of the interests of countries possessing bauxite exploited by these corporations. A communique issued by the Governments of Trinidad, Guyana and Jamaica observed that:

> '...the two governments [Guyana, and Trinidad and Tobago] regard the [tax] formula as a significant step in the direction of finding solutions to the problem of deteriorating terms of trade which is the central concern of all countries of the third world. ...the two governments are firmly in support of efforts to increase national [ownership] and control of resource industry'. [27]

Not all countries in the region would appear to be inclined to adopt a strong policy of non-alignment. Barbados, with an estimate of itself as possessing a relatively narrow range of resources to be protected, is an example of this; and the Bahamas, with its particular economic structure and location, would appear to follow this line. Thus the Prime Minister of Barbados has remarked that in the face of pressures exerted on his government to join the non-aligned group, 'I always ask who are you non-aligned against? I don't see any advantages − long or short-term − in joining the non-aligned group'. [28]

In general, however, the Commonwealth Caribbean strategy of strengthening relations with Third World countries focuses on the use of new diplomatic mechanisms towards the organisation of viable economic systems. Manley has observed that the main foreign policy aim of Jamaica is the country's economic development, and Williams has set the background of Caribbean strategy in the following way:

> Facing the traditional emphasis on links with metropolitan economies, rather than between our own individual economies, we

have learned the importance of closer ties one with another at economic and other levels — whether higher education or health, labour or shipping, examinations or meteorology, financial matters or mass communications. [29]

It is the necessity for engaging in more active, and less adaptive (to the Western world), diplomatic and foreign economic strategies that has also induced Caribbean countries towards a rationalisation of regional relations, irrespective of ideological orientations. We refer here specifically to the assumption of full diplomatic, and other, relations with the Republic of Cuba, the People's Republic of China, and the Soviet Union. [30]

But, as with other Third World countries, the new trends in international relations that are the consequence of complex United States–Soviet Union–China relations have also induced Caribbean countries to take advantage of a certain flexibility in international relations, and unhinge themselves from the frozen relations and connections of the Cold War period. But in the context of volatile domestic socio-political relations and awareness of the open character of their economic and political systems, the new active diplomacy must tend to remain subject to fears of external intervention from the dominant hemispheric power. This is so particularly because external diplomacy is in part a function of attempted internal socio-economic re-organisation, and such re-organisation relates to production structures owned by entities outside the territorial boundaries of the states. This is the policy relevance of our theoretical premise that, for the Caribbean states, 'domestic politics is international politics'.

Fears of external intervention are reinforced by the political elite's awareness that the Commonwealth Caribbean, irrespective of existing regional institutions, still possesses few political or other capabilities for sustaining the territorial integrity of the defined region as a whole. [31] The fact that this diplomatic unit consists of an archipelago exacerbates this problem.

Conclusion

The theoretical literature on the behaviour of Third World countries in the international system is still minimal, and most of it tends to analyse such countries as objects of metropolitan strategies. A recent critique has surveyed much of this theoretical literature, at least that emanating mainly from Western countries, and found it somewhat unsatisfactory. [32]

Our concern has been to stress the analysis of the structural basis of the Caribbean economic and political systems, and the response of these systems to the dynamic behaviour of international economic and political systems, of which they constitute subsystems. We have placed much less stress on the analysis of the actual making of particular decisions – what is often referred to as the range of choice problem – although this is a valid analytical approach. [33] For, as governmental elites in the region have found, foreign policy decisions have to take place in the context of an appreciation of the structures of transactions (the sets of systemic relations) which particular sectors of their state system may be involved in.

The systemic approach, however, must be placed in the context of the analytical isolation of specific issue-areas (following Rosenau) which indicate the areas of activity and decision making which elites are constrained to engage in, and which force the state as a policy making instrument to confront particular processes and institutions in the contemporary systems of international relations.

If we take this analytical approach, we perceive that states as systems (and we are forced then to consider the notion of 'state' as a discrete system) are constantly engaged in the activity of adapting, but that the important question is the identification of the particular relationships of adaptedness in which they are situated. [34] This is, in addition, the proper relevance of the concept of physical size, an important consideration in dealing with small states like those of the Caribbean area. For two states of the same size and similar resources may both be, of necessity, engaged in the activity of adapting to international processes, but their systemic contexts – the relationships of adaptedness in which they are engaged – may differ.

If we hold to the distinction between 'activity' and 'relationship', then we are much less likely to succumb to the trap into which Rosenau [35] appears to have fallen in his analysis of the notion of adaptation. The trap here is that of static analysis, and, to some degree, tautological definition.

In this chapter, however, we have been mainly concerned to isolate the specific characteristics of a number of states constituting the Commonwealth Caribbean, then to establish their location within the systems of international relations, and finally to note how these states have responded to the evolution of these relations. In other words, we have tried to establish some empirical basis for conducting the kind of theoretical exploration to which we have referred in this conclusion.

126

Bibliographical note

The systematic study of Caribbean foreign policy is, as would be expected, a comparatively new field. The following books nonetheless provide both a useful background and an indication of current work.

H. R. Brewster and C. Y. Thomas, *The Dynamics of West Indian Economic Integration*, Institute of Social and Economic Research, University of the West Indies, Jamaica 1967.

R. Crassweller, *The Caribbean Community: Changing Societies and U.S. Policy*, Praeger, New York 1972.

W. Demas, *The Economics of Development in Small Countries, with Special Reference to the Caribbean*, McGill University Press, Montreal 1965.

Basil Ince, *Decolonization and Conflict in the United Nations: Guyana's Struggle for Independence,* Schenkman, New York 1973.

Basil Ince (ed.), *International Relations of the Caribbean*, Institute of International Relations, University of the West Indies, Trinidad 1976.

Institute of International Relations, University of the West Indies, *Year-book of Caribbean International Relations*, vol. 1, Trinidad 1976.

Institute of Social and Economic Research, University of the West Indies, *Caribbean Issues Related to UNCTAD IV*, Jamaica 1976.

I Jainarain, *Trade and Underdevelopment*, Institute of Development Studies, University of Guyana, Guyana 1976.

E. de Kadt, *Patterns of Foreign Influence in the Caribbean*, Oxford University Press, London 1972.

V. A. Lewis (ed.), *Size, Self-Determination and International Relations: The Caribbean*, Institute of Social and Economic Research, University of the West Indies, Jamaica 1976.

R. Preiswerk (ed.), *Regionalism and the Commonwealth Caribbean*, Institute of International Relations, University of the West Indies, Trinidad 1968.

R. Preiswerk (ed.), *Documents on International Relations of the Caribbean*, Institute of International Relations, University of the West Indies, Trinidad 1970.

George L. Reid, *The Impact of Very Small Size on the International Behaviour of Microstates*, Sage Professional Papers, London 1974.

Notes

[1]   Lloyd Best, 'Agricultural Transformation in a Plantation Economy',

in *Proceedings of the Third West Indies Agricultural Conference*, Faculty of Agriculture, University of the West Indies, n.d.

[2] See Louis Lindsay, 'Colonialism and the Myth of Resource Insufficiency', in V. A. Lewis (ed.), *Size, Self-Determination and International Relations: The Caribbean*, ISER, University of the West Indies, Jamaica 1976.

[3] See V. A. Lewis, 'The Bahamas in International Politics: Issues arising for an archipelago state', *Journal of Inter-American Studies and World Affairs*, vol. 16, no. 2, May 1974.

[4] Quoted in Lindsay, 'Colonialism and the Myth of Resource Insufficiency', loc.cit.

[5] See Eric Williams, *Speech on Independence*, PNM Publishing Co., Port of Spain 1962.

[6] Eric Williams, op.cit.

[7] See W. Wallace, *Foreign Policy and the Political Process*, Macmillan, London 1971, and for the United States, K. Waltz, *Foreign Policy and Democratic Politics*, Little Brown, Boston 1967.

[8] In the 1962 General Election, the JLP accused the PNP of attempting to bring communism into the country. On the same theme at a later date, see 'Shearer: PNP has led Jamaica into Red Bloc', *Jamaica Daily Gleaner*, 4 December 1972. Most recently, this was an important issue in the 1976 General Election in Jamaica, in which JLP charges of communism were countered by PNP claims of 'destabilisation' directed against the USA.

[9] See for example, 'C of C [Chamber of Commerce] wants government to abandon youth trip to Cuba', *Jamaica Daily Gleaner*, 16 April 1975.

[10] There have been other reasons for this, which we shall refer to in our discussion of 'The Wider International Environment'.

[11] This is the central theme of Caribbean economists writing on the 'Plantation Economy'. See L. A. Best and K. Levitt, *Export-Propelled Economies in the Caribbean* (mimeo); and G. L. Beckford, *Persistent Poverty*, Oxford University Press, London 1972.

[12] I have explored this point at greater length in 'Linkage Politics: Foreign Policy and Domestic Political Behaviour in Third World Countries', mimeo prepared for the Seminar on Applied Social Science Techniques in Third World Countries, Institute of Social and Economic Research, University of the West Indies, Jamaica, March 1975.

[13] See Williams, op.cit., and similarly for the quotation following.

[14] *Trinidad Guardian*, 5 July 1973.

[15] In the following few paragraphs, I draw heavily on V. A. Lewis, 'Problems and Possibilities of Caribbean Community', in *Proceedings*

of the Commonwealth Caribbean Social Studies Conference, 1976, University of the West Indies, Institute of Education, forthcoming.

[16]   Michael Manley, *The Politics of Change: A Jamaican Testament*, Andre Deutsch, London 1974, pp.126–7.

[17]   *Trinidad Guardian*, 1 April 1973.

[18]   *Trinidad Guardian*, 16 June 1973.

[19]   For some discussion of the problems, see *Guyana Journal*, vol. 1, no. 3, 1969, Ministry of External Affairs, Georgetown, Guyana.

[20]   See Williams, *The Threat to the Caribbean Community*, Speech at a Special Convention of the PNW, 15 June 1976. The speech is, in the main, a denunciation of the establishment of certain types of relations between Jamaica and Venezuela, which Williams deemed harmful to Commonwealth Caribbean integration.

[21]   See 'The Commonwealth Caribbean and Self-Determination in the International System' in V. A. Lewis (ed.), op.cit.

[22]   See in addition, L. Edmondson and P. Phillips, 'The Commonwealth Caribbean and Africa: Aspects of Third World racial interactions, linkages and challenges', in B. Ince (ed.), *International Relations of the Caribbean* Institute of International Relations, University of the West Indies, Trinidad, forthcoming.

[23]   For some preliminary indications, see my 'The Commonwealth Caribbean Policy of Non-Alignment: A Note' in Ince (ed.), op.cit. See also *Main Documents Relating to Conferences of Non-Aligned Countries: From Belgrade, 1961 to Georgetown, 1972*, Ministry of Foreign Affairs, Guyana 1972.

[24]   'The Role of the Caribbean in a Hemisphere in Transition', address delivered by the Hon. Shridath S. Ramphal, Minister of Foreign Affairs and Justice, Guyana, at the Centre for Inter-American Relations, New York, 22 April 1974, mimeo.

[25]   See Williams, *PNM's Perspectives in the World of the Seventies*, Address to a Special Party Convention, Port of Spain, November 1970; 'Manley Says Third World turning to new economic order', *Jamaica Daily Gleaner*, 6 September 1974.

[26]   See *Jamaica: Ministry Paper No. 7: The A.C.P./E.E.C. Convention of Lome*, presented to Parliament by Hon. P. J. Patterson, Minister of Industry, Tourism and Foreign Trade, 8 February 1975.

[27]   'Williams and Burnham back Jamaica's new policy', *Trinidad Express*, 9 June 1974. On Jamaica's bauxite policy see L. Edmondson, 'Bauxite Diplomacy in the Caribbean and in International Relations: a preliminary exploration', University of the West Indies, Department of Government, mimeo. Also, 'Manley sees IBA as avenue for cooperation',

Jamaica Daily Gleaner, 31 December 1974.

[28] 'Barrow raps U.S. role in region', *Barbados Advocate-News*, 6 May 1976.

[29] *Trinidad Guardian*, 5 July 1973, speech on the signing of the Treaty of Chaguaramas.

[30] See for an editorial comment, 'Remaining Non-Aligned' *Trinidad Guardian*, 22 June 1974.

[31] I discuss this in my article referred to in note 21.

[32] See Bahgat Korany, 'Foreign-policy Models and their Empirical Relevance to Third-World Actors: a Critique and an Alternative', *International Social Science Journal*, vol. 26, no. 1, 1974, pp.70–94.

[33] A colleague at the University of the West Indies is currently focussing on the 'range of choice' problem. See Carl Parris, *Capital or Labour?*, Working Paper no. 11, Institute of Social and Economic Research, University of the West Indies, Jamaica 1976, which is part of a larger study in progress.

[34] I am here using a distinction derived from biological analysis, see G. Sommerhoff, *Analytical Biology*, Oxford University Press, London 1950.

[35] J. Rosenau, *Adaptation of National Societies: A Theory of Political Behaviour and Transformation*, McCaleb-Seiler, New York 1970.

6 Latin America

EDY KAUFMAN

The Latin American subsystem

Although Africa, Asia and Latin America are all generally considered to be part of the Third World, the position of Latin America [1] requires some clarification. Firstly, Latin America has on the whole a higher level of development than either Africa or Asia. Secondly, the foreign policies of the states within the area tend to be significantly more aligned with the West than with the neutralist bloc, although on economic issues raising the division along North–South lines between the rich and the poor countries Latin America would side with the developing world. When analysing the foreign policies of Latin American countries in comparison with other developing areas, a visible contradiction thus becomes apparent between the region's higher degree of development and its lower degree of independence in the international arena. This chapter aims to explain this phenomenon through the study of domestic and external variables.

A question which must first be answered is whether it is legitimate to categorise the continent as a unified entity. Many of the scholars dealing with the international politics of the region agree that it is, among them being Spiegel and Cantori, who consider Latin America to be a single subsystem, while Asia, Africa and Europe are divided into two or more units. [2] Many consider Latin America to be nothing more than a broken country of 'dismembered people, by lack of communication and feudalism since a century ago'. [3] Expressions such as 'Latin American nationalism' or 'Latin American internationalism' are often found in the writings of statesmen from the continent, emphasising the importance of Latin American unity and providing grounds for a strong case for regional nationalism.

The cohesiveness of the Latin American region can be traced back to common historical links, religion, race and culture, not only within the component states but crosscutting them. Almost all of the Latin American peoples have a similar Indo-Iberic background, which throughout the years has provided a common factor unifying the populations. The similar historical experience of emancipation from the yoke of the

Map 6 South America (for Central America see Map 5)

Spanish Empire more than a century and a half ago produces an added feeling of common identification. Generals such as Jose de San Martin or Simon Bolivar are not considered the liberators of one country only, but regional heroes who participated in the general movement of independence from Spain, and represent the ideal of continental unity. Even in the twentieth century popular leaders such as the Argentinian Che Guevara, the Mexican Lázaro Cárdenas, Fidel Castro or Salvador Allende have been considered personalities on a regional scale.

Latin America's homogeneity in various fields favours unity in action, as well as a stable regional structure. The population is 90 per cent Catholic, proportionately distributed in the same ratio in all areas of the continent. (There are more than 200 million Roman Catholics, the greatest concentration in any one area of the world.) Asia and Africa are riven by different religions and sects, which divide state from state, as well as dividing countries internally. Latin America also has cultural and linguistic homogeneity, Spanish being a unifying link. Although there is a heterogeneous ethnic population in Latin America, the existence of mixed types such as the *mestizo* and the *mulato* minimises racial tensions. In Black Africa, though radical composition within each region is basically homogeneous, strongly felt identification with sects and tribes acts as a divisive element which is stronger than the potential racial homogeneity. In Asia, where there are countries with a multiracial composition, the existing tensions are generally increased.

The Latin American continent has also experienced common political processes. It can be argued that any event in any place in the world has an impact on every other part. However, if the intensity of the actual influence could be verified, it might be said in the case of Latin America that events which occur within the same continent tend to have a greater effect on the other countries of that continent. The triumph of the Cuban revolution caused the United States to offer more aid under a new economic policy on the continent, the Alliance for Progress, which aimed to prevent the spread of communism to other countries. The anti-Cuban attitude of the OAS, the inter-American organisation, was justified by opposing all totalitarian governments, using as examples the extreme right wing dictatorships of the Dominican Republic and Haiti.

Another interesting example was the invasion of Guatemala by a US-backed military force in 1954 to depose the leftist regime. At the same time there was intensified repression of communist elements in the other countries of the continent. Martin Needler has demonstrated that certain political phenomena, such as changes from military dictatorships to civil–democratic governments, have a cyclical character in Latin

America. [4] Lately phenomena such as guerilla warfare, the radicalisation of the clergy, and an increase in military intervention in politics have affected most Latin American countries.

However, there is also heterogeneity in Latin America. Different types of government exist on the continent, but without geographical proximity. The Central American military dictatorships resemble the regimes of Paraguay and Bolivia; Costa Rica's civilian system, until a few years ago, resembled the former Uruguayan and Chilean democracy rather than any other country of the continent, and Cuba's socialist regime found its closest ally in Allende's Chile, the most distant country geographically. In the same way, the ethnic composition of states' populations is not related to their geographical location. Guatemala, Bolivia and Ecuador have a high proportion of Indians; Costa Rica, Uruguay and Argentina have an almost totally European population. Mexico, Colombia and Venezuela have a high percentage of *mestizos,* and Brazil follows Haiti in having a high proportion of blacks in its population. Neither can Latin America be easily divided into economic subregions. In spite of the fact that the countries with the highest gross national product *per capita* are concentrated in the southern area, Mexico and Costa Rica are not far behind, and Venezuela has the highest GNP of the continent.

Many of the aspects which differentiate Afro-Asia from Latin America have been developed by Martz and Williams. [5] Out of the twenty Latin American countries, we can roughly reckon that seven countries − Argentina, Brazil, Chile, Uruguay, Venezuela, Mexico and Costa Rica with a combined population of more than three-quarters of the continent − have approached in recent years socio−economic levels not distant from the mother countries, Spain and Portugal, or others such as Greece and Yugoslavia. The rest, although approaching more the standards of African and Asian nations, still present in certain cases a higher level of development, particularly in regard to variables such as individual consumption, social stratification, and university education. The differences between Afro-Asia and Latin America are not confined to economic standards, but are reflected also in the political structure, social stratification and culture. The adherence to the principles of a pluralistic Western democracy, even when military dictatorships prevail in the area, remains very strong and such regimes also attempt to provide some type of legitimation by promising elections or maintaining some sort of parliamentary facade with restricted opposition parties. The social structure presents such features as a large middle class in the more developed Latin American countries, usually accompanied by a large urban population, blue collar workers and extensive shanty-towns. The

European ingredient in the ethnic composition has left strong cultural traces in fields such as theatre, literature and art. The trade unions and student movements are powerful pressure groups in the political scene. All these points can only stress the intermediate character of Latin America between the more and less developed worlds.

Relations at the inter-regional level in Latin America are on the whole ones of limited co-operation, approaching the level of alliances in certain fields or specific cases, or the formalisation of neutral relations. A stalemate relationship between the countries at the centre of the subsystem seldom occurs, nor does the outbreak of limited crises. During the present century, apart from the Salvador–Honduras 'football war', the War of Chaco between Paraguay and Bolivia, and the Leticia border dispute between Peru and Colombia, there have not been any serious military confrontations. The few cases of conflict that arose in Latin America were basically frontier disputes, but frontiers have now been defined for over a century. Most of the conflicts are based not on latent emotions, but on principles deriving from historical claims. However, these opposing claims do not generally result in negative relations between neighbouring countries. This can be seen in the case of Chile and Argentina, and of Peru and Ecuador, whose territorial claims have not harmed their relations with each other. In the extreme case of Bolivia's demand for an outlet to the ocean, she severed diplomatic ties with Chile, but nevertheless, consular, trade, and official contacts continued. Sometimes the disputes were intensified as a result of internal problems within the countries involved, as in the case of the Chile–Bolivia, Chile–Argentina, and Argentina–Uruguay border disputes.

Another cause of antagonistic relations is when a country becomes isolated, or attacked, for ideological–political reasons. This was the case in Guatemala, which was the target of hostility from Honduras and Nicaragua in 1954. Revolutionary Cuba was also attacked during the stages leading up to the invasion in 1961, and later suffered the rupturing of diplomatic ties and an economic boycott. However, it should be pointed out that in many of these cases the initiative came from the United States, which used other Latin American countries as an indirect instrument for the attainment of its own aims.

In Latin America, the fact that nearly all the movements for national independence had the same colonial enemy to overthrow (Spain) was a unifying factor, whereas in Africa and Asia the new nationalistic movements were against various colonial powers: France, Britain, Holland, Spain, Portugal, and Belgium. Nor is it only in historical–cultural perspectives that Latin America differs from Afro-Asia; the modern economic development problems it faces are also different: its efforts to achieve political and economic emancipation today are mainly related to the creation of new relationships with one superpower, the United States. Afro-Asian states, on the other hand, are still trying to achieve full emancipation from the different former colonial powers; they now face the problem of neo-colonialism, as well as fending off penetration, economic and political, by the new superpowers.

Latin American organisational unity is not a new phenomenon; the inter-American organisation is the only regional body among the twenty-three at present existing that precedes the Second World War. In spite of the fact that many of these organisations, such as the Organization of American States, include its northern neighbour, there is a clear polarisation between the Latin American countries on the one hand and the United States on the other. J. J. Arevalo, a former Guatemalan President, referred to this relationship as 'the shark and the 20 sardines'. All the same, the Latin American group is strengthened by the existence of a wide variety of regional organisations at all levels: there are governmental economic associations, such as the Latin American Area for Free Trade (ALALC); non-governmental, cultural or political, such as the Latin American Organization for Solidarity (OLAS), which is pro-Cuban, the Latin American Center for Democratic Studies (CEDAL), which is sponsored by the democratic left parties, the Latin American Sociological Association (ALAS), etc. Even subregional organisations, based on a specific geographical unit, such as the Andean group (Venezuela, Colombia, Peru, Ecuador, Chile, Bolivia) or the smaller Central American common market, do not seriously oppose or put negative pressure on overall integration.

The external environment

The character of the post-Second World War international system has undoubtedly restricted the foreign policy options of Latin American countries. The Cold War period brought about a rigid bipolar international structure in which the superpowers received world recognition of their supremacy of power. One of the dimensions that enables them to perform their leading role is the existence of a continuous bloc or camp of unconditional followers. It provides an additional weight for the Soviet Union and the United States, whose superiority is perceived not only in terms of overall military strength but also as absolute regional powers. However, over the past few years bipolar tensions have somewhat decreased and the dangerous nuclear 'balance of terror' has reciprocally neutralised to a certain extent the superpowers' advantages over secondary powers in Western Europe or China. But although such a situation allowed for a greater foreign competitiveness in Asia and Africa, it did not affect significantly the dependence situation of Eastern Europe and Latin America on only one hegemonic superpower. The concern of the Soviet Union and the United States to maintain a tight control over their adjacent regions continues to be strong due to strategic, political and economic considerations. This principle is so far still legitimised by the other powers by a very reduced presence in the two regions. As far as Latin America is concerned neither a declared nor implemented rivalry has seriously challenged the United States' supremacy.

The Soviet Union, the expected competitor of the United States, has in fact shown very little perseverance in the pursuit of influence in Latin America. [6] Aware of the importance that the United States attaches to this part of the world and expecting a similar respect for its own sphere of influence in Eastern Europe, the Soviet Union has restricted itself mostly to maintaining normal relations with the different regimes. Increases in trade, cultural links and some forms of aid are the major instruments of Soviet policy, with little expectation of obtaining political support in exchange. The case of Cuba can only be regarded as an exception to the rule, and understood through a combination of factors which include a series of miscalculated attempts by Washington to overthrow Castro's regime, and the intense national unity that the revolutionary regime managed to create, particularly against threats of foreign intervention. Furthermore, it would be fair to say that it was more Castro's desperate attempt to avoid the undermining of his regime by the Americans than the initiative of the Kremlin that provoked in a very short period a high level of Soviet involvement in the island. [7] Later, Khruschev's adventurism led him to challenge the *status quo* to the extreme by introducing nuclear missiles in Cuba in 1962. But this episode ended in a way that re-emphasised the United States' claim to military supremacy in the area. Even now, with the exception of the military camps in the US Canal Zone, the only official American base in Latin America is to be found in Guántanamo, on Cuban soil, its continuous presence being explained not so much by its strategic importance but more as an unmistakable corroboration of its claim for supremacy.

Castro's growing influence in Latin American left wing circles at the beginning of the 1960s and his enthusiastic appeal for armed struggle all over the continent challenged the preference of a Soviet-oriented communist movement for an evolutionary change through elections. Such differences provoked a loss of support and a growing criticism of the passive role played by the Soviet Union, an argument that was vociferously echoed by the Chinese and their adherents in Latin America. Confronted with this rapid erosion the Soviet Union sought a compromise solution with the Cuban hard line, by which guerilla warfare was to be encouraged in a selected number of countries (Venezuela, Guatemala, Colombia, Paraguay and Haiti), which incidentally did not maintain diplomatic ties with Moscow or where the Communist party was banned, and where the electoral road was anyway blocked. In addition, guerillas in Guatemala, Venezuela and Colombia were already in action, strongly endorsed by the younger communist militants. In Paraguay and Haiti armed struggle never really took off, and, by the late 1960s, except for a limited force in Colombia, the communist parties abandoned the policy of armed struggle which subsequently collapsed. In broad terms, the pro-Soviet communists since the end of the Second World War have followed the 'peaceful way to socialism'. After the triumph of President Allende in Chile's 1970 elections a similar formula was tried in nearly all countries with a civilian regime (Argentina, Uruguay, Venezuela, Colombia). But the military takeover in Chile and the banning of political activities in Uruguay and Argentina have severely restricted the likelihood of the electoral option. So, by the mid-1970s, the traditional and less ambitious goal of keeping some sort of functioning relationship with Latin American regimes, however strongly pro-American and right wing they might be, remained the current policy of the USSR. With the exception of a spectacular severance of relations with the Chilean military junta, the Soviet Union has been willing to maintain relations with all other states, but still about half of the countries in the region — mainly the small Central American states — have preferred not to maintain diplomatic ties with this superpower.

The influence of China is even more drastically limited. [8] Although certain conditions are present in the infrastructure that could theoretically be attractive for radical communist policies (a large peasant population, armed insurrection, strong anti-American feelings, etc), Chinese revolutionary activities have usually been restricted to broadcasting and other means of propaganda, with virtually no help even to the few Maoist guerilla groups that were organized in Bolivia, Brazil or Colombia. Even in the verbal struggle, the major attacks were not focused on the 'paper tiger' of United States imperialism, but against Soviet revisionism and social imperialism. Furthermore, with the incipient normalisation of relations with Washington, Chinese policy has become increasingly one of keeping normal ties with any political regime, which includes the maintenance of diplomatic links with the military regime in Chile and a rather reduced relationship with socialist Cuba.

Western Europe states individually and as a Community have carried little weight in the post-Second World War era. In political terms, no challenger appeared to the hegemony of the USA with the sole exception of the visit to Latin America by President de Gaulle in 1964. This increased some francophile feelings in the continent, and in concrete terms was instrumental in the selling of Mirage planes to Peru and Brazil. It should be pointed out that at the beginning of the century many of the southern countries of the continent regarded Europe and particularly Great Britain as a primary source for livestock and agricultural exports, manufactured imports and investments. Some of these relations are still maintained in those southern countries, especially in Argentina and Uruguay, but the search to widen the European markets is not reflected in a granting of major freedom of movement *vis-à-vis* the dominating superpower. Castroist Cuba, the only real case of total emancipation, although it has succeeded in keeping trade and diplomatic relations with Western European countries, including Spain, does not find this framework a viable and strong enough guarantor of its independence, and has had to rely completely on the Soviet will to protect it.

On a political level, the European Christian Democratic parties, particularly in West Germany and Italy, provided during the 1960s some guidance and economic help to their homologue movements in Latin America, and particularly in Chile and Venezuela where they were in power. Similarly, the Social Democratic Socialist International has endeavoured to support the democratic left at present ruling Costa Rica and Venezuela. Perhaps this is best represented in the participation of Brandt, Kreisky, Palme and Mario Suarez in a summit conference that took place in Caracas in May 1976. As a whole, the political influence of Western Europe remains extremely limited. On occasions such issues as minimal respect for human rights are attached to preferential trade concessions, which are anyway unlikely to be given because of the internal economic difficulties of the European Common Market. The temporary withdrawal of the British Ambassador from Santiago, following the torture of a British doctor, no doubt had some repercussions as a symbolic warning, on Chile's image and its apparent attempt to improve its human rights record. As to Japan, its growing economic presence in Latin America does not constitute any threat to the United States' dominance in this area. Although some competition may arise between Japanese and American companies in the most modern countries of the continent, such a drive is not perceived in Washington as posing any serious threat. [9]

The presence of Asian and African countries in Latin America is indeed insignificant. However, bearing in mind the scope of this book, it may be useful to discuss the development of such contacts to the present day. The impact of non-alignment on the Latin American continent can be traced back to the end of the 1950s with the visit of leaders from both regions to each other; Sukarno visited Mexico in 1959 and Janio Quadros, who had, half a year before, been elected President of Brazil, visited India, Egypt, Yugoslavia and Cuba. It is significant that the origins of neutralism can be traced to Latin America. Latin America supported neutrality from the legal point of view in order to avoid becoming involved in conflicts of other continents. This became a doctrine with the Third Position of Perón, who, almost up to the end of the Second World War, refused to declare war on Germany and maintained a position of neutrality. With the development of the Cold War, Perón declared himself opposed to both capitalism and communism, but he failed to establish a relationship with the emerging Afro-Asian movement. At the beginning of the 1960s Presidents Quadros and Goulart in Brazil, and Prime Minister Castro in Cuba, added to this local 'neutrality' the Afro-Asian interpretation of 'neutralism'. Colonialism, and the neo-colonialism that followed it, were perceived to be a linked and common phenomenon of all three continents. However, in Brazil and Argentina the presidents did not survive for long and both countries soon returned to the old allegiance with the Western bloc.

Venezuela, because of its oil interest, has maintained close contact since 1959 with the Arab countries, and supported the Afro-Asian conference held in Cairo in 1964. Ex-President Betancourt emphasised that the 'main feature is the fact that our interest coincides with that of the Middle Eastern countries in the common objective of maintaining the price of oil in the international markets at a high price and profitable level for the producers of that raw material'. [10]

Until the middle of the 1960s there was no serious organisational connection between Latin America and the neutralist bloc. At that time, when the neutralists were undergoing a unity crisis and disagreements were growing, Cuba attempted to take over the leadership by trying to forge a link between the three continents. The difference was that Cuba attempted to organise the revolutionary elements into a new International including the subversive and extremist militants to the exclusion of a great number of government representatives (among the delegates, for example, was M. Ben Barka, main leader of the opposition to King Hassan of Morocco). The Organization of Solidarity of the People of Asia, Africa and Latin America (OSPAAAL), the 'Tricontinental', was thus created in Havana in 1965 with a mainly anti-imperialist and anti-North American philosophy. This attempt only intensified existing divisions within Afro-Asia without drawing any new elements from Latin American regimes into the movement, since with the exception of Cuba, Latin America continued to be represented exclusively by anti-government political forces. The death of Che Guevara, the collapse of the guerilla movement and the lack of revolutionary practice of most Afro-Asian participants destroyed Castro's dreams. Slowly he made his way back again to the established Third World framework.

The first neutralist conference to be organised on Latin American soil took place in Georgetown, Guyana in 1972, but the only new member from the continent to adhere fully to neutralism was Chile; the only additional guest was the Pro-Independence Movement of Puerto Rico. Argentina, Barbados, Bolivia, Brazil, Colombia, Ecuador, Mexico, Peru, Uruguay and Venezuela all participated only as observers. Another conference on Latin American soil, in Lima in 1975, showed the eager-ness of the Afro-Asian organisers of the neutralist movement to enlarge the membership with Latin American countries. In addition to Peru, so far, Panama has officially joined, viewing it as the most appropriate plat-form from which to see the reclamation of the Panama Canal applauded and approved; Argentina has adhered also, as a way of mitigating internal criticism of its move to the right, thereby loyally following the foreign policy principles established by General Perón.

Although advances have been made in relations between the neutralists and Latin America, this bloc on a more concrete basis has only attracted a few countries from the continent. The majority of the political regimes in Latin America consider themselves of the right or centre and adhere to the basic values of Western civilisation and Christendom. Spiritually the ruling elites identify themselves with the Old World and not with the Third World. For them neutralism is basically an anti-colonial expres-sion with a pro-communist connotation. [11]

At the present time unity between Afro-Asia and Latin America seems to be limited to the economic problems shared by both but to different degrees. Politically, the countries of the regions have very different out-looks. The Conference of the UNCTAD in Geneva in 1964 established the bloc of 77, which numerically encompasses the Latin American nations, whose participation is not only formal, but also active. A more recent unifying factor is Afro-Asia's production of similar raw materials, and together they seek to create a united front in the international market to control production and maintain the world price for their raw materials.

141

Table 6.1

Embassies and legations of Latin American states (1975)

	USA, Canada Caribbean	Latin America (19)	Cuba	Western Europe	Vatican	Communist countries	Asian non-communist countries	Africa	South Africa	Arab countries	Israel	Total
Argentina	4	17	1	16	1	8 (China, Yu)	12	2	1	5	1	68
Bolivia	1	9	–	5	1	2 (USSR, Yu)	–	–	–	–	1	19
Brazil	4	18	–	15	1	5 (China, Yu)	7	5	1	7	1	64
Chile	2	17	–	16	1	2 (China, Rum)	8	3	–	7	1	57
Colombia	2	18	–	13	1	–	2	–	–	2	1	39
Costa Rica	1	12	–	4	1	1 (USSR)	1 (Taiwan)	–	–	1	1	22
Cuba	4	5	–	14	1	13	7	4	–	7	–	55
Dominican Rep.	2	14	–	11	1	–	2 (Taiwan)	–	–	–	1	31
Ecuador	1	15	–	9	1	3 (USSR)	1 (Japan)	–	–	1	1	32
El Salvador	2	15	–	6	1	–	1 (Japan)	–	–	–	1	26
Guatemala	1	8	–	6	1	–	1 (Taiwan)	–	–	–	1	18
Haiti	2	8	–	7	1	–	1 (Japan)	4	–	–	1	24
Honduras	1	13	–	5	1	–	1 (Japan)	–	–	–	1	21
Mexico	7	18	1	14 (W.Germ)	–	9 (E.Ger,Chi)	9	5	–	6	1	70
Nicaragua	1	13	–	5	1	–	1 (Taiwan)	–	–	–	–	21
Panama	2	18	1	8	1	1 (Yu.)	2 (Jap.Taiw)	–	–	1	1	35
Paraguay	1	11	–	5	1	–	2 (Jap.Taiw)	–	1	–	1	22
Peru	4	18	1	13	1	8 (China)	5 (S.Korea)	–	–	4	1	55
Uruguay	2	16	–	14	1	3	2 (Aus.Jap.)	–	–	2	1	41
Venezuela	4	16	1	15	1	5 (China)	4	1	–	4	1	52
Total	48	279	5	201	19	60	69	24	3	47	17	772

Source: The original data have been compiled from *The Stateman's Yearbook, 1975–1976*, MacMillan, London, 112th edition, 1975.

A similar reference can be made to the Third Conference of the Law of the Sea that took place in Caracas in 1974, in which all participants from Asia, Africa and Latin America seemed to agree on the extension of territorial waters, safeguarding and protecting the national resources of the developing countries against the voracity of the more advanced ones.

An overall view of the external linkages of Latin American states is provided by their network of diplomatic representation (embassies and legations). Though in individual cases missions may be established due to personal, historical or circumstancial considerations, the network as a whole indicates clearly the current place of Latin American states in the international system.

A first observation should be made as to the high level of regional interaction: with an average of relations with approximately 14 out of 19 possible Latin American countries (74 per cent), it represents 36.79 per cent of their total diplomatic representation (if Cuba is excluded, the correct figure is 40 per cent). The first priority is then focused inside the subsystem, emphasised by the fact that the Latin American countries number no more than one-seventh of the world community. Within the continent, Latin American countries maintain permanent missions in countries of their immediate geographic areas: that is to say, countries of both subregions, Central America and South America, have diplomatic ties with all the countries in their respective region.

As expected, all Latin American countries but Cuba maintain an embassy in Washington, contrasting with the absence of missions in Moscow of the ten smaller and weaker states. Relations with Communist countries reach only an average of 7.77 per cent of the entire diplomatic network (corrected figures without Cuba lower it to 6.55 per cent). Relations with Taiwan are still more predominant than those with Communist China, even after the *rapprochement* between Washington and Peking. Countries considered to be the neutralists of the continent are only now timidly challenging the Western orientation of other Latin Americans. Peru continued in 1975 to maintain an embassy in South Korea and Panama's relations with the Communist bloc were confined only to a mission in Yugoslavia.

Relations with Western European countries, and particularly with the United Kingdom, West Germany and the Latin countries, remain a consistent pattern in Latin American international politics, encompassing an average of 26 per cent of their total network. Embassies and legations in Eastern Europe and the Soviet Union do not exceed one-fifth of this figure.

In the general context, the low diplomatic intercourse with Afro-Asian nations is clearly noticeable. The relatively higher numbers for the Arab countries and Israel – the country with the largest Latin American presence in Afro-Asia – can be largely explained by domestic pressures from communities related to those Middle Eastern countries, or, lately, by oil interests.

The differences in the size of the diplomatic representation maintained abroad by Latin American countries are obscured by a gradual transition. Nevertheless, the extremes are well distanced from each other. At the top we find Mexico, Argentina and Brazil with 70, 68 and 64 missions respectively. Guatemala and Bolivia close the table with 18 and 19 missions respectively, preceded by Nicaragua and Honduras with 21 each.

In all the external determinants of foreign policy of Latin American countries, the United States occupies a position of primacy. While other countries maintain only a reduced number of transactions, and are often limited to specific types of sectors (trade, cultural, etc.), the Big Brother of the North shows its presence in the continent in a multifaced form. While in other cases the external influence can be regarded basically as a government-to-government relationship, the United States has penetrated the continent in so many different ways and through such a large number of American official and private institutions that it becomes very difficult to discern the dividing line between the external and domestic settings. It is perhaps advisable then to deal with such issues in the following section dealing with the connections between the two structures.

Domestic penetration by external actors

Inherent and inter-related to its internal pluralistic structure, the United States has generally acted in Latin America through a varied number of non-governmental and official agencies, linked to different sectors and clients within the countries of the continent. With the exception of situations regarded as crises by the White House (Cuba 1962, Dominican Republic 1965, Chile 1970–73), decisions tend to be largely decentralised and in fact often seem to be contradictory. In the case of a problematic regime, it could be realistic to draw a scenario in which the State Department may opt for maintaining a policy of correct relations with a radical elite in a Latin American country, together with some low-level contacts with the more conservative opposition circles. The Department of Defense meanwhile may encourage the local military to prepare a coup – a phenomenon referred to by the ousted Dominican President Juan Bosch as 'pentagonism: namely securing the allegiance of the national army in a Latin American country to the Pentagon rather than to the national government'. [12] A multinational company may decide to support a moderate right candidate in the next elections, supplying him with money and local press coverage. The Treasury may apply an undeclared economic blockade, or try to stop other countries trading with the regime in question, or halt private and official credits to that country, cut the supply line of spare parts, or refuse to re-negotiate the foreign debt acquired during the previous pro-USA administrations. The CIA may try to maximise the use of covert operations including attempts at political assassination, training and arming extreme right terrorist groups, encouraging general strikes, creating panic and destabilising the country in general. Student organisations, trade union movements and women's associations may be stimulated or even artificially brought into being and then manipulated in order to serve American purposes. The Church may be infiltrated with elements that endeavour to prevent the winds of reform blowing too fast. The United States Information Service may work actively through the opposition mass media, projecting arguments about the danger of communism. Such a heterogeneous and conspirational picture may be assembled by combining the facts revealed in Chile about the activities investigated by the American Congress, [13] or in the testimonies of ex-CIA agents about operations in Ecuador and other countries. [14]

At least the continuous presence of some of the described elements appears to be the standard operational procedure of the United States in the continent. For example, its role in Joao Goulart's fall in Brazil in 1964 included the withholding of any direct financial assistance to his central government. This exacerbated the economic crisis by not allowing a solution to be found to the problem of its large foreign indebtedness; at the same time, it extended military support to encourage the efforts of the conspirators [15] to overthrow the civilian regime.

In any event, Latin American politicians have developed a very acute awareness of the constraints that are presented by the external impact on the domestic setting. Chalmers describes linkages that affect the system, among others, in the following ways: '1. groups with special ties abroad may emulate policies, organizations, standards of living, and so on, introducing exogenous patterns of behaviour that might stimulate chains of disequilibria; 2. unequal access to foreign resources may alter the distribution of power; 3. unstable or exceptional demands may be injected into the system by groups acting "under orders" from abroad, or by local groups seeking to compensate for deprivations experienced in their dealings abroad ...' [16]

In smaller countries one large American monopolistic company may be sufficiently strong to control political power. The name Banana Republics, applied in the past to most Central American States, described a situation in which a US-owned plantation was the main source of exports. It may also have had a servicing network of railways and telephone, telegraph, banking, internal and maritime transport, etc. In order to ensure a high margin of profit, the companies were decisive in the selection of the local ruler, generally a dictator. In Bolivia in the Chaco War competing oil companies sponsored both Bolivia and Paraguay to fight over a period of three years for a territory considered to hold rich oil fields. Nowadays we see that the influence of fruit companies seems to be on the decline, since five Central American countries under the leadership of Costa Rica (and opposed by Guatemala) have organised a cartel for a higher share in the profits of the foreign companies. Nevertheless, even in 1975 the Honduras President, Osvaldo Lopez Arellano, was forced to resign after having accepted a million dollar bribe from United Brands. The millionaires Robert Vesco and the late Howard Hughes maintained close ties with President Figueres and Somoza of Costa Rica and Nicaragua by involving them in their large business interests. In the more developed countries of thè continent the intervention of multinational companies in internal politics has been more subtle and secretive. Their investments are in fields requiring superior technology, and have represented over the last few years almost one-sixth of the total sales of all manufacturing industry in Latin America. In 1968, these amounted to eight billion dollars. [17] A perhaps more publicised case of intervention has been that of the International Telegraph and Telephone Company (ITT) in Allende's Chile. [18]

Hence, it is difficult to discern when conflict situations in foreign relations genuinely arise from a high level of outside intervention, or when they are rather created and inflated by the ruling elite as a diversionary excuse or as a means for consolidating national unity. In some cases the manipulation of alleged foreign threats càn be clearly seen. The Argentinian claim for the Islas Malvinas (Falkland Islands) or the Guatemalan demands for possession of British Honduras (Belize) have been accompanied by inflamatory speeches against British colonialism and often include the withdrawal of ambassadors. But such gestures do not provoke much of a reaction from the population. Anti-USA manifestations, though, tend to be more popular. For instance, the attempts of Kennecot – the American copper company – to embargo the shipment of

Chilean copper through legal action in France and other European countries, because of alleged debts resulting from the nationalisation of their investments, provoked unanimous condemnation in the Chilean Parliament. Even the Christian Democrats and the extreme right wing opposition party, despite their confrontation with Allende's government, stood behind the left wing regime on this issue. The appeals for Panamanian sovereignty over the Canal Zone are a major element in recruiting support for any regime in that country, with a certain expectation of a militant attitude towards the United States. The present regime of Colonel Omar Torrijos has in many ways projected a progressive image because of its clearly demanding attitude, without really changing much in the internal social structure; his continuation in power depends heavily on the results of the American election and the coming to office of a moderate administration willing to make considerable concessions in the Canal Zone.

Bunker studied cases of linkages between US economic interests and the plans for national economic growth in Peru, involving the nationalisation of the International Petroleum Company and observed that '...the pattern of United States behaviour had a number of contractive effects on the Peruvian economy. These effects caused power contenders, especially the students, to raise the issue of US economic dominance over Peru, with their power capability of threatening violence'. [19] Foreign policy as an escape when facing crucial domestic problems has been successfully employed by leaders such as Echeverría in Mexico and Perón in Argentina. In the case of Castro, there is no doubt that the element of external aggression accounts for a large amount of his popular support in Cuba.

Conversely, while the 'anti-Yankee' appeal generally could be used to attract massive support, right wing regimes can justify violations of human rights and dictatorial rule by pointing out the existence of threats of an international communist plot through internal subversion, identified usually with Cuba but also occasionally with countries such as the Soviet Union or its satellites. [20]

The range of foreign policy choice

It has already been shown that policy goals of Latin American countries are very much restricted by the hegemonic constraints imposed by the paramount superpower, the United States. It is within these narrow margins of freedom that the objectives of foreign policy are usually determined. One should, however, distinguish between the smaller and less developed states on the one hand, and the major Latin American states, the 'ABC' (Argentina, Brazil, Chile), Venezuela and Mexico. Those falling into the first category confine their aims to self-preservation, and take a secondary role in regional matters. The second group presents a more articulated and global type of foreign policy, in which national interest is defined in terms of decisions *vis-a-vis* different regions and in particular issue-areas such as the economic, political and military.

The smaller states usually follow the United States in global political matters, particularly on East–West questions, emphasising strongly the development of bilateral relations with Washington in terms of ensuring political support for their regime and improving trade figures and economic aid. In some cases, American officials have been instrumental in maintaining even horizontal co-ordination between the different ministries in the dependant countries in order to establish a more viable pattern of transaction. A typical example of this foreign policy pattern occurs in Paraguay: President Stroessner's policy of alignment is defined in terms of 'complete adhesion to the policy of the United States, the great nation which for its culture, for its strength, for its moral and material progress has earned the distinction of the First Soldier and First Arsenal of Democracies'. [21] Consequently, Paraguay was one of the first Latin American nations to support the United States in the 1962 Cuban missile crisis, contributed a 200-man military unit to the OAS Peace Force to the Dominican Republic, offered to send troops to Bolivia when Che Guevara attempted to establish a guerilla force there, and backed the policy of imposing OAS sanctions on Cuba in 1964. During a visit to Washington in March 1968 President Stroessner offered to send troops to Vietnam and was quoted in the US press as saying that he saw the American ambassador in Asuncion as a member of his Cabinet. [22] Such extreme cases of unconditional support could also be matched by many of the dictatorial or military regimes of Central America. An additional comment should be made about Costa Rica, a country which, because of a stability obtained through uninterrupted civilian regimes and by the abolition of its army since 1948, had developed an interest in the defence of human rights and has played a larger role than its tiny level of power would indicate in Central and inter-American affairs.

The continuity of the dependant status of the regimes in the small countries has been the norm; regimes with independent foreign policy orientations have had only a short life (Guatemala 1951–54, Peru since 1968 but with a self-moderating tendency). The case of Cuba is an extreme exception to this rule. From a tradition of total subordination to the

United States it has turned since 1959 into the fiercest opponent of the paramount power. By now the period of change has been long enough to be considered as an established policy. However, it should be remembered that the origins and stability of this policy can be largely attributed to a series of mistakes by the United States, including a CIA miscalculation of the military strength of the Cuban revolutionary army in the 1961 Bay of Pigs invasion. In fact, the existence of such a challenger has warned Washington against possible new cases of 'undisciplined' regimes in Latin America. In Chile and the Dominican Republic such new exceptions have been actively prevented through direct or indirect intervention.

On the other hand, a noticeably more independent pattern has been followed by the larger Latin American states: although the patterns of allegiance to the United States are predominant, several periods of change may be noticed in Brazil (1961–64), Argentina (1973–76), Chile (1970–73) and more gradually Mexico over the last five years of President Echeverria's administration.

Argentina has maintained over the years a significant European orientation in its trade relations; it subscribes to a policy of ideological pluralism, namely the principle of maintaining cordial relations with governments representing different types of social systems; it has aspired to a leading role in South America, and has in recent years actively attempted to prevent a Brazilian hegemony in the area, and it has preferred in most cases the UN forum of diversity to the more controlled inter-American framework.

Brazil, Argentina's regional rival, has opted for an energetic economic expansionist policy, playing an important role in the 1970s in smaller neighbouring countries such as Paraguay, Bolivia and Uruguay. It has shown its wish to be recognised as a military power by participation with its troops in UN peace-keeping forces; it has elaborated a balanced anti-colonialist African policy. Its traditional loyalty to the United States has been based on a particular concept of national interest: the belief that such a continuous and well founded alliance may bring about greater American support for Brazilian economic and political objectives. Economic development remains the main target, and for its sake Brazil has opted for a pragmatic international policy.

Mexico's geopolitical situation, with problems somewhat resembling those of Finland related to its proximity to the Soviet Union, has demanded a large amount of self-control in its independent attitudes towards its northern neighbours. Relying heavily on the American economy and avoiding any possible military confrontation, which in the past has provoked the loss of a great part of its territory and repeated military incursions, the Mexican government has been granted the right of dissent in specific foreign policy issues. It never severed relations with the socialist regime in Cuba and has tended to disagree with the United States more consistently than any other Latin American state in the OAS debates; it is the only Latin American country, apart from Cuba, that has broken with the military regime in Chile. The foreign policy goals of Mexico have been embodied in particular legal principles but with a somewhat flexible interpretation. [23] The Carranza doctrine restricts the right of foreign investors to use the services of their own governments in their relations with the Mexican authorities; the Cárdenas Doctrine involves the renunciation of the diplomatic protection of foreign citizens; the Estrada Doctrine stipulates that the government may decide to maintain or withdraw its diplomatic representatives whenever it deems necessary, without accepting the principle of recognition of new regimes. Mexico aims for a policy of regional economic integration but at the same time it adheres strictly to the principle of sovereignty and non-intervention to the extent of adopting an isolationist position, in particular with reference to the political problems of the adjacent Central American and Caribbean nations.

Venezuela's policy is very much determined by its oil interests. The policy of nationalisation requires it to avoid serious clashes with American interests in order not to risk retaliatory policies. Its friendly relations with Israel have to be carefully measured, in order to maintain close common economic policies with the Arab members of the OPEC. Its recent wealth has permitted Venezuela to play a large regional role patronising the fragile economies of the smaller countries in the area. Its democratic structure has gathered around Caracas other types of civilian regimes as well as leaders of moderate parties from other countries under dictatorial rule.

The Allende regime in Chile rapidly located itself in an intermediary position between the neutralist and socialist countries in world politics, but, at the regional level, the maintenance of a closer relationship with Cuba was not an impediment to friendly links with right wing regimes such as that of General President Lanusse in Argentina. It was to a lesser degree also keen to be accepted in the ranks of the social-democratic movement through its moderate wing in government, the Radical Party. While the policy of nationalisation with what was expected to be inadequate compensation brought about a confrontation with American multinationals and the Washington administration, it enjoyed a more understanding attitude from the European nations, as shown in their willingness to renegotiate the foreign debt and the continuation of businesslike transactions.

Taking the Latin American countries in their entirety, it is possible to trace some regional patterns of behaviour that have become institutionalised and through the years important in the shaping of foreign policy. Over a long period of time, principles of international law have been consolidated on bilateral and regional levels, taking the forms of binding treaties and covenants on extradition, diplomatic immunity and political asylum, and establishing a regional machinery for monitoring human rights violations. Adherence to the principle of non-intervention and self-determination has played a major role in the sharp decline of inter-state wars fought in Latin America in this century. Peaceful solutions to boundary problems have been applied in most cases, through mechanisms such as arbitration, mediation, or submission of litigation to the judgement of the tribunals of international justice.

On some foreign policy issues, groups of Latin American countries combine in opposition to the United States. A particularly large number of states aligned themselves in the early 1970s around what was then called the 'Havana–Lima Axis', claiming changes such as 200-mile territorial water limits, a halt to the intervention of multinationals in internal political affairs, supporting nationalisation of foreign companies without American official retaliatory measures, identifying with the Panamanian claims of sovereignty over the Canal Zone, criticising the United States for the decision to sell parts of its reserves of strategic minerals, demanding the restructuring of the OAS guaranteeing a lesser American dominance, and insisting on the reintegration of Cuba in the inter-American framework. On the other side, Brazil appeared to be aligned with and backed by countries such as Paraguay and Bolivia with most Central American dictatorships, claiming unity against armed insurrection allegedly instigated by international communism, and appealing for the strengthening of hemispheric security.

On the world level, on several occasions Latin America has reacted as a united entity. Such was the case in the support of the Allies in World War II, the demand for greater limitations on the prerogatives of the great powers at the United Nations, the endorsement of the 'Uniting for Peace' resolutions in the case of Korea and Congo, the submission of draft proposals related to the Israeli–Arab conflict in 1961, 1962 and 1967, and in ascribing to the principles of disarmament and collective security.

The decision making process and the domestic environment

As the previous section indicates, it would be wrong to ignore the differences which arise from the various degrees of development and levels of power between Latin American countries. Certainly, a more articulate and complex domestic setting, which would be reflected in foreign policy issues, may be looked for in the advanced countries such as Brazil and Venezuela, rather than in the more traditional societies of Paraguay and Nicaragua. Furthermore, the extent to which a particular regime is authoritarian or competitive bears a direct relation to the domestic constraints influencing foreign policy. In states ruled by a dictatorial government, the role of the opposition is concentrated on the chief national issues. On the other hand, as Alker and Russet put it with reference to Latin America, 'An authoritarian government without a solid mass is likely to depend on the endorsement of commercial interests, both foreign and domestic, who would not look kindly on a Southern (neutralist) or Eastern (communist) foreign policy.' [24] Their observation derived from the fact that the more democratic regimes, in their voting at the United Nations on East–West or Cold War issues, have tended to be more in the middle of Latin American group voting behaviour rather than the authoritarian regimes, which generally deviated toward the West, or in the case of Cuba, to the East.

It follows then that the more developed and pluralistic the society the larger the importance of the domestic structure's actors on the making of foreign policy. The inverse can be said about the smaller, less developed and autocratic type of regimes. This has been the case with most of the 'banana republics' in Central America, where the internal setting could be understood as a unitary actor represented in the power of the President, and largely manipulated by the regional superpower, the United States. In the wider regional context, foreign policy formulation, in theory and practice, resides largely in the hands of the Executive Power, and the President in particular. The general feature of a strong executive system in Latin America becomes even more acute in this domain; major decisions on international problems, appointments of the Foreign Minister and in most cases also the majority of high-ranking foreign services personnel, and direct involvement in diplomatic activities are characteristic of the functions of the Señor Presidente. However, often the personality, political orientation and interest of the President in foreign affairs may determine the degree of his involvement in such issues and the desire to use it as a major tool of government. Innovators such as President Echeverría in Mexico, Allende in Chile and Perón in

Argentina have tended to be more concerned with foreign affairs, whereas more conservative rulers in the same countries at other times were inclined to be more isolationist and detached from the international community.

The Minister of Foreign Affairs – usually ranking fourth in importance in the Cabinet, after the Ministers of the Interior, Defence and Economy – has command over the more routine type of activities and the administrative side of supervising the Ministry's personnel. The institutionalisation of regional gatherings of foreign ministers in the Organization of American States and other frameworks has increased his representational function. Still, his position remains mostly a consultative one, the President being the sole person authorised to finalise the result of bilateral and multilateral discussions at the ministerial level.

The diplomats themselves are in most cases political appointees, fluctuating rapidly with the unstable character of the administrations in most countries. [25] This category also quite often includes important political figures in disgrace, confined to an elegant exile in a diplomatic post. However, it should be pointed out that a higher degree of professionalism can be found in larger countries such as Argentina, Mexico and Chile (until the military coup of 1973). Brazil's foreign ministry – Itamarati – presents the most outstanding case in which recruitment for the diplomatic corps involves strict selection processes and extensive training, allowing also for a high degree of continuity and gradual promotion. But the rule in the continent would be that, excluding the appointments in a few major capitals and particularly in Washington and the United Nations, it would be hard to attribute much importance to the role of the diplomat in the field. In some cases, the exile–politician diplomat, while abroad, continues to be active in the internal political issues of his own country, an explanation that was given for the murders in 1974 and 1976 respectively of the Uruguayan Colonel Trabal and Bolivian General Anaya, both ambassadors in Paris. As a rule no strong inputs are to be expected from ambassadors in foreign countries, even in matters of bilateral relations with the country to which they are accredited. At home, the higher echelons of the foreign ministries may include veteran diplomats who, more by virtue of their qualities and experience rather than the official power they exercise, may be instrumental in pursuing or recommending certain courses of action.

Parliaments in general have an insignificant influence on the foreign policy decision making process. [26] Ratification of treaties, declarations of war, confirmations of diplomatic appointments, reception of official guests from abroad in the House and commemoration of the national days of foreign countries are typical of the kind of formal and solemn functions fulfilled by the legislative power. However, in matters related directly to internal economic policies, such as nationalisation, foreign investment and concessions, etc., the parliaments provide room for polarised and vigorous debates. The general weakness of the legislative control over foreign policy is made even more salient by the fact that parliamentary democracy, particularly in the last few years, has disappeared from most Latin American countries – Venezuela, Colombia, Costa Rica and, to a certain extent, Mexico being the outstanding exceptions. Very much as an expression of their own self-preservation, congressmen have condemned the destruction of parliamentary democracy in countries such as Chile, Uruguay or Brazil. Since in such cases there was no contradiction with the President's line, it is hard to consider such declarations as a powerful input.

Public interest in international issues is generally low, but a somewhat higher sensitivity exists towards continental problems and in particular those related to the relationship of Latin American countries with the United States. The serious press provides quite extensive coverage of international problems, maintaining some correspondents in the major world capitals and syndicating articles mostly from Western sources. Foreign policy at large remains the domain of the elite and of particular groups, organised for general purposes or with the intention of influencing specific foreign policy issues.

Within the party political spectrum, the extremes put more emphasis on foreign policy issues: communists, [27] Castroists and other Marxist movements tend to focus on the USA as the major target, and specialised campaign committees organise activities in solidarity with liberation movements concerning both continental and extra-continental issues (Vietnam, Greece, etc.). Right wing movements, often virulently anti-communist, do not always confine themselves to persecuting left-wingers in their own country, but may act as a force against relations with the Soviet Union, or as a source of aid to right wing para-military organisations in other neighbouring countries. A perhaps even more marked spirit of continental solidarity can be found among the left wing guerilla fighters, the most outstanding example being the attempt of Che Guevara to establish a force in Bolivia with a handful of Cuban and other Latin American revolutionaries. Parties in the centre of the political spectrum tend to be less interested and more divided in foreign policy issues.

Among extra-continental problems, the Middle East conflict in particular excites a considerable degree of attention, in terms of a steady and prolonged interest, throughout most of the countries in the region. The controversy about such a remote problem can perhaps be explained by the existence of both the Jewish and to a lesser extent the Arab communities and their involvement with their related kinsmen in the Middle East. These two communities are spread throughout the continent in quite large numbers: there are about one million Jews and one and a half million Arabs in Latin America.

In the past, the power base of most Latin American countries was considered to be formed by a triangle: the landowners, the Catholic Church and the military. This coalition was strongly allied with the United States and with Great Britain in the southern part of the continent, both of which traditionally favoured the strengthening of these groups. In the 1960s, however, a number of factors destroyed the mololithic character of these institutions. Today the Church is deeply divided, with the progressive sector taking the lead in suggesting reforms with clear implications which run contrary to US economic interests and have a nationalistic and Third World connotation. The military have provided from within their ranks some social reformers as in Peru, and even a few of the leaders of the left wing guerilla movements (Lamarca in Brazil and Yon Sosa in Guatemala). Still the Chilean coup of 1973 can only confirm the opinion that the army as an institution remains by and large a staunch defender of the *status quo,* even at the price of subscribing to the use of most repressive methods.

The landowners or oligarchy have gradually lost influence in countries where industrialisation has created a new native entrepreneur, a force interested in not only widening the external markets but also aiming at enlarging the number of domestic consumers. This process has resulted in some land owners who resented the modernising trends encouraged by consumer-oriented local foreign and especially American interests exploiting nationalistic feelings in order to prevent changes which affect their traditional interests. Nevertheless, it can be shown that on balance land owners have proceeded to invest in the private industrial sector, making it difficult to differentiate them as a separate group. [28]

The growing influence of state-controlled economic enterprise, which now accounts for approaching 35 per cent of commercial activity in the continent as a whole, has relegated private local business to third place, after foreign-owned enterprise. [29] This trend has also produced a new class of technocrats with a high degree of interest in development. They relate in a perhaps more pragmatic and non-ideological way to the different prospects of foreign trade and alternative sources of aid.

Although they accept the basically paramount role of the United States, they have attempted to develop trade relations with the Soviet Union and other, secondary, powers.

Intellectuals and artists, mostly to the left of the political spectrum, are active in politics in general and have endorsed positions on external issues. Trade unions and student movements, although highly politicised, tend to concentrate their efforts on professional and national problems. Still, a continental crisis can provoke strong reactions among the militant sectors of these movements, often acquiring 'anti-Yankee' overtones during visits of high-ranking officials from the USA.

Conclusions

I have tried to show that it is highly questionable to categorise Latin America with Asia and Africa as part of the Third World. Foreign policy is low in the priorities of most Latin American countries as far as world politics are concerned.

Investigating the domestic structure of the more developed countries, and referring specifically to Mexico, Blanksten believes that since the developmental 'take-off point' has already been achieved, an international crisis could be of fatal consequence to the economic standards so far reached, and that therefore in many ways they have become the *status quo* or introverted type of society. [30] This observation is made in contrast to the energetic and more militant foreign policy of Indonesia which may be explained by its state of under-development and its need for a serious international crisis to hold the country together. Cohesion in society, including the economy, is vital for development. The different stages of development of Latin America as compared with Asia and Africa could no doubt be considered an important explanatory variable of newly-born states. However, abstracting a particular case from the characteristics of the international system does not allow us to understand the different foreign policies of states in Latin America with a similar level of development to the average Afro-Asian state. Bolivia, the Dominican Republic, Ecuador or Honduras present approximately similar standards in socio-economic indicators to Cameroon, Ceylon, Egypt or Nepal, and yet the character of the foreign policies of the first group differs drastically from that of the second. Perhaps the major determinant is the lack of independence in the orientation of Latin American countries, the hegemonic presence of one superpower, legitimised by the characteristics of a bipolar international system preventing Latin American countries to a great extent from seeking alternative external sources of support. The lack of great power competition in the area forces upon the Latin American political leaders serious limitations in the search for alternative strategies. Their freedom of action is severely restricted by the margins imposed upon them by the United States, although even here the possibilities for manoeuvre might indicate interesting differences among the dependant countries. Hence regimes in Brazil broadly perceived their national interest in terms of an absolute loyalty to the United States, while Argentina has been interested in maintaining relations with the superpowers in a way not very different to the attitude shown by Western European countries, thus slotting itself into the wider framework of the Western World. But is is useful to point out that, although they represent the largest and strongest countries in South America, they have never, except for short-lived waverings, found a way of presenting a united stand against American hegemony in the area. The superpower has consistently isolated any deviant country, and if necessary undermined its political regime. In the regional context, Cuba should be considered more as a peripheral element rather than an integral part of the Latin American subsystem, with most of its transactions now being with other continents and particularly with the Soviet bloc. Excluded from the OAS in 1962, it maintained diplomatic relations only with Mexico, and the formal re-opening of the regional gates in 1975 has so far not brought it full integration in the area. Most of the Latin American countries have not yet established diplomatic ties, even after Cuba abandoned the idea of promoting guerilla warfare throughout the continent. Paradoxically, the mere existence of such a zealous opponent of the United States as Castro has in fact restricted even more the freedom of action of other Latin American regimes; now any serious departure from the traditional pro-American stand is regarded as dangerous because of the possibilities of a gradual alignment with Cuba's militant position.

Another element which must be emphasized is the high level of regional institutionalisation. Although the military and political frameworks present an inter-American dimension, in the economic, social and cultural fields the Latin Americanist idea prevails. The existence of bilateral and multilateral ties and the intensity of interactions characterise this subsystem as a very cohesive unit. In many ways, such a consolidated picture serves occasionally to enhance a greater freedom of action *vis-à-vis* Washington.

In Latin America foreign policy decisions made by the President are usually influenced by the constraints of the external setting rather than a response to domestic cleavage. This would be the case in the usual extra-continental matters, while in problems related to the United States or neighbouring countries the presence of internal influences would tend to be rather higher. Similarly, internal politics might be highly relevant when the issue-area concerns economic measures such as nationalisation or foreign investment. Moreover, it should be pointed out that, unlike areas with a lower level of development, Latin America is characterised by the existence of well-organised pressure groups such as trade unions, student movements, the Church, political parties, professional and economic interest associations, and so forth. Notwithstanding this, their activities are mostly related to domestic policies. One can observe situations in which pressure groups may be influenced to a large extent by an external power (USA, Cuba) attempting to de-stabilise the ruling regime in one way or another. It is therefore difficult to present a clear-cut distinction between the influences emanating from the external and internal setting, since the linkages among them are distinctively important in such a penetrated subsystem as Latin America.

Clapham's analysis of sub-Saharan African countries ends with a note about the disparity between the opportunities and greater freedom that these countries enjoy in the domain of foreign policy, in contrast with a fragmented domestic structure and their weak status in the international economic system. In his own words: 'Liberty in one respect is constantly tempered by impotence in the other' (see Chapter 4). May I be allowed to paraphrase this and conclude by stating that the lack of liberty of Latin America in its international relations is one of the major causes of a general feeling of impotence and resignation, perceived in terms of stagnation, economic foreign exploitation and a growing sense of purposelessness.

Bibliography

There have been few attempts to study Latin American foreign policy at a comparative level. Studies in international relations in Latin America have mostly been undertaken by Western scholars, and these have tended to focus on United States influence in Latin America, and to a lesser extent on the Latin American policies of other outside powers. Contributions made by Latin Americans have for many years approached the subject from a legalistic or historical angle, though recently an emphasis on economic factors has become apparent. Very few scholars have integrated internal and external variables in the study of foreign policy in Latin America. The reason for the overwhelming emphasis on external determinants of policy is undoubtedly related to the fact that for most countries the domestic setting does not seem to play an important role in foreign policy decisions. Correspondingly, studies of domestic politics and government scarcely touch on foreign policy decision making. It is also symptomatic that crises involving some degree of United States intervention are particularly well documented, including Guatelama (1954), Cuba (1961–2), Dominican Republic (1968), and Chile (1973); periods of stability tend to be neglected.

The following list does not pretend to be exhaustive. It is restricted to books published in English during the past ten years. Any serious study of the subject would also need to take account of the literature in Spanish.

General studies

Agor, Weston T., 'Latin American Inter-State Politics', *Inter-American Economic Affairs,* vol. 26, no. 2, 1972–1973, pp.19–34.
Bailey, Norman, *Latin America in World Politics,* Walker, New York 1967.
Davis, Harold E. et al., *Latin American Foreign Policies,* Johns Hopkins, Baltimore 1975.
Dillon, M. (ed.), *Latin America in World Affairs: The Politics of Inequality,* Barrons, New York 1973.
Ferguson, Yale H. (ed.), *Contemporary Inter-American Relations,* Prentice-Hall, Englewood Cliffs 1972.
Frank, A. Gunnar, *Capitalism and Underdevelopment in Latin America,* Monthly Review, New York 1969.
Goldheimer, Henri, *The Foreign Powers in Latin America,* Princeton, New Jersey 1972.
Gregg, R. W. (ed.), *International Organization in the Western Hemisphere,* Syracuse University Press, Syracuse 1968.
Hellman, Ronald, and Rosenbaum, Jon (eds), *Latin America: the Search for a New International Role,* Sage, Beverly Hills 1975.
Kaufman, Edy, *The Superpowers and their Spheres of Influence: A Comparative Analysis of the Foreign Policies of the Soviet Union and the United States in Latin America and Eastern Europe,* Croom Helm, London 1976.
Theberge, James D., *Latin America in the World System: the Limits of Internationalism,* Sage, Beverly Hills 1975.
Wionczek, M. S., *Latin American Economic Integration,* Praeger, New York 1966.

Great powers in Latin America

Bronheim, David, 'Relations between the United States and Latin America', *International Affairs*, vol. 46, July 1970, pp.501–16.

Burr, Robert N., *Our Troubled Hemisphere: Perspectives on United States–Latin American Relations*, Brookings, Washington 1967.

Commission on United States–Latin American Relations, *The Americas in a Changing World*, Quadrangle, New York 1975.

Gil, Frederico, *Latin American–United States Relations*, Harcourt Brace, New York 1971.

Grunwald, Joseph et al., *Latin American Economic Integration and United States Policy*, Brookings, Washington 1972.

Slater, Jerome, *The OAS and United States Foreign Policy,* Ohio State, Columbus 1967.

Wagner, Robert H., *United States Policy toward Latin America: A Study in Domestic and International Politics*, Stanford 1970.

Johnson, Cecil, *Communist China and Latin America, 1959–1967*, Columbia, New York 1970.

Clissold, Stephen, *Soviet Relations with Latin America 1918–1968*, Oxford University Press, London 1970.

Dinerstein, Herbert S., 'Soviet Policy in Latin America', *American Political Science Review*, vol. 61, 1967, pp.80–90.

Oswald, Gregory and Strover, Anthony, *The Soviet Union and Latin America,* Praeger, New York 1970.

Studies of individual states

Astiz, Carlos Alberto (ed.), *Latin American International Politics: Ambitions, Capabilities and the National Interest of Mexico, Brazil and Argentina*, Notre Dame UP, Notre Dame 1969.

Conil Paz, Alberto and Ferrari, Gustavo, *Argentina's Foreign Policy, 1930–1962*, Notre Dame UP, Notre Dame 1966.

Selcher, W.A., *The Afro-Asian Dimension of Brazilian Foreign Policy*, Florida UP, Gainesville 1970.

Storrs, K. L., *Brazil's Independent Foreign Policy, 1961–1964*, Cornell, Ithaca 1973.

Petras, James and Morley, Morris, *The United States and Chile*, Monthly Review, New York 1975.

Uribe Arce, Armando, *The Black Book of American Intervention in Chile*, Beacon, Boston 1975.

Veliz, Claudio, 'The Chilean Experiment', *Foreign Affairs*, vol. 49, no. 3,

1971, pp.442–53.

Bonsal, Philip W., *Cuba, Castro and the United States*, Pittsburgh UP, Pittsburgh 1971.
Jackson, D. Bruce, *Castro, the Kremlin and Communism in Latin America*, Johns Hopkins, Baltimore 1969.
Wolpin, C., *Cuban Foreign Policy and Chilean Politics*, Lexington, 1971.

Archer, Jules, *Mexico and the United States*, Hawthorn, New York 1973.
Blanksten, George I., 'Foreign Policy of Mexico', in R. C. Macridis (ed.), *Foreign Policy in World Politics*, Prentice-Hall, Englewood Cliffs 1967.
Poitras, Guy E., 'Mexico's New Foreign Policy', *Inter-American Economic Affairs,* vol. 28, no. 3, 1974–1975, pp.59–78.
Smith, Arthur K., *Mexico and the Cuban Revolution: Foreign Policy-making in Mexico under President Adolfo Lopez Mateos, 1958–1964*, Cornell, Ithaca 1970.

Bunker, Rod, 'Linkages in the Foreign Policy of Peru', *Western Political Quarterly*, vol. 22, no. 2, June 1969, pp.280–97.
Sharp, Daniel A., *United States Foreign Policy and Peru*, Texas UP, Austin 1972.

Liss, Sheldon B., *The Canal: Aspects of United States–Panamanian Relations*, Notre Dame UP, Notre Dame 1967.
Mellander, G. A., *The United States in Panamanian Politics*, Interstate, Danville, Ill. 1971.

Whitehead, L., *The United States and Bolivia,* Haslemere, Beckenham, Kent 1969.

Notes

[1]   For the purposes of this work the core of Latin America does not include the following countries: Trinidad and Tobago, Jamaica, Barbados, Guyana and the French, British and Dutch colonies. These are located on the periphery and their inclusion would impair the unitary character of the region. This distinction is a result of their different historical tradition and experience, and resulting linguistic, ethnic, religious and cultural differences.
[2]   Cantori, Louis J. and Spiegel, Steven L. (eds), *The International Politics of Regions: A Comparative Approach*, Prentice-Hall, New Jersey 1970. While Latin America is considered to be a single subsystem,

Africa is divided into five and Asia into four such units.

[3] Herrera, Felipe, *Nacionalismo Latinamericano*, Editorial Universitaria, Santiago de Chile 1967, p.21. Alba summarises this point by stating that 'Latin American unity is first of all the result of human action, it is a social product. Latin American diversity is a product of nature, of geographic and climatic factors that man cannot influence even with the most modern technique.' Alba, Victor, *The Latin Americans*, Praeger, New York 1969, p.5.

[4] Needler, Martin C., *Political Development in Latin America. Instability, Violence and Evolutionary Change*, Random House, New York 1968.

[5] Martz, John D., 'The Place of Latin America in the Study of Comparative Politics', *Journal of Politics*, no. 28, Fall 1966, pp.57–80; and Williams, Edward, 'Comparative Political Development: Latin America and Afro-Asia', *Comparative Studies in Society and History*, vol. II, Cambridge University Press, 1969, pp.342–53. In both cases, the authors point out the differences existing between Latin America and the underdeveloped Afro-Asia, stressing as well certain similarities between the first continent and Europe.

[6] For a further development of the subject see Kaufman, E., 'La Politique de l'Union Sovietique en Amerique Latine: échec ou réussite', *Res Publica*, vol. XIV, no. 3, 1972, pp.567–90.

[7] Dinerstein, Herbert S., 'Soviet Policy in Latin America', *American Political Science Review*, vol. 61, March 1967, p.84.

[8] See Halperin, Ernst, 'Peking and the Latin American Communist', *The China Quarterly*, vol. 29, Jan–March 1967.

[9] For a controversial article claiming that a greater economic interaction between Japan and Latin American countries helps to reduce the dependence of the latter countries upon the United States, see Barsukov, Yuri, 'El Japon en Latinoamerica', *Panorama Lationamericano*, no. 212, Novosti Press Agency, October 1975.

[10] Betancourt's speech published in *El Nacional*, Caracas, 13 January 1960, mentioned in Zea, Leopoldo, *Latin America and the World*, University of Oklahoma Press 1969, p.40.

[11] See Reisky de Dubnic, Vladimir, 'Brazil's New Foreign Policy: From Non-Alignment to Solidarity with the West', in Astiz, Carlos A. (ed.), *Latin American International Politics*, University of Notre Dame Press, Indiana 1969, pp.274–88.

[12] 'Pentagonism has established a governmental schizophrenia, a double power in the United States: that of the civil government and that of pentagonism. The American armed forces obey the latter. Latin American

armed forces – with only rare exceptions – will also obey the pentagonist power rather than their national governments.' Bosch, Juan, *Pentagonism: A Substitute for Imperialism*, Grove Press, New York 1968, p.121.

[13] See 'Covert Action in Chile 1963–1973' in *Hearings on Covert Action* before the select Committee to Study Governmental Operations with Respect to Intelligence Activities of the United States Senate, vol. 7, December 1975, Washington, as well as many other documents related to USA–Chile relations published by the Congress.

[14] Marchetti, Victor and Marks, John D., *The CIA and the Cult of Intelligence*, Dell Publishing, New York 1974; and Agee, Philip, *Inside the Company – CIA Diary*, Penguin, Harmondsworth, Middlesex 1975.

[15] Skidmore, Thomas E., 'The U.S. Role in Jao Goulart's Fall', in Fagen, Richard R. and Wayne, Cornelius A. Jr, (eds), *Political Power in Latin America*, Prentice-Hall, Englewood Cliffs, New Jersey 1970, pp.217–23.

[16] Chalmers, Douglas A., 'Developing on the Periphery: External Factors in Latin American Politics', in Rosenau, James N. (ed.), *Linkage Politics*, The Free Press, New York 1969, p.75.

[17] These and other figures can be found in Council for the Americas, *The Effects of U.S. and Other Foreign Investments in Latin America*, New York 1969.

[18] Sampson, A., *The Sovereign State of ITT*, Fawcett Crest Books, Connecticut 1973; and *Multinational Corporations and United States Foreign Policy*, Hearings before the Subcommittee of Multinational Corporations of the Committee on Foreign Relations, United States Senate 1973.

[19] Bunker, R., 'Linkages and the Foreign Policy of Peru – 1958–1966', *Eastern Political Quarterly*, vol. XXII, no. 2, June 1969, p.287.

[20] *Libro Blanco del Cambio de Gobierno en Chile*, Santiago de Chile, 1973. A meticulously documented and controversial version of a 'Plan Zeta', aimed at eliminating the military leadership by the left wing revolutionaries with Cuban and North Korean help, scheduled for a week after the 11 September coup, is used to legitimise it as a pre-emptive action.

[21] Bourne, R., *Political Leaders of Latin America*, Penguin, Harmondsworth, Middlesex 1968, p.122.

[22] Amnesty International, *Paraguay in the Seventies*, London, October 1971, p.3.

[23] For an extensive analysis of the different doctrines see Seara Vazquez, Modesto, *La Politica Exterior de Mexico*, Esfinge Mexico 1969.

[24] Alker, Hayward R. and Russet, Bruce M., *World Politics in the*

General Assembly, Yale University Press, New Haven 1965, p.266.

[25] 'With one or two possible exceptions, true career diplomats have existed or exist in Latin American countries only by accident and in spite of the procedures employed in their selection, promotion and assignment.' Astiz, Carlos Alberto (ed.), *Latin American International Politics: Ambitions, Capabilities and the National Interest of Mexico, Brazil and Argentina*, University of Notre Dame Press, Notre Dame 1969, p.7.

[26] One can easily trace the absence of references to foreign policy matters in Agor, Weston H. (ed.), *Latin American Legislatures: Their Role and Influence*, Praeger, New York 1971.

[27] The total figure for members of the pro-Soviet communist party in Latin American countries can be estimated for the second half of 1973 as approximately 400,000 (figures compiled from data about individual countries from Hoover Institute for Peace, War and Revolution, *Yearbook on International Communist Affairs*, 1973, pp.283–400). But with the military takeovers in the Southern countries, the functioning of the large communist parties (Chile with 200,000 members, Argentina 126,000 and Uruguay 30,000 members) was seriously affected by imprisonment of its members, enforced exile and dismantling of the organisational apparatus. Other Marxist groups present a very fragmented picture and a not insignificant part of its efforts are spent in combating the 'revisionist' pro-Soviet communists.

[28] Zeitlin, Maurice and Ratcliff, Richard, 'Research Methods for the Analysis of the Internal Structure of Dominant Classes: The Case of Landlords and Capitalists in Chile', *Latin American Research Review*, vol. X, no. 3, Fall 1975, pp.5–55.

[29] Goldhamer, Henri, *The Foreign Powers in Latin America*, Princeton University Press, New Jersey 1972, p.284.

[30] Blanksten, George I., 'The Developed-Underdeveloped Dichotomy', in Farrell, Barry R. (ed.), *Approaches to Comparative and International Politics*, Northwestern University Press, Evanston 1966, p.129.

7 Conclusion: comparative foreign policy and developing states

CHRISTOPHER CLAPHAM

The five regional chapters have gone a long way towards confirming the validity of the basic premise from which Chapter 1 started: that, while it is certainly fallacious to treat the foreign policies of developing states as though they were industrialised (and particularly Western) ones, nonetheless all states share common features and problems, and any comparison of their foreign policy making should be able to call on a common set of concepts. This concluding chapter will seek to take the discussion further, combining material from Chapter 1 and the regional chapters to examine to what extent, and in what ways, it may be useful to compare foreign policy making in developing or underdeveloped states.

The first format for comparing foreign policies is simply the taxonomic one, and in this sense policies must be comparable, unless the categories selected are particularly culture-bound or otherwise unilluminating. Each of the regional chapters starts from the assumption that it will be useful to say something about foreign policy making under each of a handful of headings: the historical and geographical setting of the states concerned; the nature of the external environment in which they operate, and the constraints which it places on policy makers; the form of the domestic society and political structure, and the pressures which this too creates for external policy, together with the linkages which inevitably arise between internal and external factors; the decision making apparatus, with the composition, perceptions and goals of the groups or individuals who control it. Any analysis of foreign policy must say something about all these things, whether it employs an elaborately articulated scheme such as Rosenau's, [1] or whether it proceeds more directly from consideration of what is most important in any particular case. Equally, taxonomy is a necessary preliminary to any further comparison, since this requires information to be collected and codified in comparable form.

It is only when one comes to look at the data that the taxonomic enterprise reveals, therefore, that it becomes possible to identify significant differences in foreign policy behaviour, and to order the different variables in such a way as to clarify the quest for explanations. At this point, differences become apparent not only between developing and industrial states, but equally between the developing states themselves, at both regional and individual levels. This is not surprising. Any category for generalisation in the social sciences tends to fragment under close investigation, or at best is found to possess a coherence at one level of analysis which it lacks at another. The task of comparative analysis is then to select the most significant categorisations, and to distinguish the levels at which they have something useful to say.

This book has − as it must − to some extent prejudged the issue, first of all by selecting the foreign policies of developing states as a worthy subject for comparison, and then by choosing the region − or the sub-system, as the current terminology would have it − as its principal comparative category. These choices are justifiable: the first in that the gap between rich and poor nations, between industrialised and under-developed, between the great power blocs and the 'peripheries' of the international system is, and is increasingly recognised by policy makers in underdeveloped states to be, one of the most important facts about the current international system; the second in that with the decline of the western colonial empires and the weakening of the bipolar superpower system characteristic of the late 1940s and 1950s, 'the dominant traits of international politics in the peripheries arise from characteristics of subsystems in the peripheries'. [2]

Certainly the regional approach has been useful, in that it has revealed important variations between regions and indicated the extent to which the regional context shapes the nature of foreign policy. The regions them-selves are not mere geographical conveniences, but are marked by a considerable though varying degree of internal coherence. For the most part, member states of the regional subsystem display common historical, social and economic backgrounds, and appreciable intra-regional inter-action. Except in South East Asia, regional members share a high degree of cultural identity, whether as Arabs, Africans, West Indians or Latin Americans, and view the region as a whole which is intimately related to their perceptions of international affairs. In some regions, notably the Arab states and Black Africa, core issues − the Palestine/Israel and Southern Africa questions respectively − help to intensify the sense of regional solidarity and appreciably shape individual states' foreign policy options. [3] In Latin America and the Commonwealth Caribbean, though the domestic political systems are perhaps too penetrated to permit the emergence of solidaristic foreign policies in the same way, the sense of common identity is nonetheless strongly felt.

One of the most important factors which these regional variables help to shape, then, is the degree of conflict or co-operation between states within the region. Thus all Middle Eastern states need to take account of the highly conflictual nature of international relations in the region, since a degree of Arab solidarity is largely the result of the conflict against Israel, and is subject to a great many internal tensions. Sub-Saharan Africa, Latin America and the Commonwealth Caribbean, on the other hand, all possess a high degree of internal solidarity which greatly increases the safety of the international environment. In South East Asia, after the Middle East the most explosive area of the globe, any sense of regional solidarity is very much weaker, and many states have to reckon in addition with a marked lack of internal solidarity which affects their approach to international issues and opens them to external penetration.

Thus the regional environment in turn helps to determine the importance of particular functional areas of foreign policy to states within each region. In the Middle East, states have had territory violently wrested from them (Syria, Jordan, Egypt), or have been convulsed by civil wars in which their neighbours took an active part (Yemen, Lebanon), or need to remain constantly on guard to protect their existence (Israel); not surprisingly, then, the security area is salient, and considerable emphasis is placed on military alliances and arms supplies. In sub-Saharan Africa, by contrast, small states like Togo or The Gambia may maintain only the most derisory armed forces, in the belief that subsystemic norms will inhibit their more powerful neighbours from attacking them, while the most salient areas of foreign policy relate to continental aspirations and the control of the domestic economy. In any region where regimes are weak, however, and this goes for most of the areas with which we are concerned, one important goal of foreign policy will be to help bolster the government against its domestic opponents; this is perhaps most evident in South East Asia, but it is true in varying degrees of the Middle East, sub-Saharan Africa and Latin America as well. Only in the Commonwealth Caribbean have governments not, so far, been liable to extra-constitutional overthrow, and even there foreign policy is one element in inter-party rivalry.

Another important variable which depends significantly on the regional level is, paradoxically perhaps, the nature and degree of external great power involvement and penetration. All foreign policies, of course, are shaped to a significant degree by the general global allocation of power. The very existence of independent Third World states is due in some measure to the declining international status and military capability of the European colonial powers, though it is more the result of the growth and effectiveness of their own nationalist movements. Likewise, the movement away from bipolarity, though partly a consequence of the emergence of Third World actors, has had appreciable effects in most areas of the developing world, and has made itself felt to a limited extent even in Latin America. Nonetheless, the regional chapters have shown some very marked differences. Some regions have configurations of great power impact which result from common historical experiences, especially of colonialism. This is most marked in the Caribbean, where both the domestic society and the regional subsystem are the creations of the colonial period, and where the economy can be viewed only as an extension of external market forces. Some of the same features are present, though to a markedly less intense degree, in sub-Saharan Africa. In Latin America and to some extent the Middle East, external involvement is a function more of geographical location: in Latin America because of the presence of the North American superpower, and in the Middle East because of its strategic importance. Intense intra-regional conflict almost inevitably increases superpower involvement through the tendency of conflicting parties to seek patrons outside; South East Asia and the Middle East provide very clear examples, as does the Angolan civil war. Thus different regions of the developing world vary between great power hegemony (Latin America, Caribbean), great power confrontation (Middle East, South East Asia) and a fair degree of autonomy (sub-Saharan Africa), with enormous effects on the opportunities and constraints for foreign policy makers.

The regional level of analysis, then, tends to emphasise differences. If, however, we are concerned with possible common features of foreign policy making in developing countries as a whole, then it becomes necessary to shift our unit of analysis, and to look for variables of a different kind. On this much larger scale, comparisons will inevitably be more highly generalised, but it is possible to distinguish three areas in which they might usefully be sought. The first, development, relates to the similarities in internal structure which developing countries may be supposed to possess; the second, dependence, relates to common aspects of their position within a stratified global economic and political order; the third, identity, relates to features of foreign policy which may follow from their identification of themselves as belonging to a Third World international community.

Though political scientists have for the most part abandoned the concept of 'development', there is a fair degree of consensus, most clearly articulated by Huntington, [4] on what the characteristic features of developing political systems are. These are, firstly, an increase (due to social and economic change) in the number and range of interests making demands on the political process, and, secondly, a persistent difficulty in relating these demands to governmental activity within a stable and institutionalised political order. Both features can illuminate, at least to some extent, the aspects of foreign policy making outlined in previous chapters. The growth of public demands and expectations which bear on external relations is a constant though often unexamined backdrop to Third World foreign policy making. It is implicit, for example, in the competing nationalisms which fuel international conflict in the Middle East; in the internal conflicts which lead both established regimes and their opponents to look for external support in South-East Asia; in the intensity of African states' reactions to apartheid in South Africa; in the ambivalence of Caribbean and Latin American attitudes to the United States; and, most of all, in the desperate search to fulfil their peoples' economic expectations which leads regimes throughout the developing world to seek increased control over economic resources and flows both within and outside their own frontiers. In a world in which foreign policy was totally the concern of decision making elites, these pressures on the international system need scarcely arise.

At the same time, the previous chapters have almost invariably emphasised the individualism, not to say idiosyncrasy, of the actual decision making process within their respective regions. Whatever the general aspirations of groups within the society, the principal decision maker usually seems able to operate within very few specific domestic constraints. Idiosyncratic behaviour on a global scale calls for more than an idiosyncratic explanation. In this case it is to be found in what Huntington has termed 'praetorianism': the excess of demands over governments' capacities to satisfy them, which leads to political instability, the decay of institutional links between social pressures and political action, and the constant shifts to which those in power are put in order to remain there. The prevalence of military governments is one aspect of the phenomenon, even though in many cases these are not so very different from their civilian equivalents. Where foreign policy making is not highly personalised, as for example in Israel and some of the Latin American states, this reflects the existence of an effective range of domestic institutions through which policy makers have to work.

The existence of developing or Third World states can be defined not only by their internal characteristics, but also by reference to their economic weakness and historical dependence in a stratified international system. As the 1960s concern for 'development' has increasingly (and perhaps prematurely) been abandoned, so in the 1970s 'dependence' has taken its place. The resulting tendency to look at Third World countries through their role in the international system should, on the face of it, be particularly fruitful for the comparative analysis of foreign policy. It is not surprising, therefore, that the themes of penetration and dependence have been emphasised in all of the regional chapters, or that this penetration should critically affect the nature of foreign policy, and the range of foreign policy choice, throughout the Third World. In many cases, this amounts to much more than the 'linkage politics' between domestic and international systems which Rosenau has made famous. [5] It reflects the fact that for many purposes systemic boundaries between internal and external environments simply do not exist, a point made most clearly for the Caribbean, though indicated also in the discussions of Latin America and, to a lesser extent, sub-Saharan Africa. South-East Asia, on the other hand, ranges between highly penetrated societies such as the Philippines, and states such as Burma and post-war Cambodia and Vietnam which have cut themselves off from external contacts to the greatest possible degree.

Thus the autonomy of the state is itself very much a variable, and much of the foreign policy behaviour of state leaders may correspondingly be interpreted either as attempts to increase this autonomy (as in the South-East Asian cases cited above, the expulsion of Soviet advisers from Egypt, or the nationalisation of foreign companies in Africa and the Caribbean), or as a recognition of its non-existence, as most markedly in some of the statements of President Stroessner of Paraguay quoted in the chapter on Latin America. It is here, perhaps, that the 'uses of foreign policy' discussed by Weinstein, [6] or the 'situation-role' model suggested by Korany, [7] come into play. Both concentrate on the predicaments faced by rulers confronted by multiple and generally conflicting pressures, for whom foreign policy is one instrument among several that may be brought into play. While this viewpoint is obviously not restricted to Third World leaders, the immediacy of the problems which they face, and the weakness of the accepted conventions and institutional links which place much of foreign policy beyond the immediate control of leaders in developed industrial states, make it specially relevant to them. Both Weinstein and Korany offer an interesting sketch rather than a fully articulated approach; both of them, too, in concentrating on the situation facing the policy maker, may tend to over-emphasise the importance of formal foreign policy and the amount that the individual leader can do. Nonetheless, starting as they do from the study of foreign policy in developing states, they offer rather greater insights into that policy than do the models devised for highly institutionalised societies which, in a rather laboured fashion, they criticise.

It is worth noting, though, that just as there are 'issue areas' in foreign policy, which may call for rather different treatment, so also there are areas of autonomy or dependence, which to some extent may be distinct from one another. Cultural penetration, for example, is at its most extreme in the Commonwealth Caribbean, followed perhaps by Latin America and the elite sections of African society. In the Middle East, however, Arabic Islam (and even, to a much lesser extent, Judaism) help to preserve a barrier against western or eastern communist incursions, and make possible the emergence of an Islamic radical such as Qadhafi. Economic penetration is again most marked in the Caribbean, Latin America and Black Africa, and thus places constraints on any form of foreign policy designed to alter trade and capital flows. Yet political penetration − the existence of powerful political actors within the country whose interests are linked to those of external powers − is very much more salient in Latin America than in either of the other two. In Guyana, where American support was instrumental in securing the success of the general strike which helped overthrow the explicitly Marxist Jagan government, the successor regime has moved steadily leftwards in its turn. There are fewer constraints on the political orientation of African regimes. Thus a non-aligned foreign policy is compatible with economic penetration to a far greater degree in Africa than in Latin America. Military penetration, to take another area, is most obvious in the Middle East and South East-Asia.

Another problem with the concepts of dependence and penetration is that of selecting a yardstick by which they are to be assessed. If one measures them against the extreme of dependence represented by direct colonialism, then it becomes clear that Third World countries can acquire an appreciable (though very variable) freedom of action simply by virtue of being formally independent states. Botswana is not like the Transkei, just as Jamaica (to say nothing of Cuba) is not like Puerto Rico. When one looks at Egypt, or Nigeria, or Argentina, the difference is still more marked, and it is by no means obvious that their foreign policies are vastly more constrained than those, say, of the United Kingdom. If, on the other hand, one measures dependence against an ideal representing a total freedom of action, then it soon becomes clear that such freedom is enjoyed by no one, least of all perhaps by thoroughly penetrated small industrial states such as Holland or Belgium. Dependence, like develop-ment, helps to distinguish some characteristic features of foreign policy making in Third World states, but only by placing them within a conceptual frame of reference which they share with every country on the globe.

The third way in which one can look for common themes in Third World foreign policies is through the common identities of the policy makers themselves, and especially through the sense of solidarity expressed in the movement for non-alignment and its associated institutional forms such as the UNCTAD Group of 77 and the non-aligned conferences. One immediate problem with this approach, as the Latin America chapter most clearly shows, is that not all the states with which we are concerned would consider themselves part of a non-aligned group, even though most of them join in seeking more favourable economic terms from the industrialised states. A unit of analysis which depends on leaders' perceptions may change unpredictably with the leaders themselves. Nor does this approach have any comparative conceptual focus to offer in seeking to explain how foreign policies are made. One can say, however, that the group of Third World states as a whole appears to be becoming, in practice, an increasingly important reference group by which its individual members set their foreign policies, comparable to, though as yet by no means so influential as, the regional groupings which help to set the foreign policies of Arab, African or Latin American states. It may equally be useful to see a sense of Third World identity, compounded of the aspirations, solidarities and resentments resulting from under-development and dependence, as constituting an important part of the psychological framework within which decision makers operate. Even so idiosyncratic a figure as President Amin can thus be seen to exemplify certain common attitudes towards the external – and especially the colonial – world, a point which goes far to explain the approval with which he appears to be regarded by individuals (rather than governments) in Third World countries outside his own. [8]

Another level at which one can look for comparisons is simply that of the individual state and its decision makers, and here another set of variables comes into play. Capability analysis is an obvious and very useful tool, both for distinguishing between different states within the Third World or a particular region of it, and for relating Third World and other states on a common scale. Most of the regional studies have indicated significant differences between states within the region which can be ascribed to their populations, natural resources, gross national products, military capabilities and so forth. Latin American states, for example, fall into two distinct divisions, with Argentina, Brazil, Chile, Mexico and Venezuela in one, and all the smaller states in the other; in

Black Africa, Nigeria's population is more than twice, and its gross domestic product more than three times, that of the next largest state; in the Middle East, the military capabilities of Egypt, Iran and Israel rank them clearly as the three major states of the region. The possibilities for national comparison tend to be under-emphasised by an approach which, as in this book, concentrates on the regional and global levels; but foreign policy analysis has tended so much to concentrate on the state that the deficiency is more than made up elsewhere, for example in work on the foreign policies of small states. [9] The fact that the great majority of Third World states are small, in population as well as in economic and military capabilities, particularly suits them to this approach.

One intriguing approach to state-level comparison might be to look at the foreign policies of mavericks in the regional subsystems: states whose internal dynamic is such as to lead them to define themselves and their relationships with the external world in a different way from their neighbours. North Vietnam, Israel, Somalia and Cuba are all examples of states which do not fit easily into their regions because their national or regime goals are different from, and hard to reconcile with, those of other regional actors. Examining them helps to illuminate not only the states themselves, but also the unspoken assumptions of the subsystems from which they differ. The nature of subsystemic constraints may also be illustrated by looking at 'marginal' states at the edges of regional subsystems, perhaps the classic case being the Sudan, in its relations with both the Arab world and Black Africa. One recent unpublished study suggests that the desire to be identified with each subsystem by its core members has markedly affected the Sudan's foreign policy behaviour. [10]

This study of states within their regional context takes us a little closer to one famed foreign policy concept about which this book has said very little, the 'national interest'. Perhaps this hoary phrase is best left to linger in that limbo to which modern analysis has tended to consign it, particularly as the newness of many developing countries, added to the weakness of national integration and accepted institutional procedures, makes it even more difficult to define there than in the long-established states. Yet the problem of goals in foreign policy remains, and can only effectively be studied at the state level — except for those who would claim that developing countries have so little foreign policy choice open to them that it cannot usefully be studied at all. One can only expect lasting goals to be articulated as the immediate aftermath of independence recedes. For the new state, the most urgent problems after independence are likely to be domestic ones, unless — like Israel or the now defunct South Vietnam — it accedes to nationhood under intense external threat. [11] New state foreign policies are therefore characteristically put together from the institutional hangover of the imperial connection, the requirements of domestic political identification and security, the rhetorical ideology of leaders, and the need to announce and articulate a presence on the international scene. Only later, as leaders and circumstances change, does it become possible for political elites to appraise what is relatively permanent about their countries' situation, both domestically and externally, and thus to reach a consensus about what is practicable and desirable in their foreign policies. The need for this appraisal is particularly evident for states, such as those of the Commonwealth Caribbean, which have historically been most closely linked to the imperial power.

Eventually, some elements of national – or at any rate of state – interest do generally emerge. Any state, as such, has an interest in maintaining its territorial integrity, and an idea of national interest is most consciously articulated when this is threatened. Governing elites equally have an interest in strengthening the state apparatus which they control against penetration from without and overthrow from within, and they can frequently identify this interest with defence of the nation against external imperialism or internal disunity. But beyond that, both governments and peoples do tend to acquire, in time, a set of attitudes and identities which constrain responses to the outside world. It is thus not surprising that many of the foreign policy stances of Haile-Selassie's government in Ethiopia should be duplicated, often in intensified form, by the military regime which replaced it, since they shared a sense of Ethiopian nationhood and a commitment to defend the existing frontiers which, granted the continuity of the regional and global systems within which they had to operate, pushed them into a number of very similar responses. It is perhaps more surprising, but nonetheless understandable, that an analoguous continuity should obtain in some respects in Cambodia. But even in Nigeria, one of the most culturally diverse of Third World states and the recent victim of a bitter civil war, foreign policy may now be seen as firmly linked to a national perspective, derived from the country's oil revenues, development policies, and desire to take a leading role in the regional subsystem, rather than to the colonial connections and ethnic divisions which were so important before 1970. [12]

There are, however, difficulties about studying these emergent national policies in the same way as has been usual for the industrialised states. It would on the whole be true to say that studies of foreign policy in the more developed world tend to approach the subject by way of process: how policy is made. They identify the continuities of policy, and the enduring interests which it needs to take into account, by identifying the bureaucracies, political parties, interest groups, public attitudes, external influences and so forth which impinge on a regularised pattern of policy making. [13] In many developing countries, these approaches fail simply by virtue of the fact that such regularised patterns can scarcely be discerned. Studies of foreign policy tend therefore – in an equally broad generalisation – to approach it by way of function: what it is supposed to do. This approach enables the analyst to proceed by directly linking the perceptions of the decision maker to the overall national and global environment, skipping over the mechanisms which lie between; such an approach, for example, is implicit in the work of Weinstein and Korany already referred to. It may be argued that regular functions must in time generate regular processes through which they can be performed, but it is still premature to generalise about what these processes might be. They may eventually come to operate in a way familiar to foreign policy analysts in industrialised states, but it is more likely that they will need to be elucidated through the mechanisms, such as patronage and brokerage, which are found most useful in the analysis of domestic politics.

Shifting, then, from levels of comparison to specific techniques of comparison, it becomes evident that these must be adapted to the circumstances in which they are to be used. Familiar techniques such as the detailed reconstruction of decisions or bureaucratic processes cannot be excluded from consideration, but it must be recognised that they may not yield very useful results in states where decision making is idiosyncratic and bureaucracies are unimportant. But, wherever systematic information can be collected on variables connected with foreign policy making, it can be made to yield useful results. Capability analysis has already been touched on. Investigation of the psychological environment of decision makers is an open field, which because of the greater personalisation of decisions could prove more valuable than in more institutionalised systems. Events analysis has been used to show, and to indicate reasons for, marked differences in foreign policy conflict in different regions of Africa, and within the same regions over time. [14] Diplomatic linkage analysis has been used to indicate degrees of external alignment and regional integration. [15] Analysis of trade and aid flows can give meaning to generalisations about 'dependence', and assess the resulting constraints on foreign policy. [16] Even though there are important empirical differences between states in the functions of foreign policies, the ways in which they are made, and the constraints under which they must operate, the methodologies which one may pursue in order to uncover those differences are essentially the same. It is only, indeed, a common methodological concern which makes it possible to draw meaningful comparisons at all.

Notes

[1] James Rosenau, 'Comparative Foreign Policy: Fad, Fantasy or Field?', in Rosenau, *The Scientific Study of Foreign Policy*, Free Press, New York 1971, pp.67–94; and see Chapter 3 of the present work.

[2] J. I. Dominguez, 'Mice that Do Not Roar: Some Aspects of International Politics in the World's Peripheries', *International Organization*, vol. 25, no. 2, 1971, pp.175–208.

[3] A. M. Elhassan, 'Dual Marginal Membership in Overlapping Regional Sub-Systems: The Foreign Policy Behaviour of the Sudan', unpublished dissertation, University of Lancaster, 1976.

[4] See S. P. Huntington, 'Political Development and Political Decay', *World Politics*, vol. 17, no. 3, 1965, pp.386–430; and *Political Order in Changing Societies*, Yale, New Haven and London 1968.

[5] James Rosenau (ed.), *Linkage Politics*, Free Press, New York 1969.

[6] F. B. Weinstein, 'The Uses of Foreign Policy in Indonesia', *World Politics*, vol. 24, no. 3, 1972, pp.356–81.

[7] B. Korany, 'Foreign-policy Models and their Empirical Relevance to Third-World Actors: a Critique and an Alternative', *International Social Science Journal*, vol. 26, no. 1, 1974, pp.70–94.

[8] A point which comes out particularly in African readers' letters to newspapers; see, for example, *West Africa*, 26 July 1976, p.1070.

[9] See, for example, R. P. Barston (ed.), *The Other Powers: studies in the foreign policies of small states*, Allen & Unwin, London 1973; A Schou and A. O. Brundtland (eds), *Small States in International Relations*, Almqvist, Stockholm 1971; and D. Vital, *The Survival of Small States*, Oxford UP, London 1971.

[10] Elhassan, op.cit.

[11] See R. L. Rothstein, 'Foreign Policy and Development Policy', *International Affairs*, vol. 52, no. 4, October 1976.

[12] For a recent case study which brings this out, see O. Aluko, 'Oil at Concessionary Prices for Africa: a case study in Nigerian decision-making', *African Affairs*, vol. 75, no. 301, October 1976.

[13] Most of the relevant literature has already been cited in the Introduction, but see also W. Wallace, *The Foreign Policy Process in Britain*, RIIA, London 1975, for a classic study in this genre.

[14]   R. W. Copson, 'Foreign policy conflict among African states, 1964–1969', *Sage International Yearbook of Foreign Policy Studies*, vol. 1, 1973, pp.189–217.

[15]   See D. H. Johns, 'Diplomatic activity, power and integration in Africa', *Sage International Yearbook of Foreign Policy Studies,* vol. 3, 1975, pp.85–105, and tables 4.1 and 6.1 of the present work.

[16]   See P. J. McGowan, 'Economic Dependence and Economic Performance in Black Africa', *Journal of Modern African Studies*, vol. 14, no. 1, 1976, pp.25–40.

Index

Abboud, General 89
Abu Musa Islands 60, 63
Acheampong, Colonel 83, 84, 89
Afar and Issa Territory (TFAI) 93
Afghanistan 44
Africa 36, 76–109, 114, 116, 123, 133, 135,
  136, 140, 142, 149, 156, 158, 166–73
Africa–Caribbean–Pacific group (ACP) 92
Aid 58, 79, 85, 86, 90, 96, 104, 175, see also
  Military aid
Alexandretta 51
Algeria 44, 46, 49, 57, 59
Aliens 29, 30, 32, 78, 83, 86, 87, 100, 101
Alker, H. R. 152
Allende, President 133, 134, 138, 146, 147,
  150, 152
Alliance for Progress 133
Allison, G. 2
Ambassadors 34, 88, 148, 153, see also
  Diplomatic relations
Amer, Marshal 65
AmericanIndians 134
Amin, President 3, 83, 84, 87, 90, 94, 97, 100,
  172
Anaya, General 153
Andean group 136
Angola 81, 85, 91, 92, 94, 95, 168
Ankrah, General 89
Antigua 116
Arabs 48–51, 56, 57, 60, 81, 140, 142, 144,
  150, 151, 155, 166, 167, 172, see also
  individual Arab states
Arab League see League of Arab States
Arellano, President 146
Arevalo, President 136
Argentina 134, 135, 138–42, 144, 146–50,
  153, 157, 171, 172
Arusha agreement 92
Asaad, President 61, 65
Asia see Middle East, South-East Asia
Association of South East Asian Nations
  (ASEAN) 24, 33, 36, 37
Attaturk 51, 63
Australia 18, 142

Bahamas 110, 113, 116, 117, 120, 124

Bahrain 44, 51, 53
Banana republics 146, 152
Banda, President 85, 88–90, 94, 100
Bangladesh 26, 81
Barbados 110, 113, 116, 117, 120, 124, 141
Barka, Ben 140
Bauxite 124
Belgium 135, 171
Belize 113, 119, 120, 146
Ben Gurion, David 65
Benin see Dahomey
Bermuda 120
Betancourt, President 140
Bhutto, Prime Minister 5
Biafra 81, 92, 93, 95–7
Billiard ball model 35
Blanksten, G. I. 156
Bolivar, Simon 133
Bolivia 134–6, 138, 141, 142, 144, 146, 149,
  151, 153, 154, 156
Bosch, President 145
Botswana 97, 100, 102, 171
Brandt, Willy 139
Brazil 113, 120, 122, 134, 138–42, 144, 145,
  148, 149, 151–5, 157, 172
Brazzaville group 92
Brecher, M. 9, 56
Britain 2, 4, 9, 19, 22, 37, 46, 52, 59, 77, 81,
  83, 84, 86, 87, 90, 91, 95–7, 100, 110, 113,
  114, 116, 119, 124, 135, 139, 143, 146, 155,
  171
British Honduras see Belize
Brokerage 79, 104, 175
Brunei 37
Bunker, R. 147
Bureaucracy 2–4, 34, 36, 63, 88, 115, 153, 175
Burma 22, 25, 29, 30, 32, 34–6, 86, 170
Burham, Forbes 118
Burundi 77, 100, 102
Busia, Kofi 94, 104

Cabinets 64, 65, 153
Cambodia 4, 5, 22, 23, 25, 27, 28, 34, 35, 86,
  170, 174
Cameroon 80, 102, 156
Canada 117, 142

Cantori, L. J. 131
Capabilities, capability analysis 5, 53–60, 100, 125, 172, 175
Cardenas, Lazaro 133
Caribbean 75, 77, 99, 104, 110–30, 142, 166–71, 174
Caribbean Common Market (CARICOM) 110, 119–23
Caribbean Free Trade Area (CARIFTA) 116
Casablanca group 92
Castro, Fidel 133, 137, 140, 141, 147
Central African Empire 101, 102
Central African Federation 89
Central Intelligence Agency (CIA) 145, 149
Central Treaty Organisation (CENTO) 47
Ceylon see Sri Lanka
Chad 82, 95, 102
Chalmers, D. A. 145
Charisma 6, 9, see also Leaders, Personality
Chile 10, 134–6, 138, 139, 141, 142, 144–50, 152–5, 172
China 4, 18, 21–3, 29, 30, 37, 38, 45, 86, 90, 95, 125, 137, 138, 142, 143, see also Taiwan
Christianity, Churches 31, 55, 61, 133, 141, 145, 155, 158
Cocoa 78, 101
Coffee 101
Cold War 29, 114, 125, 136, 140, 152
Colombia 110, 120, 134–6, 138, 141, 142, 154
Colonialism 7, 18–20, 24, 52, 75–9, 98, 99, 110, 115, 135, 140, 168, 171
Communism 21, 25, 112, 117, 118, 133, 137, 141, 147, 151, 154, 171
Communist parties 3, 4, 30, 117, 138
Communist states 82, 95, 102, 142, 143
Comparative analysis 1–11, 44, 67–9, 165–76
Congo (Brazzaville) 95, 102
Congo (Leopoldville/Kinshasa) see Zaire
Copper 9, 78, 101, 146, 147
Costa Rica 120, 134, 139, 140, 146, 148, 154
Coups d'etat 63, 84, 94, 96, 98, 138, 145, 155, see also Military regimes
Cuba 94, 95, 99, 112, 113, 120, 125, 133–5, 137–44, 147–52, 154, 157, 158, 171, 173
Cultural factors 1, 19, 62, 65, 131
Cyprus 44, 47, 65

Dahomey 102
Dayan, General 66
Debts 58, 83, 96, 145
Decision making 6, 32–6, 62–7, 87–90, 114–16, 152–6, 169, 172, 175

Defence analysis 5, see also Military factors
Demographic factors 53, 54, 100, 102, 172, 173
Dependence 7, 8, 11, 21, 56, 86, 96, 101, 104, 112, 118, 137, 168–72, 175
Destler, I. 2
Development 10, 131, 134, 156, 168–70
Diamonds 78
Diplomatic relations 30, 91, 92, 95, 100, 102, 116, 117, 125, 135, 138, 139, 142–4, 150, 153, 157, 175
Domestic environment 26–32, 38, 52–62, 68, 79–87, 104, 116–18, 144–56, 158
Dominican Republic 112, 133, 142, 144, 145, 148, 149, 156

East, M. 2
East African Community 92, 122
Echeverria, President 147, 149, 152
Economic factors 5, 7, 37, 56–8, 77, 78, 85–7, 89, 90, 96, 101, 102, 112, 115, 119, 124, 134, 146, 147, 155, 169, 171
Ecuador 134–6, 141, 142, 156
Education 25, 77
Egypt 4, 44, 46, 47, 49, 50, 53–5, 57–61, 63–6, 68, 140, 156, 167, 170, 171, 173
Elites 3, 10, 24, 25, 62, 64–7, 77, 79, 81, 95, 104, 113, 125, 141, 154, 169, 174
El Salvador see Salvador
Entente Council 92
Entrepreneurs 32, 78, 155
Eritrean Liberation Front 81
Eshkol, Prime Minister 66
Ethiopia 44, 75, 81, 85, 88, 90, 92, 93, 96, 99, 100, 102, 116, 117, 174
Ethnic divisions 29, 30, 54, 78, 80, 82, 83, 116, 133, 134, 174
Europe, Eastern 137, 143; see also Communist states
Europe, Western 137, 139, 142, 143, 157; see also EEC, individual states
European Economic Community (EEC) 45, 57, 92, 116, 119, 121, 124, 139
Events analysis 175
External environment 36–8, 45–52, 68, 90–8, 122–5, 136–44, 158, 167, 168

Falkland Islands 146
Figueres, President 146
Finland 149
Foreigners see Aliens
Foreign ministries 33, 34, 88, 152, 153

France 5, 19, 22, 25, 46, 51, 53, 77, 81, 82, 85, 93, 95, 96, 135, 147
French Guiana 120
Frontiers *see* Territorial disputes
Functions of foreign policy 7, 27, 121, 175

Gabon 85, 93, 101, 102
Gambia, The 100, 102, 167
Gandhi, Mrs Indira 4
de Gaulle, President 93, 139
Germany 65, 139, 140, 142, 143
Ghaddafi *see* Qadhafi
Ghana 78, 82, 83, 88–90, 94, 97, 98, 100–2, 104
Global system *see* External environment
Gold 9
Good, R. 7
Goulart, President 140, 145
Grenada 110
Greece 10, 44, 47, 134, 154
Group of 77 141, 172
Guatemala 113, 120, 133–6, 138, 142, 144, 146, 148, 155
Guerilla movements 49, 134, 138, 141, 154, 155, 157
Guevara, Che 133, 141, 148, 154
Guinea 82, 85, 94–6, 99, 102
Guyana 110, 112, 113, 116–20, 122–4, 141, 171

Hafaz, Brigadier 63
Haile-Selassie, Emperor 81, 85, 174
Haiti 133, 134, 138, 142
Halperin, M. 2
Hassan, King 140
Herzl, Theodor 51
Ho Chi Minh 35
Holland *see* Netherlands
Honduras 120, 135, 142, 144, 156
Houphouet-Boigny, President 82, 94, 95, 104
Hughes, Howard 146
Huntington, S. P. 169

Ideology 34, 36, 50, 51, 85, 86, 92, 117, 118, 122, 123, 135
Imperialism *see* Colonialism, Neo-colonialism
Independence 20, 23, 25, 78–80, 82, 83, 113, 135
India, Indians 4, 5, 18, 30, 77, 78, 116, 117, 123, 140
Indochina 20, 21, 28, 33, 35, 36, 38, *see also* Cambodia, Laos, Vietnam

Indonesia 2–4, 7, 20, 23–6, 28, 30–7, 156
Intellectuals 156
International Petroleum Co. 147
International system *see* External environment
International Telephone & Telegraph Co. (ITT) 146
Iran 5, 44, 46, 47, 49–51, 53–5, 57–60, 63, 68, 173
Iraq 44, 46, 49, 52, 53, 55, 57, 59, 60, 63, 64
Islam 27, 31, 50, 55, 61–3, 93, 171
Israel 3, 9, 44, 46–50, 53–62, 64–9, 92, 142, 144, 150, 151, 166, 167, 169, 173
Italy 139
Ivory Coast 82, 91–5, 101, 102, 104

Jagan, Cheddi 171
Jamaica 110, 112, 113, 115–18, 120, 121, 123, 124, 171
Japan 9, 19, 24, 28, 32, 45, 56, 57, 139, 142
Jews, Judaism 54, 56, 155, 171, *see also* Israel, Zionism
Jordan 44, 46, 49, 54, 57, 59, 60, 167
Jordan, River 50

Kampuchea *see* Cambodia
Kassem, General 52, 63
Kaunda, President 84, 89, 90, 92, 93
Kennecot 146
Kenya 3, 92, 93, 97, 100–2
Khieu Samphan 34
Khmer Republic *see* Cambodia
Khruschev, Nikita 137
Kissinger, H. 6
Korany, B. 170, 175
Korea 4, 143, 151
Kreisky, Otto 139
Kurds 54, 60
Kuwait 44, 52, 58

Lamarca 155
Landowners 155
Lanusse, President 150
Laos 23
Latin America 75, 89, 95, 104, 121, 123, 131–64, 166–72
Latin American Area for Free Trade (ALALC) 136
Latin American Center for Democratic Studies (CEDAL) 136
Latin American Organization for Solidarity (OLAS) 136
Latin American Sociological Association (ALAS) 136

Leaders, leadership 6, 34, 35, 63, 64, 78, 87, 89, 90, 115, 170
League of Arab States 48, 50, 93
Lebanon 44, 49, 55, 58, 60, 63, 68, 78, 167
Le Duan 35
Legislatures 4, 33, 63, 66, 67, 153, 154
Lesotho 100–2
Liberia 75, 87, 88, 92, 101, 102
Libya 44, 46, 47, 57, 59, 63, 64
Linkage 31, 77–9, 100, 170, see also Penetration
Lome Convention 4, 92
Lumumba, Patrice 83

Macapagal, President 35
Makarios, President 6
Malaysia 20, 23, 25, 27–31, 33, 35, 36
Malawi 85, 88–90, 92–4, 96, 100–2
Mali 95, 102
Malik, Adam 4
Malvinas see Falkland Islands
Manley, Michael 120, 124
Mao Tse Tung 30
Marcos, President 32, 35
Martz, J. D. 134
Marxism see Communism
Mauritania 44, 53, 102
Mba, President 85
McGowan, P. 3
Menon, Krishna 9
Mexico 134, 140–2, 144, 147–50, 152–4, 156, 157, 172
Middle East 42–74, 81, 89, 91, 95, 99, 104, 140, 144, 154, 155, 167–9, 171, 173
Migdal, J. S. 2
Military aid 42, 46, 47, 81, 82, 93, 96, 97
Military factors 37, 48, 49, 58–60, 65, 66, 69, 94, 95, 135, 137, 167, 171–3, see also Strategic factors, Violence, Wars
Military regimes 10, 25, 29, 32, 35, 65, 66, 81, 84, 89, 104, 133, 134, 150, 155, 169, 174, see also Coups d'etat
Misperception 9
Modernisation see Development
Mohammed, Murtala 84
Monrovia group 92
Morocco 44, 49, 53, 140
Mosca, G. 10
Moslems see Islam
Mozambique 85, 90, 92
Multinational companies 9, 37, 78, 86, 87, 101, 112, 124, 145, 146, 151, 170

Nasser, President 6, 47, 55, 58, 64, 65
Nation-building see Ethnic divisions, Separatist movements
National interest 34, 123, 148, 173, 174
Nationalism 5, 22, 23, 50, 51, 80, 82, 83, 89, 99, 131, 137, 168, 169
Needler, M. 133
Nehru, Pandit 6
Neo-colonialism 7, 9, 94, 100, 136, 140, see also Multinational companies, Penetration
Nepal 156
Netherlands 19, 25, 26, 113, 135, 171
Neto, President 3
Neutralism see Non-alignment
New Emerging Forces 28
Ne Win, President 32, 35
Nicaragua 120, 135, 142, 144, 146, 152
Niger 102
Nigeria 4, 5, 81, 83, 84, 88, 91–7, 100–2, 116, 171, 173, 174
Nixon, President 84
Nkrumah, Kwame 6, 83, 88, 90, 98, 100, 104
Non-alignment 27, 28, 95, 124, 131, 140, 141, 150, 172
North Atlantic Treaty Organisation (NATO) 47
Numeiry, President 3, 89
Nyerere, President 6, 92–4

Obote, President 87, 100
Oil 37, 56, 57, 97, 101, 144, 146, 150, 174
Oman 44
Organisation of African Unity (OAU) 91–3, 97, 114
Organisation of American States (OAS) 114, 133, 136, 148, 150, 151, 153, 157
Organisation for Economic Co-operation and Development (OECD) 5
Organisation of Petroleum Exporting Countries (OPEC) 5, 48, 49, 150
Organisation of Solidarity of the People of Asia, Africa and Latin America (OSPAALA) 140, 141
Ottoman Empire 50, see also Turkey

Pakistan 3, 5, 26, 81
Palestine, Palestinians 49, 54, 61, 166
Palestine Liberation Organisation (PLO) 49
Palme, Olaf 139
Pan-Africanism 78, 80, 94
Panama 120, 141–3, 147, 151
Panama Canal Zone 137, 141, 147, 151

Paraguay 134, 135, 138, 142, 146, 148, 149, 151, 152, 170
Pareto, V. 10
Parliaments *see* Legislatures
Patron–client relations 28, 37, 42, 46, 47, 175
Penetration 9, 32, 37, 42, 52, 77, 79, 110, 112, 118, 136, 144–7, 158, 167, 170, 171
People's Democratic Republic of Yemen (PDRY) *see* Yemen, South
Peron, President 140, 141, 147, 152
Personality 6, 32, 34, 35, 62, 63, 87, 89, 152, 169, 175
Peru 135, 136, 139, 141–3, 147, 148, 155
Philippines 20, 24, 27, 32, 35, 37, 170
Policy analysis 8
Policy making *see* Decision making
Political parties 64–7, 82, 83, 97, 117, 118, 122, 123, 139, 147, 154, 158, 175; for individual parties *see* countries
Population *see* Demographic factors
Portugal 19, 26, 85, 90, 92, 98, 100, 134, 135
Praetorianism 169
Press 33, 154
Pressure groups 4, 60, 61, 135, 145, 154, 158, 175
Psychological environment 8, 9, 45, 112, 172, 175
Puerto Rico 141, 171

Qadhafi, President 6, 63, 64, 171
Qatar 53
Quadros, President 140

Rabin, Prime Minister 61, 67
Rational actor approach 4
Ras al-Khayma Sheikdom 60
Regional environment 18–26, 36, 42–4, 48–52, 67, 68, 75–9, 91–4, 110–14, 118–22, 131–6, 143, 157, 166–8, 173
Religion *see* Christianity, Islam, Jews
Rhodesia 83, 89–91, 97, 98, 100
Rosenau, J. 44, 123, 126, 165, 170
Rumania 142
Russet, B. M. 152
Russia *see* USSR
Rwanda 102

Sabah 27, 37
Sadat, President 46, 47, 58, 63, 64
Sallal, Brigadier 63
Salvador 120, 135, 142
San Martin, Jose de 133

Saudi Arabia 5, 44, 46, 49, 50, 53, 55, 57–60, 68
Senegal 4, 85, 93, 94, 100–2, 104
Senghor, President 85, 93, 94, 104
Sekou Toure, President 82, 94
Separatist movements 20, 26, 27, 81
Shapiro, H. 3
Sharja Sheikdom 60
Sierra Leone 78, 83, 85, 102
Sihanouk, Prince 27, 28, 34, 38
Singapore 20, 23, 27, 29, 30, 33, 35
Somalia 44, 80, 81, 90, 93, 95, 96, 99, 101, 102, 173
Somoza, President 146
South Africa 9, 83, 85, 90–2, 97, 98, 101, 142, 166, 169
South-East Asia 17–41, 75, 95, 99, 104, 166–71
Sovereignty 9, 22, 27, 32, 87, 118, 150
Soviet Union *see* Union of Soviet Socialist Republics
Spain 10, 19, 133–5, 139
Spanish Sahara 49, 53
Spiegel, S. L. 131
Sri Lanka 156
Stereotypes 9
Stevens, President 85
Strategic factors 21, 37, 47, 52, 53, 137, 168
Stroessner, President 148, 170
Students 83, 85, 135, 145, 147, 156, 158
Suarez, Mario 139
Subsystems *see* Regional environment
Sudan 3, 44, 89, 99, 100, 102, 173
Suez Canal 63
Suharto, President 3, 32, 35
Sukarno, President 3, 25, 28, 34, 35, 38, 140
Surinam 113, 120
Swaziland 77, 100–2
Syria 5, 44, 46, 49, 51, 53, 54, 57–60, 63–5, 167

Taiwan 142, 143
Tanaka, Prime Minister 57
Tanbs Islands 60, 63
Tanzam Railway 90, 100
Tanzania 92–4, 101, 102, 104
Taxonomy 2, 44, 165
Territorial disputes and integrity 26, 27, 37, 51–3, 60, 80, 81, 93, 113, 114, 123, 135, 174
Thailand 3, 18, 22, 28, 29, 33, 35, 36
Thanom, Marshal 35

183

Timor 26, 37
Togo 102, 167
Torrijos, Colonel 147
Trabal, Colonel 153
Trade unions 83, 135, 145, 156, 158
Transkei 171
Transnationalism 9
Tricontinental 141
Trinidad and Tobago 110, 112, 113, 115, 116, 119, 120, 123, 124
Tshombe, Moise 94
Tun Abdul Razak 30, 35
Tunisia 44
Tunku Abdul Rahman 29, 35
Turkey 44, 46, 47, 50, 51, 53, 57, 59, 62–5

Uganda 2, 3, 83, 86–8, 90, 92, 94, 95, 97, 100–2
Union of Soviet Socialist Republics (USSR) 2, 4, 8, 9, 21, 37, 38, 45–7, 58, 63, 81, 86, 93, 94, 96, 112, 114, 125, 136–9, 143, 147, 149, 154, 156, 157, 170
United Arab Emirates (UAE) 44, 53
United Arab Republic (UAR) 63, see also Egypt
United Brands 146
United Kingdom see Britain
United Nations (UNO) 7, 88, 91, 98, 104, 149, 151–3
United Nations Conference on Trade and Development (UNCTAD) 98, 141, 172
United States of America (USA) 2, 5, 9, 19, 21, 22, 24, 25, 28, 29, 32, 33, 37, 38, 45–7, 54, 56, 58, 59, 61, 82, 84, 95, 96, 112–14, 117, 125, 133, 135–9, 142–51, 154–8
U Nu, Prime Minister 35
Upper Volta 96, 101, 102
Uruguay 134, 135, 138, 139, 141, 149, 153, 154
Uses of foreign policy 7, 28, 31, 170, see also Functions of foreign policy

Vatican 142
Venezuela 110, 113, 120, 122, 134, 136, 138–42, 148, 150, 152, 154, 172
Vesco, Robert 146
Viet-Minh 28
Vietnam 22, 23, 26, 28, 34, 35, 37, 99, 154, 170, 173
Violence 48, 49, 89, 135, 151, 167

Wars: Algeria-Morocco (1963) 49, 53; Angola (1975–76) 85, 91, 92, 94, 168; Iraq (1968–75) 49, 54, 55, 60; Indochina (1946–54) 28; Jordan (1970) 49, 50, 54; Lebanon (1975–77) 49, 61, 63; Middle East (1948) 48; Middle East (1956) 48; Middle East (1967) 48, 50, 53, 65; Middle East (1973) 45–8, 54, 56, 63, 64; Nigeria (1967–70) 91, 95, 97; Sahara (1975–76) 49, 53; Vietnam (1964–75) 22, 38, 98, 148, 154; World (1939–45) 18, 19, 21, 25, 28, 42, 140, 151; Yemen (1962–67) 49, 50
Weber, M. 6
Weinstein, F. B. 2, 7, 170, 175
West Indies see Caribbean
West Indies Associated States 100, 115
West Indies Federation 114–16, 119
West Irian 20, 26
Williams, E. 134
Williams, Dr Eric 115, 116, 119, 121, 124

Yaounde Conventions 92
Yemen, North (Yemen Arab Republic) 44, 49, 50, 53, 63, 167
Yemen, South (PDRY) 44, 53
Yon Sosa 155
Yugoslavia 134, 140, 142, 143

Zaire 83, 88, 94, 100–2, 151
Zambia 9, 78, 83–5, 89, 90, 92, 93, 97, 100–2, 116
Zionism 50, 51, 56

Other SAXON HOUSE publications

Hopwood, A. G.	*An accounting system and managerial behaviour*
Black, I. G., et al	*Advanced urban transport*
Pollock, N. C.	*Animals, environment and man in Africa*
McLean, A. T.	*Business and accounting in Europe*
Rogers, S. J., B. H. Davey	*The common agricultural policy and Britain*
Hermet, G.	*The communists in Spain*
Klingen, J. S.	*Company strategy*
Chrzanowski, I.	*Concentration and centralisation of capital in shipping*
Bailey, R. V., J. Young (eds)	*Contemporary social problems in Britain*
Mack, J. A.	*The crime industry*
Sjølund, A.	*Daycare institutions and children's development*
Lewis, C.	*Demand analysis and inventory control*
Jambrek, P.	*Development and social change in Yugoslavia*
Macmillan, J.	*Deviant drivers*
Richards, M. G., M. E. Ben-Akiva	*A disaggregate travel demand model*
Teff, H.	*Drugs, society and the law*
Snickers, F. et al (eds)	*Dynamic allocation of urban space*
Ellison, A. P., E. M. Stafford	*The dynamics of the civil aviation industry*
Birnbaum, K. E.	*East and West Germany*
Masnata, A.	*East-West economic co-operation*
Ghosh, D.	*The economics of building societies*
Richardson, H. W.	*The economics of urban size*
Starkie, D. N., D. M. Johnson	*The economic value of peace and quiet*
John, I. G. (ed.)	*EEC policy towards Eastern Europe*
More, W. S. (ed.)	*Emotions and adult learning*
Grassman, S.	*Exchange reserves and the financial structure of foreign trade*
Thompson, M. S.	*Evaluation for decision in social programmes*
von Geusau, F.A.M.A. (ed.)	*The external relations of the European Community*
Bergmann, T.	*Farm policies in socialist countries*
Ash, J. C. K., D. J. Smyth	*Forecasting the U.K. economy*
Blank, S.	*Government and industry in Britain*
Buttler, F. A.	*Growth pole theory and economic development*
Richardson, H. W., et al	*Housing and urban spatial structure*
van Duijn, J. J.	*An interregional model of economic fluctuations*
Brittain, J. M., S. A. Roberts (eds)	*Inventory of information resources in the social sciences*
Fukuda, H.	*Japan and world trade*
Jackson, M. P.	*Labour relations on the docks*
Stephenson, I. S.	*The law relating to agriculture*
Hess, H.	*Mafia and Mafiosi*
Vodopivec, K.	*Maladjusted youth*
Hovell, P. J., et al	*The management of urban public transport*
Funnell, B. M., R. D. Hey (eds)	*The management of water resources in England and Wales*
Martin, M. J. C.	*Management science and urban problems*
Rhenman, E.	*Managing the community hospital*
Giddings, P. J.	*Marketing boards and ministers*
Klaassen, L. H., P. Drewe	*Migration policy in Europe*
Chapman, C. B.	*Modular decision analysis*

Hodges, M.	*Multinational corporations and national governments*
Liggins, D.	*National economic planning in France*
Friedly, P. H.	*National policy responses to urban growth*
Madelin, H.	*Oil and politics*
Tilford, R. (ed.)	*The Ostpolitik and political change in Germany*
Friedrichs, J., H. Ludtke	*Participant observation*
Fitzmaurice, J.	*The party groups in the European parliament*
Brown, J., G. Howes (eds)	*The police and the community*
Lang, R. W.	*The politics of drugs*
Denton, F. T., B. G. Spencer	*Population and the economy*
Dickinson, J. P. (ed.)	*Portfolio analysis*
Wilson, D. J.	*Power and party bureaucracy in Britain*
Wabe, J. S.	*Problems in manpower forecasting*
Willis, K. G.	*Problems in migration analysis*
Farnsworth, R. A.	*Productivity and law*
Shepherd, R. J.	*Public opinion and European integration*
Richardson, H. W.	*Regional development policy and planning in Spain*
Sant, M. (ed.)	*Regional policy and planning for Europe*
Thorpe, D. (ed.)	*Research into retailing and distribution*
Dickinson, J. P.	*Risk and uncertainty in accounting and finance*
Hey, R. D., T. D. Davies (eds)	*Science, technology and environmental management*
Britton, D. K., B. Hill	*Size and efficiency in farming*
Buchholz, E., et al	*Socialist criminology*
Paterson, W. E.	*The SPD and European integration*
Blohm, H., K. Steinbuch (eds)	*Technological forecasting in practice*
Piepe, A., et al	*Television and the working class*
Goodhardt, G. J., et al	*The television audience*
May, T. C.	*Trade unions and pressure group politics*
Labini, P. S.	*Trade unions, inflation and productivity*
Casadio, G. P.	*Transatlantic trade*
Whitehead, C. M. E.	*The U.K. housing market*
Balfour, C.	*Unions and the law*